As I Have Loved You

AS I HAVE LOVED YOU

The Challenge of Christian Ethics

by James P. Hanigan

Paulist Press ■ New York and Mahwah

Library of Congress
Catalog Card Number: 85-61740

ISBN: 0-8091-2734-2

Published by Paulist Press
997 Macarthur Boulevard
Mahwah, New Jersey 07430

Printed and bound in the
United States of America

Contents

for

MECH

always

importance of the Bible for both Catholic piety and Catholic theology. The Catholic faithful in general and Catholic theologians in particular were urged to make the sacred Scriptures the major source nourishing their minds and hearts. This was especially emphasized for those who practice the discipline of moral theology or Christian ethics.

> Special care should be given to the perfecting of moral theology. Its scientific presentation should draw more fully on the teaching of holy Scripture and should throw light on the exalted vocation of the faithful in Christ and their obligation to bring forth fruit in charity for the life of the world (*Optatam totius* 16).

Ironically, this immersion in the teaching of holy Scripture as the primary source of moral theology does not seem to have produced a new unity in moral conviction and practice. It has spawned new debates about the proper use of Scripture for moral decision-making. It does not seem to be all that clear as to just what the Scriptures do and do not say about the moral existence of the Christian believer.

The second major event, the publication of *Humanae Vitae,* stands in sharp contrast to the decrees of the Council in at least one respect. The encyclical does not introduce or advocate change in the Church or even an openness to the new trends and aspirations of people in the secular world. On the contrary, it stands against change and the desires of many contemporaries for a new view of human sexuality and for more convenient and effective methods of birth control. The letter reiterates in unmistakably clear language a traditional Catholic moral teaching that could be expressed in the form of a specific moral prohibition: "Thou shalt not practice artificial contraception for any reason."

Needless to say, the encyclical generated a hitherto unknown degree of debate and dissent in the Church, leaving many people in confusion about the moral teaching and moral authority of the Church. It was not a question of the Pope's words being ambiguous or uncertain, for they were luminously clear and definite. But when the atmosphere of debate and dissent surrounding the letter was joined to the uncertainty provoked by the changes coming from Vatican II, and was further linked to the transformation of values occurring in the secular society at large—think of the revolution in sexual mores, the civil rights movement, the anti-Vietnam protests, the women's movement, and all the talk about the new morality—the confusion in regard to Catholic moral teaching and its relevance to the appropriate conduct of one's life became understandably great.

As one moral theologian who does not think that the differences in the moral perceptions of Christians are, in fact, as wide as they often appear to be, nor that people's moral confusion need be as great as it sometimes is, I have attempted in the following pages to present a clear over-view of what appears to me to be a consistent and coherent tradition of moral thought and reflection. The book presents the problems, procedures and insights of moral theology, of Christian ethics, from the perspective of a Roman Catholic theologian. In the first chapter I indicate what the problems of moral theology are precisely as they emerge from the effort to start one's moral reflections from a serious and attentive reading of the New Testament text. The next seven chapters explore these problems and discuss the ways that have been developed for their possible resolution. The first eight chapters, therefore, present an understanding of what morality is all about as faith sees it, or, in more personalist terms, what it means to be a moral person who makes moral decisions with the freedom of God's children.

The final two chapters attempt to put some flesh on the formal or skeletal outline of moral theology presented to that point. By examining the traditional Catholic emphasis on the evangelical counsels of poverty, chastity and obedience, one comes up against the basic human relationships to material wealth, to sexuality, and to social power and authority. Finally, a reflection on the call to divine-human friendship enables us to glimpse the deepest meaning and purpose of the moral life.

To assist the reader and to promote the possibility of shared discussion of the central issues of our moral existence, I have placed a few study questions at the end of each chapter. For more ambitious readers I have also added a brief, annotated bibliography to aid in further study and research. The bibliography inevitably reflects my own perspectives and preferences on the issues.

Hence it makes no pretense to being exhaustive or fully representative of the work being done today in the field of moral theology. But it is sufficiently balanced, I believe, to provide a fair introduction to the issues.

On the wall of my office at Duquesne University there hangs a framed saying done in needlepoint by one of my former students. The saying reflects both the inspiration and the hope for this book. "All the beautiful sentiments in the world weigh less than a single lovely action." We read a similar idea in the Scriptures: "Our love is not to be just words or mere talk, but something real and active" (1 Jn 3:18). I have been privileged to have students over my years of teaching who have both stimulated and challenged me to live what I teach even as I sought to challenge them. It is with gratitude to my students past and with hope for my students present and future, among whom I count the readers of this book, that I offer the present work as a help to responsible and loving action.

I wish to add a special word of thanks to Laurie Gormley who helped to type the manuscript and to Mr. Edward Scheid for his assistance with the study questions and bibliography. My colleagues at Duquesne are an unfailing source of encouragement and friendship. And above all there is MECH.

1 The Problems of Christian Ethics

Anyone who takes the time to read the New Testament with a degree of serious attention will quickly come to recognize that love of neighbor is the most characteristic and insistent moral demand made upon those who would be followers of Jesus. It is, of course, not the only moral demand, nor is it the first demand from which all other demands flow. That honor belongs to the invitation to "repent, and believe in the good news" (Mk 1:15). But love of one's neighbor has the distinction of being by far the most common requirement of Christian discipleship.

LOVE AND THE NEW TESTAMENT

The demand to love one's neighbor can be found in such well-known parables as the good Samaritan (Lk 10:29–37), the last judgment (Mt 25:31–46), and the sower of the seed (Mk 4:1–9), to mention only a few. We find the same demand for love of neighbor in numerous sayings attributed to Jesus himself by the Gospel writers. Among these sayings the two great commandments of love of God and love of neighbor (Mk 12:28–34; Mt 22:34–40), the golden rule (Mt 12:7), and the new commandment given to the disciples by Jesus at the Last Supper (Jn 13:34–35; 15:12), from which this book takes its title, are, perhaps, the most familiar. We can also find the demand to love one's neighbor dramatized in the example of Jesus himself as he is portrayed in the Gospel stories which tell about his relationships with other people. We need only think, for example, of the numerous healing stories (Mk 1:21—2:12), the multiplication of the loaves and fishes (Mt 14:13–21; Mk 6:30–44; 8:1–10), the invitation to Zacchaeus (Lk 19:1–10), or the changing of water into wine at the wedding feast at Cana (Jn 2:1–12). Most dramatically presented is the example of Jesus' own sacrificial death on the cross. "A man can have no greater love than to lay down his life for his friends" (Jn 15:13).

So characteristic of Christian morality is the demand to love one's neighbor that Paul and the other authors of the New Testament epistles never tire of urging it upon their readers. Paul himself is but one clear example of this repeated insistence. For him love is the greatest of all human capacities (1 Cor 13:1–13). He urges the Christians at Corinth never to do anything to offend anyone (1 Cor 10:32), but to let everything be done in love (1 Cor 16:14). The new Christians in Galatia are exhorted to carry one another's burdens (Gal 6:3) because love of neighbor exhausts the whole law (Gal 5:13–15). He admonishes the Christians in Ephesus not to allow the sun to set on their anger (Eph 4:25–32) and to give way to one another in love (Eph 5:21), while the message to the Philippians includes the demand to think always of other people's interests first (Phil 2:4).

Other authors of epistles are equally insistent on love for one's neighbor. The author of the Letter to the Hebrews, for instance, urges them to love one another like brothers and to welcome strangers into their midst (Heb 13:1). The Letter of James informs its readers that love for one's neighbor as oneself is the supreme law (Jas 2:8–9). The author of 1 Peter repeats the admonition that Christians are to love one another (1 Pet 1:22–23) and further advises that they are never to pay back one wrong with another wrong (1 Pet 3:8–12).

The most vigorous and direct advocate of neighbor-love as the chief ethical demand of the Christian life, however, is the author of the Johannine epistles. He insists that Christians live a life of love (2 Jn 6), for only by living in love can they live in the light and avoid death (1 Jn 2:9–10). In what must be the clearest and most pointed statement about the importance of neighbor-love for Christian life in all of Christian literature, the same author has written:

> Anyone who says, "I love God," and hates his brother, is a liar, since a man who does not love the brother that he can see cannot love God, whom he has never seen. So this is the commandment that he has given us, that anyone who loves God must also love his brother (1 Jn 4:20–21).

In the light of biblical texts like the above, and many others too numerous to cite here, it is abundantly clear why Christians have come to understand that love for one another is the most basic, most truthful, most compelling witness to their faith that they can offer. For, "by this love you have for one another, everyone will know that you are my disciples" (Jn 13:35). It is also understandable how a theologian of the unsurpassed stature of a St. Augustine could rightly summarize the whole of Christian ethics in the pithy phrase, "Love, and do what you will." Such a phrase is entirely consistent with the report in Christian tradition about John, the beloved disciple. It is reported that he never wearied of repeating to his own disciples that they should love one another. When asked why he did not say something else or something more than this, he is said to have replied that there really was nothing more to say. "Love one another" said it all.

Almost twenty centuries later, having learned much from both the testimony of the biblical authors and the long experience of the Christian theological tradition, we must acknowledge that "love one another" continues to say it all. Faithful Christian living is now, as it was then, as simple as that. We may explain the importance of this demand to love one another after the manner of a medieval theologian like Thomas Aquinas who saw the virtue of charity or love as the inner, life-giving form of every virtue. Or we may prefer the explanation of a modern ethician like Joseph Fletcher who simply sees love as the ruling norm of all Christian behavior. But whatever the explanation, it remains the case that Christian discipleship comes down to loving one another as Jesus has loved us.

PRACTICAL PROBLEMS

But when we human beings are confronted with the demand to love one another in the course of our daily activities in ways that are real and concrete, the demand does not always appear to be so simple after all. It poses very real problems for us, problems that are both theoretical and practical in nature, or, if one prefers, problems of both head and heart.

Motivation and Sin

On the practical level we sometimes find that it is very hard, if not impossible, for us to love others and that in the depths of our hearts we really do not wish to love them or involve ourselves in their problems and in their lives. We do not always find it to be the case that, as the Second Vatican Council insisted should be the case, "The joy and hope, the grief and anguish of the men of our time, especially of those who are poor or afflicted in any way, are the joy and hope, the grief and anguish of the followers of Christ as well" (GS 1).

All that is to say that in our human experience we sometimes discover we have a problem with our motivation, with finding convincing, deeply felt reasons for expending our time and energy to care for others. It might not strike us, for example, as always being either fair or sensible that we should "love our enemies and pray for those who persecute us" (Mt 5:44), or that we should forgive a person who has wronged us seventy-seven times (Mt 18:21–22). Such a course of action may not be merely difficult but impossible because it appears to throw prudence and good sense to the winds. It does not always sit well with our hopes and ambitions and hard work that the greatest or first among us is the one who is the slave to all the others (Mk 10:43–44). The slave may well appear to us to be simply lacking in ambition or diligence or seriousness of purpose. Consequently, we find that we do not always have the heart for such love, even if we have been taught and dimly believe that such loving is what we ought to want and ought to do. As the great Danish thinker, Søren Kierkegaard, once expressed it, the human problem is not that we do not know what we should do, but that we do not want to know and do not want to do it. Thus it is clear to us that a simple act of the will is not sufficient to move us toward this kind of loving. For in the world as we experience it, such loving does not make a great deal of sense.

While Kierkegaard's observation may well be something of an exaggeration—surely there are times when we do want to know and do the good—there is certainly a degree of experienced truthfulness in what he said. Anyone who has struggled to remain patient and kindly toward an insensitive neighbor, an over-bearing parent or teacher or boss, a boorish acquaintance, a recalcitrant child or student, knows how hard it is not only to love the other person, but even to want to love him or her in certain circumstances. Indeed, we even feel justified in our annoyance. Loving others seems to be even more of a challenge when we have to deal with neighbors who have betrayed a trust, violated a friendship, physically injured or even killed one of our family or friends, insulted, degraded or humiliated us in front of others. At such times it may be all we can do to hold ourselves back from striking out in anger to avenge the hurt or the wrong. To love our enemies might well seem to exceed the reach of our hearts, to ask for more than human flesh is capable of giving. Even worse, such forgiveness may well appear to be a violation of what justice demands and a sign, not of divine love, but of callous human indifference to the pain and suffering of others. Surely there is some truth to the idea that morality begins in the human resentment that arises in the face of injustice.

The problem of motivation, then, shows itself to have two faces. Both faces can be illustrated by Jesus' act of forgiving those who nailed him to the cross (Lk 23:34). What would a similar act of forgiveness on our part require? Surely it would require that we see our enemies as Jesus saw his, as unwitting, unaware slaves of sin, blind to the real evil they were doing. It would also require that we feel about them as he did, full of compassion and mercy, rather than anger and revenge. But would either requirement be a possibility for us if we did not also share his understanding of God and the human condition? Would his kind of love be possible for us if we did not also share his faith and hope, his Spirit? The problem of motivation to love one another, as it is faced in moral theology, therefore, takes in both the question of the interior attitudes appropriate to Christian faith and hope and also the question of sin, its meaning, its manifestations, its consequences for ourselves and others.

Human Finitude

Motivation, however, is not the only practical problem we human beings have when faced with the demand "to love one another as I have loved you." We may very well want to do just that, but in trying to do so we come up against certain inabilities in ourselves; we recognize certain limits to the human condition.

We discover that we lack the energy, the time, the skills, or even the material resources necessary to love our neighbors as we would wish and as they need. Who among us would not want to feed the starving children of the world, or bring peace and reconciliation to quarreling and hostile relatives, classes, ethnic groups or nations? Yet we find ourselves quite limited in our ability to do these things. Sometimes the limit is in ourselves; we do not have what the neighbor needs. We want to help but we cannot do what is required. At other times we could help but that help is not received, is not welcome, is rejected. So we must make choices to care for some neighbors to the neglect of others, to try to remedy some human hurts even while tolerating or ignoring others. Even with a heart willing to expend all one's energies and resources in the service of others, we ourselves must take time to eat and sleep, pray and study, relax and recreate, if we are to have anything to give to others.

So it is that our human finitude confronts us with the necessity of establishing priorities in our loving others. If we are to be truthful, we must come to grips with the limited nature of human freedom and human responsibility. We must choose both whom we will serve and the ways in which we will serve. For not everyone has the same gifts or has received the same calling. As Paul reminded the Corinthians, "Now you together are Christ's body; but each of you is a different part of it" (1 Cor 12:27). So each one of us must learn the limited ways in which to contribute his or her loving service in cooperation with others, while avoiding the corrosive effects of envy or contentious rivalry. For the biggest temptation arising from the fact of our human finitude is to do nothing because we cannot do everything, to reject our own proper, limited responsibility because we are not fully and finally responsible for everything. Some will experience the opposite temptation, to assume too much responsibility and to try to do too much. In doing this they fall prey to either messianic delusions or overwhelming guilt and despair. Hence, moral theology concerned with love for one's neighbor must face the problem of human finitude and the limits of human freedom and responsibility.

Human Development

There is one last practical problem we all encounter in accepting the challenge to love one another. Even with a heart and mind set on loving, and a clear sense of our priorities and possibilities for doing so, we do not remain unchanged and unchanging in our earthly pilgrimage. As human persons we are unfinished creatures; our bodies, our minds, our emotions, our spirits, develop or regress. What appeared clear and certain to us at the age of ten often seems complex and confusing at the age of twenty. What we valued so highly in our teenage years is counted of only minor worth as we enter our forties. What I was sure was a simple matter of right and wrong requiring only moral courage when I was without responsibility takes on the appearance of great ambiguity requiring high moral wisdom now that I am to be held responsible for a decision. Just as our physical bodies and emotional states develop, or fail to develop, over time, so also does our moral awareness and sensitivity.

Most of us recognize this to be the case, at least implicitly, if not always explicitly. We do not, for example, expect the same degree of responsible freedom from a child or even from a teenager as we expect from a man or woman of more mature years. We do not ask young children to embrace abstract ideals of justice, truth and equality because we know they are incapable of understanding such ideals. We discourage teenagers from premature sexual liaisons and early marriages because we recognize that few, if any, of them are emotionally and intellectually ready for the full responsibility that interpersonal commitment entails. Loving one another, then, is something each one of us must grow into, not something that comes ready-made, or just happens, or is settled once for all. Just as there is something called physical maturity and emotional maturity, so there is something called moral maturity for which we all bear a responsibility. Moral theology, therefore, must attend to the process of moral growth and development, to the human movement into more mature forms of loving and responsible freedom.

In summary, the practical problems associated with the challenge to love one another can be identified as the following: the problem of motivation; the problem of sin; the problem of finitude; the problem of moral development. The next four chapters of the present book are designed to speak to these problems, to shed such light on them as is available from reflection upon and experience in living out the scriptural and historical tradition of the Christian faith.

The following chapters, however, do not attempt to solve these problems, still less to explain them away. Practical problems, once understood with whatever degree of clarity, remain problems. Understanding sin, for instance, more adequately than before does not lessen or negate the power of sin in human life. Moral theology or the discipline of Christian ethics is not a problem-solving discipline which produces a mechanical means for arriving at answers or solving problems. It might more properly be compared to the construction of a map which seeks to indicate the lay of the land to be traversed on the human journey. The map can reveal where certain pitfalls are likely to be encountered, where helpful resources for the journey may be expected, where safe passage through dangerous waters may be found. But we are well-advised at the outset to recognize that there are no short-cuts along the journey of human life and Christian discipleship. To paraphrase the famous Lutheran theologian, Dietrich Bonhoeffer, the free grace of the living God is available for us as we live the human journey, but while that grace is free, it is not cheap.

THEORETICAL PROBLEMS

In addition to the practical problems which arise from the demand to love one another in deed and truth, there are other problems to be faced. These are practical in the sense that they have a bearing upon the practice of the Christian life, but they are more immediately theoretical or intellectual in nature. That is to say, they require some sort of theoretical framework for their resolution. They are all aspects of the basic human problem of how we know what is morally good or evil, of the method we use to decide that an action is morally right or wrong. In technical language these problems are the issues of ethical epistemology to which philosophers devote much time and effort. Some Christian traditions simply refuse to face this kind of problem, believing that human reason has been so corrupted by sin that it is incapable of arriving at truth. Other traditions, like that of Roman Catholicism, which preserve a high esteem for human reason, see philosophy as an indispensable tool of theological reflection and ethical wisdom. It is not a matter of setting theology and faith aside to pursue philosophy, but of employing the tools of philosophy to understand the demands of faith more fully and more responsibly.

Conscience

Once again there are four specific problems that can be identified which moral theology needs to address. The first may be called the problem of conscience. By definition, the moral person is the conscientious person. To act in accord with one's conscience is to act morally. What, then, is the problem of conscience? The problem can be indicated in a series of questions. How do we know when we are being conscientious and not merely rationalizing or acting in accord with subjective whim or social prejudice? Even granting that we should follow our consciences, what is this conscience we are to follow, where is it located, what does it do, how is it formed? And most importantly, what is the extent of its authority? For instance, what do we do when our conscientious judgments about the proper ways to love our neighbors come into conflict with the judgments of others, particularly others who hold places of authority in the family, or school, or state, or Church?

There are, then, a range of questions about conscience which will require a separate chapter for their discussion. These are questions which simply cannot be addressed without taking into account important data from such behavioral sciences as psychology and sociology, as well as reflecting upon the biblical and theological data. The central importance of conscience for the moral life deserves to be emphasized, however, from the outset. For if properly understood, conscience may rightly be called the voice of God, the secret sanctuary where we are alone with God, as the Second Vatican Council expressed it (GS 16–17).

Love and Law

The second and the third of our theoretical problems are related in interesting ways and will have to be treated together.

Simply put, these two problems may be called the problem of love and the problem of law. A major, ongoing concern of Christian theology has been how love and law are to be related to one another. For the moment we may simply ask the question this way: what do the ten commandments have to do with the great commandments of love of God and neighbor, or with Jesus' command to love one another as he has loved us?

As a theoretical matter, in contrast to the practical problem of motivation, the problem of love is a matter of definition and also of identifying and describing an experience. The word love is used in the English language to refer to such a wide variety of experiences and relationships that it tends to lose any precise meaning. Love, it is said, is wonderful, lights up our lives, makes the world go round, and many other enjoyable things. Yet most of the great love stories in western literature are tragedies, with sad and sorry consequences for the lovers. Love seems to break as many hearts as it heals, to inflict equal amounts of joy and pain. In our culture sexual intercourse is often referred to as "making love" or as an act of love. But there would appear to be nothing loving about such acts of sexual intercourse as occur in rape, prostitution or incest. It is of great importance, therefore, to express as clearly as possible the meaning of the word "love" in Jesus' command to love one another.

It is equally important to identify and to describe the experience the word points to so as to distinguish the authentic experience of Christian love from its many possible counterfeits. For not all our experiences of loving are of a piece. People tell us that they love flowers, love their dog or cat, love baseball, love their children, love their country, and love ice cream. We often distinguish different experiences of loving in the English language by using adjectives in front of the noun, love. We speak, for instance, of maternal love, brotherly love, sexual love, platonic love, to indicate very real differences both in our feelings and in the nature of the relationships into which love moves us. For a second instance, we recognize that parental love has, and properly should have, significant differences from marital love. The love we bear toward close friends has different features from the love we bear toward distant relatives, though both may be called love. We expect celibate love to manifest itself differently than sexual love. For this reason we must ask about the features that are proper to the love Jesus invites us to show to our neighbors and inquire how this love relates to our other experiences of loving and being loved. It is obvious that not everything that calls itself love is to be counted as love in Jesus' sense of the term.

The third theoretical problem, the problem of law or moral rules, is directly related to the problem of love because it is through moral rules that we first come to some sense of what love requires. All societies teach their members some moral rules or lay down some framework of law to guide the behavior and relationships of their members. From a very early age all of us are instructed that we should do this and not do that, that it is nice to behave in this way and nasty to behave in that way. Moral rules become the carriers of a society's values, of its perceptions about what is morally good and morally evil. In this way moral rules become our first clue as to what is loving action and what is not. At the same time that we experience the obligatory demand made upon us by law, we also experience the limitations and occasional conflicts that are inescapably related to law. These limits and conflicts can be illustrated through popular proverbs which are one way in which moral advice is transmitted from generation to generation. What is a person to do when confronted with the following two proverbs: "Look before you leap" and "He who hesitates is lost"? The briefest of reflections on human experience reveals that we cannot have it both ways. It may be that neither proverb fits the occasion, or that both do and are in conflict.

Moral theology finds itself forced to inquire into both the value and the limits of moral rules, and to ask about the relationship of our inherited rules to the more fundamental obligation to love the neighbor. Are rules a dependable guide to the loving form of action in a particular situation or do they stand in the way of love? Do they turn us into cold-hearted legalists concerned only with the letter of the law and not its spirit? Do we become so concerned with keeping the rules that we forget the persons who are the point and purpose of our activity? Most crucially of all, are there any absolute rules which are obligatory at all times and places so that we know there are some actions we should always do and others we should never do under any circumstances? Are there intrinsically unthinkable deeds for Christian

love? Or is the love Jesus demands so unique, so creative, so
formless that it can never take the form of rules? As we shall see,
this question of absolute rules is an important, difficult question
that is highly debated by theologians and non-theologians alike.

Moral Method
The final theoretical problem associated with the command
to love one another has to do with the method of moral reasoning
we employ in making moral decisions. It might also be called the
problem of objective norms of morality, or the question as to
whether there are objective norms and, if so, what they are. Is
there something beyond one's own integrity to appeal to in
defense of moral decisions? Again this problem can be unfolded
in a series of questions. When you make a moral decision, what
evidence do you take into account? What standards or criteria do
you use to weigh the evidence? When you are asked, to what do
you appeal as a justification for your decision? Putting the matter
more concretely, how do you know, for example, that it is right
to keep your promises and wrong to commit adultery? How do
you know that some moral rules, such as the prohibition on lend-
ing money at interest, no longer apply in the modern world, and
other rules inherited from the past, such as paying a fair wage for
fair work, still apply? From the perspective of the future, as we
face new questions about human behavior arising from the new
possibilities afforded us by our technological achievements, how
do we know whether or not we should produce test-tube babies?
Can we make moral rules about this new possibility, and what
should those rules say? How do we know? Certainly the Bible does
not tell us in so many words. If we rely on someone else's judgment, how do they know?

In approaching these questions of ethical method or epistemology, it is important not to lose sight of the question motivat-
ing or underlying the methodological concern. We want to know
what love demands. It is because we want to do the loving thing
in this situation that we ask these hard questions. To enter into
the questions of moral methodology, and so into the question of
the sources of moral theology, is not to abandon the basic command of Jesus to love one another, but rather to take that command with full seriousness. If, for example, one were struggling

with the question of whether or not to place a sick, elderly parent in a nursing home, love for one's parent itself demands that we consult a variety of sources in order to arrive at a decision that could be called both responsible and loving. Surely I would want my decision in this matter to be informed by the biblical and historical tradition of Christian faith. But I would also want it to be informed by sound medical knowledge, by the best resources of human reason and knowledge. In addition I would call upon the experience of others I trust and love who have had to face the same decision. I would call upon the wisdom of my community of shared faith. Finally I would consult the integrity of my own heart that seeks in love what is best for my sick parent.

Reflection on this example, in the context of the problem of moral reasoning, reveals two final important considerations. First, it reveals the basic sources of our moral knowledge, the traditional sources of moral theology, all of which must be consulted if we are to make any claim to being conscientious. In traditional language these sources are the Bible, Christian tradition, human reason and experience, and the authority of the Church's teaching office, whatever form it takes. For Roman Catholics this form is sometimes the magisterial office of Pope and bishop. But as the example also indicates, we do not consult these sources in a mechanical fashion, expecting automatic answers to appear. The sources are informing or formational in nature, requiring that we work through the problems already mentioned in this chapter and bring our reflections to prayer, if the final decision which is ours is to lay claim to being a conscientious, loving decision. (More will be said about prayer and the moral life in the final chapter of this book. May I merely add here that prayer is not a source of moral knowledge in the objective sense with which we are presently concerned.)

The second important consideration which the example about the sick parent reveals has to do with the kind of certainty attainable in moral matters. No matter what decision one makes in regard to the sick parent, I will never be able to prove it was the right decision or the best decision. At least I will never be able to prove it in the same way that I might be able to show that it was the most economically efficient decision. Moral decisions can be defended both religiously and rationally. Indeed, they deserve such defense. But they cannot be scientifically proven in the same way that a mathematically based theory or a chemical experiment can be proven to be valid. As Aristotle pointed out long ago, one should not expect more certainty in human affairs than the matter in question allows. But having no reasons for a moral decision is not the same thing as having good, defensible, but not absolutely certain reasons. Moral decision-making may not be an entirely logical business, but it can be and ought to be a reasonable business.

Our moral existence in Christ is, then, a project of our human freedom. It is not a problem to be solved and set aside, but a continuous, always unfinished self-creation, impelled and guided by the Holy Spirit of God. The full implications of this statement will be explored in more concrete terms once the basic problems have been addressed. But again I remind the reader that the problems are the problems of trying to love as we have been loved by the Lord. For now let us turn to the basic relationship of religious faith to our moral practice.

STUDY QUESTIONS

1. Are there specific ways in which we can love one another as Jesus loved us? Are there examples in your life of how other people have shown such love to you?

2. Are there specific obstacles to loving the neighbor in your own life of motivation, sin and finitude?

3. Are you aware of and can you indicate signs of your own moral development?

4. Do love and law come into conflict in your own experience? Which one guides your conscience?

5. Describe the method you think you follow in making moral decisions. For example, how would you go about deciding what to do with a sick, elderly parent?

BIBLIOGRAPHY

Birch, Bruce C. and Larry L. Rasmussen. *The Bible and Ethics in Christian Life.* Minneapolis: Augsburg Publishing House, 1976. A fine introduction to the limits and positive uses of the Bible for the moral life by two Protestant theologians.

Curran, Charles E. "Dialogue with the Scriptures: The Role and Function of the Scriptures in Moral Theology," *Catholic Moral Theology in Dialogue.* Notre Dame: Fides Publishers, Inc., 1972, pp. 24–64. An excellent chapter by an eminent Catholic theologian suggesting the way in which the Scriptures can shape a vision of life.

Gustafson, James M. *Christ and the Moral Life.* New York: Harper & Row, Publishers, Inc., 1968. A classic work by America's outstanding Protestant ethician, indicating the ways Christ is, can be, and should be related to the moral life. Difficult reading for a beginner in the field.

Perkins, Pheme. *Love Commands in the New Testament.* New York: Paulist Press, 1982. An excellent, exegetical analysis of the various commands to love by a fine biblical scholar.

2 Faith and Practice

Most people who profess some sort of religious beliefs are strongly convinced that their religious beliefs make a significant difference in the way they behave and conduct their lives. Historically, most people have been convinced that some kind of religious beliefs are necessary if any sense of morality was to be developed and respected in society. To cite but one example, both Thomas Jefferson and John Adams, two of the chief architects of the United States of America's form of self-government, were convinced that citizens would not freely obey the laws of the land unless they believed in a God who punished evil and rewarded virtue. In some way or other morality needed, if not a God, at least belief in a God.

No doubt people who are convinced of the importance of religious beliefs for moral practice are quite sincere in this conviction and are at least partially correct. For religious beliefs can and do provide reasons why people should act in some ways and avoid acting in other ways. Most religions with which we are familiar seem to think that certain patterns of behavior, certain ways of life, certain ethical obligations follow almost naturally, as it were, from their particular understanding of and convictions about the Divine Being and his purpose.

Christianity is certainly no exception to this common phenomenon, as the New Testament writings already make clear. The speeches attributed to Peter in the early chapters of the Acts of the Apostles are a good illustration of the perceived relation between faith and moral behavior (Acts 2:14–36; 3:12–26). In these sermons Peter proclaims his belief in what God has done in Christ and his conviction that in the divine action the promise to Israel has been fulfilled. The conclusion drawn from this proclamation of faith, in one form or another, is a recommended form of action. Paul follows the same pattern repeatedly in his epistles.

First he proclaims the faith, teaching what God has revealed in Christ. Then, on the basis of the proclamation, Paul draws ethical conclusions and engages in ethical exhortation. Particularly clear examples of this procedure can be found in his discussion about eating meat that has been offered to idols (Rom 14:1–21) and his discussion of the immorality of consorting with prostitutes (1 Cor 6:12–20). In both cases the reasons given for the recommended course of action would be simply unintelligible outside the context of his religious beliefs.

THE PROBLEM

This widely-held conviction that certain forms of moral behavior are either sanctioned or proscribed by specific religious beliefs reveals itself in a number of ways. Many of us are quick to question the sincerity of a person's beliefs when the expected moral action is not forthcoming. Many of us simply take for granted that people who share our religious beliefs will also share our moral values and our convictions about what is morally right and wrong behavior. Conversely, we also tend to assume that people whose values and behavior are similar to our own probably have similar religious beliefs, while those people whose values and moral practice differ markedly from ours most likely have very different religious beliefs as well.

In making these kinds of assumptions we make moral practice a test of the sincerity or depth of a person's faith. How often do we hear remarks such as, "If you really believed that God loved all people, you wouldn't be prejudiced." Or again, "If you are willing to give that much money to the Church, you must really be serious about your faith." We also incline to make specific moral practices a requisite sign of membership in and identity with a specific religious community. For example, Quakers do not join the military, Catholics do not practice birth control, Mormons do not smoke or drink, Baptists do not play cards or dance, and so on. In this way the prohibition or advocacy of certain moral practices itself becomes an article of faith, so that to say one believes that abortion is wrong, for instance, seems to be on a par with saying one believes in God.

Of course, the relationship between religious faith and moral practice is neither this direct nor this simple, despite appearances to the contrary. Nor can certain moral practices serve as an adequate identification of a person's religious sincerity or church membership. There are very sincere Baptists who do dance and very sincere Catholics who do practice birth control. There are people who do not share Mormon religious beliefs who neither smoke nor drink as a matter of ethical conviction. There are non-Quakers who reject all participation in military service as a matter of conscience. Shared moral convictions and practices are simply not a sign of shared religious beliefs. The search for ethical practices, or even principles, that are unique to or distinctive of a particular religion has proved to be an unrewarding one. The line between religious faith and moral practice does not turn out to be a straight one, however much it may seem so to religious believers themselves.

In recent years the relationship between religious faith and morality has been of particular concern to a fair number of Christian ethicists. Their interest has taken a variety of forms and been motivated by a number of different interests. But one of the predominant forms this interest has taken is a debate over whether or not there is or even can be a distinctively Christian ethic. Expressed in a more concrete way, the concern has been to learn whether there is a pattern of life or a set of moral obligations that is, or should be, unique to Christian faith and life. If there is such a distinctive pattern or set of obligations, presumably it would not make sense to and would not be shared by anyone who did not share the faith.

This debate has not been of merely academic interest or importance, although specific theoretical concerns about ethical method have had a central place in the debate. We will attend to some of these theoretical concerns in Chapter 8. Quite pressing moral issues are also very much at stake. Is overt homosexual behavior, for example, compatible with Christian faith or should it exclude the actively homosexual person from membership in the Church? Can the Christian community remain faithful to its own beliefs and mission and at the same time tolerate or even approve practices like abortion, divorce and remarriage, or various forms of artificial contraception? In the context of the proliferation of nuclear weapons, the question of a Christian's participation in war and preparation for war has become a matter of great concern. Can a Christian be a soldier? A nuclear scientist? A weapons maker? The theologians of liberation have been urging the same kind of question upon us from the perspective of economic and social justice.

It is not to the point here to enter fully into this debate, interesting and important as it is. I have mentioned it only to underline the fact that the relationship between faith and moral practice is by no means a simple one and, therefore, needs some careful consideration here. One way to enter into this consideration is through the door provided by the sociology of religion which seeks to understand the function of religion in human life and the social purposes it serves. I am going to propose one such functional definition of religion, compiled from various sources, and then explore the meaning of the definition in order to clarify the relationship between religious faith and moral practice.

RELIGION—A SYMBOL SYSTEM

Religion, understood from a sociological perspective, may be defined in the following way. Religion is a symbol system which (a) illuminates the ambiguities of human existence and (b) expresses the *ultimate* meaning and value of life, thereby (c) generating deep and abiding convictions and attitudes, which in turn (d) produce a commitment to action and to a special way of life. This definition requires that we investigate what a symbol system is and how it does, in fact, perform this fourfold function.

To call religion a symbol system is to make two important assertions. First, religion, as a human reality, deals in symbols. While its focus is reality, indeed even ultimate reality, its vehicle for that focus is symbolic reality, or symbols. A symbol is a reality that points to something beyond itself. We all have a great deal of experience with symbols and we understand them almost without conscious effort. All words, for example, are symbols and a language is the most obvious example of a symbol system one can mention. Flags are symbols of the country or organization which creates them. Our gestures, like smiling, saluting, bowing, and genuflecting, are symbols. Many of our heroes and heroines, both

historical and legendary, are symbols. And, of course, there are
the numerous religious and secular symbols germane to feasts like
Christmas, Easter, Thanksgiving and Memorial Day.

The critical thing to note about symbols is that, while they
have a reality of their own and so are real in their own right, their
full meaning and worth comes from the reality they point to or
symbolize. Symbols are properly understood and valued only to
the degree we understand and value their referent. The flag of a
country I know nothing and care nothing about is merely a piece
of colored cloth to me, but it is really more than that. The cross,
one of the major symbols of the Christian faith, is treasured only
to the degree that it is understood and valued as symbolic of
God's infinite mercy and compassion. To see it only as a piece of
wood is to miss the greater part of its reality. To define religion
as a symbol system, then, is to claim that religion is concerned
with the symbolic nature of reality, with reality as it points beyond
itself.

No religion limits itself to or is exhausted by a single symbol.
Religion is a system of symbols, like a language. Hence the second
important assertion that is made in calling religion a symbol system is that religious symbols are linked to one another, are inter-
related to one another in a way that is coherent and mutually illuminating. One symbol helps make clear the meaning of another
so as to form a whole system of meaning. In terms of our patriotic
symbols, it is not sufficient for a country simply to have a flag.
The flag expresses a coherent meaning and symbolizes the nation
in the light of other symbolic realities like national heroes, holidays, songs, stories and places. A Christian symbol like the cross
becomes fully intelligible, and in turn contributes to the intelligibility of other symbols, only in the light of such symbols as
Adam and Eve, the fall, resurrection, heaven, hell, Church, Spirit,
and so forth. Religion, then, is not a collection of unrelated symbols, but a symbol system.

Symbols—Their Function

The symbol system that is religion, if it is still a living religion,
exercises a fourfold function which accounts for the importance
and staying power of religion in human experience. A particular
religion can die because its symbols lose their expressive power

and no longer fulfill their function. Whatever else can be said about religion, a religion lives because it fulfills a profound human need, and, when it ceases to do so, another symbol system will displace it.

Ambiguity

The first function of religion is to illuminate the ambiguities of human existence. Religious symbols shed light upon, make sense out of, enable understanding of, help the traveler see where he or she is headed. The image of illumination is that of a flashlight shining into a darkened room. The darkness of the room is not entirely dispelled, but some light is shed which makes entry possible. Religious symbols, then, are not so much what we see as they are the light by which we see what would otherwise be totally dark. And what they illuminate or shed light upon are the ambiguities of human existence, enabling us to see them precisely as ambiguous.

An ambiguity is any event or experience which confronts us in a two-sided way, as something that is at one and the same time good and bad, happy and sorrowful, promising and threatening, welcome and burdensome. The result is that we do not know what to make of the event or the experience. It is ambiguous. An ambiguity is not a dilemma, not an either-or experience, but a both-and experience. In meeting an ambiguity it is not a matter of choosing one side or the other. We inescapably get both sides or nothing at all, the good and the bad, the joy and the sorrow, or plain emptiness. That is why our human experience is often so difficult and perplexing, for it is full of ambiguities.

Among the more common ambiguities of human existence three may be mentioned here for purposes of illustration: death, love and success. The ambiguous nature of death is readily evident in the death of a loved one who has been suffering through a long, painful illness. Death comes as something that is both welcome and regretted. We regret the end and the loss of our loved one even as we welcome death as a release from pain and a passage to final rest. We really do not know how to feel in such a situation; our feelings are a mixture of sorrow and gladness which confuses us and often troubles us. But it is not only this kind of death that has an ambiguous character; all death does. For all death is loss and to be regretted. Yet it is also the one inescapable path to the discovery of what, if anything, lies beyond death.

Love and success are likewise ambiguous experiences. They bring joy, satisfaction, a sense of fulfillment and the promise of a brighter tomorrow. But they also inevitably bring added worry and responsibility, fear of losing what has been gained, the need to work harder in order to preserve their blessings, the ultimate prospect of one day losing what is so dear. It is not surprising in the least that we human beings both desire and fear love and success, for we know of their ambiguous nature. In the face of their ambiguity we ask ourselves "Is it worth it? Do I dare risk it?" and we remain unsure of how we really feel about all this.

It is one of the functions of religious symbols to shed light on these ambiguities, not by making the experiences in question unambiguous, but by helping us see the experiences in their full ambiguity and by helping to answer our questions about the ambiguity. To illustrate the point briefly, the cross and resurrection of Jesus does not make death any less ambiguous as a human experience. Note the popular, and wise, saying common enough among Christian believers: "Everybody wants to go to heaven, but nobody wants to die to get there." What the symbols of cross and resurrection do illuminate is the ambiguous nature of death by insisting that death, while a consequence of sin and an enemy of human life (1 Cor 15:20–26), is neither as final nor as fatal as it may appear. It cannot be loved or rejoiced in, but it can be faced with quiet courage and with hope. For in the resurrection death has been conquered. It has lost its victory and so it has lost its sting (1 Cor 15:55).

Meaning

A second function of religious symbols, closely related to the first function, is to express the *ultimate* meaning and value of life. All symbols are expressive of meaning and value. Religious symbols are religious because they express the ultimate, the final, the most fundamental meaning and value. All symbols express the meaning and value of something. Religious symbols express either the meaning and value of the whole, or the meaning and value of something in relation to the whole. They deal directly, not in what this or that particular experience or event or reality means, but in what it all means together, in what human life as a whole means and is worth. Religious symbols mediate the ultimate to us in reference to ourselves. They point beyond themselves to the meaning and value for us of the ultimate mystery surrounding and suffusing all reality and existence, which we call God.

The first two functions of religious symbols pertain to the order of religious beliefs. They work through stories, creeds, ritual enactments, and even catechetical instruction and prayer. In explicitly Christian theological language, these two functions work by symbolizing what and who God is, what his character is like, what he has done, is doing and intends to do, what he can be counted on for. It has traditionally been the work of dogmatic theology to devote itself to the illumination and coherence of these symbols. It is one of the advantages of the definition of religion proposed here that it makes clear that religious beliefs and dogmatic theology are not without direct relevance to moral behavior and moral theology.

Attitudes

Whenever a symbol system, whatever it may be, performs these first two functions for its adherents, it may properly be called, from a sociological perspective, a religion, and two additional functions will be found to follow. Because the symbol system is effective in illuminating ambiguities and expressing meaning, it will also generate or give birth to deep and abiding convictions and attitudes in the human person. The word generation is an apt word, for, like physical generation, the birth of attitudes and convictions is a long, slow, often hidden process that is dependent for success upon a number of different factors. Attitudes and convictions do not spring full-blown into life in a moment or by magic. They are formed slowly over years in interaction with the formative symbol system.

The words "deep and abiding convictions and attitudes" have also been chosen with care for a purpose. They point to convictions and attitudes that are not only strong enough and stable enough to last over considerable periods of time in the midst of changing circumstances, but which are so deeply rooted in us that we may not even be consciously aware that they are ours. As

dimensions of our unconscious awareness, it may take special
events or unusual circumstances to reveal them to our conscious
selves. Is it not the case, for example, that we are sometimes sur-
prised by the depth of our own anger, or passion, or love, or loyalty when some exceptional event elicits it in us? We did not know
we felt that way about a particular cause or so deeply about this
particular person. At other times we surprise ourselves by acting
on principle in the face of temptation, for we did not realize previously that our conviction was so strong or so deeply rooted in
us.

As has long been recognized by students of symbolic communication, symbols often operate at the pre-conscious or
unconscious levels of human awareness, which is why I have spoken here of attitudes and convictions rather than of ideas and
ideals. Few people could honestly make an explicit list of all their
attitudes and convictions, or begin to measure their depth and
tenacity. To take but one example, how deeply does the basic attitude of hope that life is finally and fully worth living run in you,
the reader? How consistently and profoundly does such an attitude shape the way you see, feel and respond to life? None of us
can really say for sure. But such questions do make clear that the
religion or the symbol system we are speaking of throughout this
chapter is not the one we nominally say we embrace or give mere
lip-service to. It is rather the symbol system we really are formed
by, the one that is in fact operative in us. While we might *say,* for
example, that a saint like Francis of Assisi or a contemporary like
Mother Teresa is the symbol of a holy, dedicated Christian life, it
may well be that more secular symbols of worldly success are far
more formative of our convictions and attitudes about the good
life. Since we have no direct access to what is, in fact, so deeply
operative in us, we are led to the fourth function of religion as a
symbol system. Our external manner of life is the clue to our real
convictions and attitudes.

Way of Life

The attitudes and convictions generated by a religious symbol system produce in turn a commitment to action and to a special way of life. It is because we think and feel in certain ways at
the deepest levels of our being that we are moved to act in certain

ways. We judge some experiences, some goals to be worthwhile, so we commit ourselves to their pursuit. Other goals and experiences we feel to be of little or no worth and so we are not moved to seek them. The language of commitment to action is not meant to be restricted to exceptional actions or radical commitments. We human beings only get out of bed in the morning and start on our daily rounds because we are moved by the conviction that for one reason or another it is worthwhile to do so. Students study, workers work, teachers teach, parents parent, children play, because of the interior attitudes and convictions that have been formed in them by one or another symbol system.

The notion of a commitment to a special way of life, finally, is not intended to refer to a particular calling in life, for example, to be a priest or a nun or an engineer or a doctor. Rather it indicates that we all strive for a degree of consistency and coherence in our lives in accord with the formative or operative symbol system to which we adhere. This consistency and coherence gives us a pattern or structure of life to pursue, not merely a number of unrelated actions to perform. In deciding that certain goals have meaning and are worth pursuing, we commit ourselves to a way of life, on either a temporary or a permanent basis, that is built around and structures our pursuit of these goals. The person who is convinced of the importance of a formal education enters, for a time, upon the student's way of life. The couple who value their mutual love as unifying and life-giving enter upon the more permanent commitment to the married way of life.

In entering upon any way of life, it is not merely this action or that action that is seen to have meaning and value. It is a structured existence, a way of life that is embraced, even while the details or particulars of that way of life may remain unknown and unknowable. For one who is formed in reality by the Christian symbol system, the commitment to a way of life is the commitment to follow Jesus, to be his disciple, or to live something that may be loosely called the Christian way of life. It remains unclear, even after the commitment has been made, what in its entirety that way of life will entail. Nor does the commitment itself answer the question about the rightness or wrongness, morally, of all specific human decisions and actions. The sincere, authentic commitment to "love one another as I have loved you" does not settle or put an end to ethical questions. It does, however, provide a context or framework for asking such questions.

Symbols—Their Dynamics

The foregoing definition and discussion of religion and its multiple dynamics can be usefully summarized in the following diagram.

$$
\begin{array}{ccccccc}
 & \text{SYMBOL} & \text{HUMAN} & & & \\
\text{GOD} \leftrightarrow & \text{SYSTEM} \leftrightarrow & \text{PERSON} & \leftrightarrow \text{ACTS} & \leftrightarrow \text{WORLD} \\
\end{array}
$$

$$
\left\{\begin{array}{l}\text{Attitudes} \\ \text{Convictions} \\ \text{Intentions} \\ \text{Motives}\end{array}\right\}
\left\{\begin{array}{l}\text{Physical} \\ \text{Verbal}\end{array}\right\}
\left\{\begin{array}{l}\text{Situation} \\ \text{Consequences}\end{array}\right\}
$$

By placing the human person in the center of the diagram, I am not trying to make a case for an anthropocentric ethic that would make the human the measure of all things. But the human person, with his or her interior attitudes, convictions, intentions and motives, is the starting point for understanding the relationship of faith and practice, for it is in the human person that the two intersect. These interior attitudes, convictions, and so on are shaped in the person by the symbol system operative in his or her life. Hence the arrow points away from the symbol system toward the person to indicate the direction of influence.

The symbol system, in its turn, points beyond itself to ultimate reality. But in religions of revelation, like Christianity, it is ultimate reality that reveals itself in and through the symbols. In a real sense the symbols of the faith are given in revelation. Christians are given Jesus; they do not invent him. Hence the arrow points away from God toward the symbol system to indicate again the direction of influence.

The human person is moved interiorly to action that may be verbal or physical or both. Because action flows from the interiority of the person, the arrow once again points away from the person toward the person's acts. But action is always action in a world. It takes place in time and space, occurs in a specific situation and always has definite consequences. To a greater or less degree human action changes the world in which it occurs. So once again the arrow points away from the person's acts toward the world. The world is created and shaped anew by human action in accord with human attitudes, convictions and intentions.

An interesting thing happens to human beings, however, as they act in the world. Things do not always work out as planned; intentions are not realized; actions do not achieve the desired consequences. The world does not prove to be as malleable as first thought. As a result, the direction of influence begins to reverse itself and to flow in the opposite direction. The world dictates action and the intentions which guide action. Action and its consequences have an impact upon the interior attitudes and convictions of the human agent. So the arrows on the reader's right side of the diagram must point in both directions.

When attitudes and convictions are challenged by the experience of acting in the world, they in turn raise questions about the validity and worth of the person's symbol system. And once the symbol system is subjected to question, this forces a further question about the nature of ultimate reality itself. The existence and character of God become problematic. The relationship between religious belief and moral practice, therefore, is not one-way or uni-directional. It is, rather, dialectical, a relationship of reciprocal and corrective interaction. The understanding and feeling of faith shapes behavior; the experience of acting in the world reshapes the understanding and feeling of faith in a continuous process.

Given the vast variety of human experience as we act in the world with its equally varied situations and consequences, it is little wonder that the human understanding of ultimate reality has assumed a multitude of forms and produced a number of symbol systems. Given this variety of symbol systems, it is also little wonder that there is a great plurality of attitude, conviction and judgment among human beings in regard to morality.

The plurality of symbol systems and moral views in the world clearly poses a considerable and fundamental moral question. For if we are formed in our interior depths by the symbol system we embrace, then the religion we choose to be formed by is among the most fateful choices we can make. Nor can any of us now living in a pluralistic world avoid being influenced by the competing symbols of other religions, some of which will be in sharp conflict with our consciously chosen religion. It becomes a struggle to achieve consistency and coherence in our religious symbol system, and so also in our interior life and external behavior. If the crusaders of medieval Christianity who murdered and pillaged in the name of Christ strike modern-day Christians as bizarre and aberrant, they may be no more odd than twentieth century Christians whose major energies are devoted to the pursuit of wealth and pleasure. Discrepancies between faith and practice are not surprising.

Symbols—Their Challenge

There is one more feature of the relationship between faith and practice which requires attention here, since it again highlights the fundamental role of human responsibility for both faith and practice and their relationship. This feature is best illustrated by a concrete example drawn from experience. In my youth I was taught that the worst evil in the world was mortal sin. It was better that the whole world should cease to exist than that I should ever commit one mortal sin. In addition, I was instructed as to the kinds of actions that constituted mortal sin. Sin took a prominent place in my symbol system and had a deeply formative impact upon me. I strove to avoid the kinds of actions that were labeled mortal sins, and if I did something that even resembled a mortal sin, I hurried to confession to repair the evil and to avoid eternal damnation.

Let us imagine, for the moment, a young boy with the same outlook as just described who arrives in his teenage years with all the natural curiosity and feelings of any adolescent. One day he comes upon a group of his classmates while they are looking furtively at a copy of *Playboy* magazine. To look at magazines like this is, he has been taught, one of those actions that constitute mortal sin. But these classmates are his friends; he likes them and thinks that they are good people. Being a fairly alert youth, he knows about wars, terrorism, economic poverty and exploitation, environmental pollution, racial and sexual prejudice, and any number of other terrible things. He finds it somewhat hard to be convinced that looking at pictures in a magazine could be the worst evil in the world. At this point his human experience, his action in the world with its varied situations and consequences, poses a distinct challenge to the validity and worth of his symbol system, and so also to his understanding of God and his will. A person in this situation has four choices, though it may not be explicitly clear to him what those choices are.

The first choice is to decide on the basis of his human experience that the symbol system by which he has been formed is simply wrong at this point. What it calls mortal sin is not nearly as bad as the symbol system has made it out to be. Indeed, it is not bad at all. Furthermore, if the symbol system is wrong about something as basic as what is good and evil, it is likely to be wrong about the other things it has formed him to think and feel. The symbol system must be rejected as a matter of personal sincerity. A new set of symbols must be found, which will most likely require a time of search and experimentation with a variety of symbol systems. Our youth will be lost and confused for a while, not knowing what he thinks or feels, not sure about what is morally good and morally evil. In short, he has gone through the process known as losing one's faith, though he may still retain some of his previously established moral attitudes and convictions.

There is, however, a second possible response when experience challenges one's symbol system. Instead of deciding that his symbol system is simply wrong, he can decide that it needs to be reinterpreted or understood in a new way. This choice is a live possibility precisely because of the multivalent character of symbols which, unlike concepts and words, have no exact and fixed meaning. So our teenager may still accept as true that mortal sin is the worst evil in the world, but decide that what counts as mortal sin needs to be redefined. New meaning also has to be found for symbols like the cross, heaven, hell, and so on, and new attitudes will develop in regard to love and sex and work and play. This path of reinterpretation was the direction many students took during the Vietnam era. Obscenity, for example, was still held to be a negative moral value, but it was not sex that was obscene but war. Hence the slogan, "Make love, not war."

In taking the path of reinterpretation one is able to hold on to one's symbol system, so that the language of faith and the meaning and value of life to which it points are not simply lost. But by giving a new meaning to the symbols, one is able to meet the challenge posed by the experience of acting in the world. By relating the old symbols to one another in new ways, by emphasizing some symbols to the neglect of others, the person creates a new structure of meaning and value based on the sole norm of his or her own personal experience. In the process of doing this, the symbols lose their cutting edge, their ability to challenge and correct the way one has of seeing and feeling the world. The symbols cease to mediate ultimate reality, becoming instead a means by which one explains and justifies one's own limited experience as normatively human.

Consequently, this process of reinterpretation involves a certain degree of bad faith, though the inauthenticity may well be hidden for a time from the person doing the reinterpretation. What happens, in effect, in this process is that the person's nominal symbol system remains the same. Lip-service is paid to traditional religious beliefs. But there is a change in the operative symbol system. This change is manifested by the evident changes in one's moral commitments and moral behavior.

For people whose religious beliefs and moral convictions have been challenged in the way I have described there is also a third choice. They can refuse to face the challenge in any conscious, deliberate way. The challenge is not perceived as an invitation to growth, as an opportunity for a more mature faith. It is perceived simply as a temptation to be rejected and fled from. To take this path also involves a degree of bad faith which again may be hidden for a time from the person making this choice. But what takes place is a deformation of experience, a denial of what one knows or suspects to be true. There is a kind of pseudo-innocence about this process which is manifested in the acceptance of trivial obligations as crucially important and the dismissal of fundamental moral demands as non-essential or unrelated to religious beliefs. One is reminded of Jesus' indictment of the Pharisees in Matthew's Gospel (Mt 23:13–36): "Alas for you, scribes and Pharisees, you hypocrites! You pay your tithe of mint and dill and cummin and have neglected the weightier matters of the law—justice, mercy, good faith. These you should have practiced, without neglecting the others. You blind guides, straining out gnats and swallowing camels" (Mt 23:23–24).

To illustrate this choice in the present context of our example, and by contrast to the first two choices, we might note that it is only this choice which continues to regard looking at *Playboy* magazine as a matter of serious moral wrong. The first two choices, albeit for different reasons, have rejected that view. But the third choice has also denied that the grave evils in the world which provoked the challenge in the first place are really as bad as they are made out to be or have anything to do with morality. To do this requires the person to develop a kind of moral fundamentalism in which reason has no role to play in determining what is morally good and evil, and in which moral behavior is reduced without qualification to being obedient to what has been revealed once for all as God's will. One simply believes that it is wrong to look at *Playboy* magazine as a matter of faith, and faith is not to be questioned.

Finally, there is a fourth choice for the person whose symbol system has been challenged by his lived experience. He can decide, not that his symbol system is wrong, not that it needs some kind of radical reinterpretation, and not that his experience of the world is irrelevant and to be ignored but that he is not seeing the world in full accord with his symbol system. Symbols foreign to or incompatible with his religious symbol system are distorting his vision. He, therefore, needs to re-examine his own way of seeing his behavior and to understand it more deeply in the light of his symbol system's opposition to the slick pornography that *Playboy* presents. In making this re-examination, in allowing himself to be challenged not only by experience but also by his symbol system, he may come to understand how the sexual exploitation of women, their objectification as things to satisfy male curiosity and lust, is foreign to the human dignity of both women and men. He may come to see that, while there is no great consequence to the single act of looking at this magazine here and now, the single act is part and parcel of a larger pattern of moral evil and a consequence of sin.

In following this path, in allowing his symbol system to challenge him to see the world in deeper and more truthful ways, not only does our teenager keep the faith; he grows in his understanding of the faith and its ethical depth and implications. His religious beliefs, his symbol system, does not mechanically dictate his behavior. Nor does his limited human experience simply become the norm of all that is true and good. Rather faith and practice exist in healthy, dialectical relationship to one another. Faith guides and challenges practice; practice challenges and enhances the understanding of faith. They mutually enlighten and confirm one another and in the dialectical process the human person grows in religious and moral maturity.

THE CHRISTIAN SYMBOL SYSTEM

It is the task of moral theology to inquire into the specifically Christian symbol system, seeking for the attitudes and convictions appropriate to those symbols as well as for the way of life that flows from the attitudes and convictions. Initially, it is not so much specific forms of behavior that are the focus of interest in moral theology, as it is a vision or a pattern of life. While it is hardly possible here to investigate all the symbols of the Christian faith, a brief look at some of the major symbols will provide us with an understanding of the basic pattern of life and the attitudes and convictions that sustain and nourish that way of life.

The Revelation of God

The God revealed in the life, death and resurrection of Jesus of Nazareth, whom Jesus addressed as "Abba, Father" (Mk 14:36), is not fully intelligible apart from the religious experience of the people of Israel. For the God Jesus called Father, he also called the God of Abraham, Isaac and Jacob (Lk 20:38). This God is, above all else, beyond human understanding and imagining. His thoughts are not our thoughts; his ways are not our ways (Ps 139). He is mystery, which is not to say God is unknowable, but that he is inexhaustible, unfathomable depth. What is known about God always falls far short of the reality, always leaves more to be known. Like all mysteries, knowledge of them requires revelation. God, if he is to be known at all, must make himself known. Graciously in his goodness and love he has done so.

From the perspective of Catholic theology this revelation has four main locations. God has made himself known in the work of creation. As St. Paul expressed it: "what can be known about God is perfectly plain . . . since God himself has made it plain. Ever since God created the world his everlasting power and deity—however invisible—have been there for the mind to see in the things he has made" (Rom 1:19–20). In his creation God is revealed as good, indeed as perfectly good, since everything he made was good (Gen 1:31). It was good precisely because God had made it, so that God is, as the Letter of James expressed it, the Father and source of all that is good (Jas 1:16–17).

A second major place where God has made himself known is in the history of the people of Israel. As he did in creating, so also here, God initiates action by entering into a relationship with them that is covenantal in nature, a relationship of mutual pledge and promise. Its simplest expression is: I will be your God and you will be my people. The covenant is activated and renewed through a series of covenantal promises to Abraham, Isaac, Jacob, Moses, David, Solomon and so on. In this relationship God is revealed as the initiator of the relationship, as jealous for his people, as stern and just, as quick to punish sin and quick to show mercy. But through all the vicissitudes of history he is revealed above all else as faithful to his promises so that the chief characteristic of God, what marks him as God in Israel's eyes, is his everlasting, steadfast love (Ps 136).

Throughout the Hebrew Scriptures, however, there is a persistent tension in Israel's relationship with God. The tension is not on Israel's side, for the people can and do recognize their own weakness and need for mercy well enough. The repeated cycle of Israel's apostasy, punishment, repentance and deliverance which characterizes the Deuteronomic historian's account of Israel's history shows this recognition. The tension is in their understanding of God's part in the relationship. Is God's fidelity to Israel and to his promises conditional or absolute? Is it dependent upon Israel's fidelity to the covenant so that God will love his people and continue to be for them only if they earn his love by their obedience? Or is his love plainly and simply absolute,

without conditions of any kind, so that God will be true to his
word no matter what Israel does?

The New Testament resolves this tension in its understanding of God's revelation in Christ. Jesus as the Word made flesh,
as the Lamb of God, as Lord and Christ and Savior, is the one
who most fully and definitively reveals to us what God is like in
his attitude toward us. God is like Jesus. Whoever sees Jesus gets
the clearest glimpse of God. In him we have the best clue to the
character of God.

At this point it would seem important to remind the reader
that Jesus is not to be simply equated with God. To say without
qualification that Jesus is God is theologically inaccurate. The
Christian God is Trinitarian, Father, Son, and Holy Spirit. Even
Jesus does not remove or exhaust the mystery that is God. He is
himself in his humanity a symbol that points beyond himself to
the one he called Father and with whom he is one in the unity of
the Holy Spirit. Or, in the phrase of the eminent Dutch theologian, Edward Schillebeeckx, Jesus is the sacrament of the encounter with God.

Briefly recall what was said above about symbols, for there is
an important point to be understood here. Symbols have reality
in and of themselves. They are not nothing; they are not empty
signs or imaginary things. Jesus was truly a human being, a man
in history about whom a number of factual things can be said.
But symbols have their full meaning, their true worth only in reference to that which they symbolize and make present to us. Symbols, then, participate in and make present that which they symbolize. As the primary symbol of God, Jesus can truly be called
divine because he participates in the divine life. To encounter him
is to encounter God symbolically or sacramentally, which is to say
in a real, but mediated way. But, as is the case with any symbol,
one can encounter Jesus and miss the point, fail to see the symbolic meaning. That is why the critical question in Christian faith
and ethics is the question Mark has Jesus address to his disciples
in the very center of his Gospel: "Who do you say that I am?"
(Mk 8:29). If that is the central question, then the attitude central
to the ethical existence of the Christian is what is called conversion or repentance and faith. For when one is confronted by

Jesus and asks: "What should I do?" the answer always is, "Repent, and believe the good news" (Mk 1:15).

The God, then, that Jesus reveals to us and symbolizes in his own person is a God with a single, unrelenting attitude toward human beings. He loves them unconditionally, without limits, freely, without distinction. He is a God of unlimited graciousness who loves his creatures, not because he finds something attractive or worthy in them which draws his love, but because of who and what he is in himself. God is not a reactor to goodness, truth and beauty as we human beings are, but the initiator of them. God does not respond to or reward love and goodness; he originates them. His love is totally free and without strings attached. It is what, theologically, we call grace—a pure gift. But this love is not a form of indifference, not a love that loves everyone because it loves no one in particular, or that cannot be offended because it does not really care. God's love as revealed in the covenant with Israel and in the person of Jesus is intensely personal and passionate, so much so that blindness to or rejection of that love can move Jesus to tears and to anger (Lk 19:41; Jn 9:39–41). While God's love is clearly a demanding love, it is no *quid pro quo*. There is literally nothing God wants from us for his own benefit. His love is for us, so that the early Church Fathers could rightly affirm *gloria Dei, vivens homo*—the glory of God is the fully alive human being.

The Revelation of the Human

In revealing God to us as a loving, saving God, Jesus at the same time reveals to us the true human condition before God. He reveals us to ourselves, both as to what we are and what we may become. We are sinners, lost sheep who have gone astray, prodigal sons who have left their father's house and fallen into slavery, blind people led by blind guides, people of deaf ears and hardened hearts, children of the evil one who prefer darkness to light. This is no trivial matter, for it may result in everlasting darkness, in being lost forever. It is not God's desire for us to be lost: "He wants everyone to be saved and reach full knowledge of the truth" (1 Tim 2:4). Jesus came, according to the Gospel of John, "that they may have life and have it to the full" (Jn 10:10). He is the door that opens unto life; indeed he is himself "the way, the truth and the life" (Jn 14:6).

There is also a fourth place or source of the revelation of God. Jesus, of course, is no longer among us in the flesh. But he has not left us alone. His Spirit has been poured out on all those who believe in him. His Spirit, the life-giving Spirit, gives life to the community called Church, inspires its Scriptures which bear witness to what God has done in Christ, and continues to guide and instruct the community of the faithful on its pilgrimage through history. The Spirit does not reveal new or additional things, for the Spirit does not speak of himself. Rather the Spirit enables us to penetrate ever more deeply into the basic mystery of God in Christ. The Holy Spirit of God both challenges and comforts, disciplines and enlightens us, individually and collectively, leading us always toward the fullness of divine and human unity for which Jesus prayed at the Last Supper: "May they all be one. Father, may they be one in us, as you are in me and I am in you" (Jn 17:21).

The Structure of the Moral Life

Since religion and morality draw their dominant themes and overall structure from the articulated experience of God which has inspired them, we are now in a position to indicate the basic structure of the moral life as portrayed for us in the sacred Scriptures. We find a pattern of divine action and human reaction. God initiates in creation, in history, in Jesus, in the Church through the Spirit, a relationship of love. He offers himself and continues to offer himself to us. We respond in freedom. That is the essence of Christian morality. The human choice is fundamentally a choice to say yes or no to God's offer of himself in love.

This basic structure of the moral life may be called covenantal or dialogic. It is a structure for which human conversation is a useful analogy for gaining insight into the divine-human relationship. While human conversation serves many particular purposes, one general note about it is that it always seeks some kind of communion, a oneness of mind, of feeling, of purpose, of outlook. In conversation that is authentic, the dialogue partners seek to understand and be understood, to come to, as we say, a meeting of the minds. We share our thoughts, our feelings, our fears and aspirations, as a way of arriving at this oneness. So it is in the divine-human dialogue, as the Scriptures see it. In giving his gifts to us, God seeks to give himself. In creation, in history, God speaks his mind and heart to us. In this context we can understand the wisdom of the Gospel writer in calling Jesus the Word of God.

One basic difference between a human dialogue and the dialogue with God lies in the nature of God. God is always the initiator of the dialogue and is always faithful to it. This difference has two important implications. First, the mutual expressions of sorrow and forgiveness which are essential in human dialogue are one-sided in the dialogue with God. The words of sorrow and repentance, of inadequacy and failure to be less than truthful, are always ours. The words of forgiveness and reconciliation are always God's and are available to us for the asking. In the technical sense of the matter, the previous description is correct. From the perspective of practical spiritual growth, however, and moral and psychological honesty and well-being, it is often necessary for us to fight with God, to complain about his ways, and even to forgive him for our griefs and hurts and disappointments, as the example of the prophets and saints can teach us. If we do this with sincerity and perseverance, we will, of course, find ourselves in the long run joining in with the prayer of Job.

> I know that you are all-powerful: what you conceive, you can perform. I am the man who obscured your designs with my empty-headed words. I have been holding forth on matters I cannot understand, on marvels beyond me and my knowledge. . . . I knew you then only by hearsay; but now, having seen you with my own eyes, I retract all I have said, and in dust and ashes I repent (Jb 42:2–6).

The second important implication of God's initiative and fidelity in the divine-human dialogue has to do with the reactive nature of the human response. We human beings do not, as we often do with one another, take the initiative in the dialogue with God. We do not do things or say things before God to which God can be asked or expected to respond. No deeds, no words of ours can demand a response from God. No prayer, no fasting, no promise, no good work can place a claim upon God for a response. For in encountering God, we encounter the One who is supremely free and sovereign, offering to us a love that is so selfless and so free that it can in no way be manipulated or coerced. It is here that we discover the demanding, obligating nature of the divine love. To experience the divine love and freedom, even in our limited human and mediated way, is to experience the divine claim on our total loyalty and obedience. The blinding holiness of God before which humans bow in awe and reverence is no abstract quality, but a feature of the supremely free love that has given us to ourselves, given itself totally to be for us, and will settle for nothing less. It is to find oneself caught up into a conversation that is without limit and without end.

To this point I have been trying to describe a model or pattern of the Christian life as a profoundly personal dialogue with God which God initiates and to which we, in our freedom, respond. The basis of this life is God's self-communication to us in creation, in history, and most fully in Jesus. In turn, Jesus' own totally faithful response to the Father, accepted and confirmed in the resurrection, serves as the model for our own response. The foundation or basis of all moral obligations in the Christian life is, then, the gift of faith sealed in baptism and nourished in the Church through word and sacrament. Faith in Jesus tells us who we are before God and leads to the most basic of all moral demands: Be and become who and what you are.

The life of dialogue with God is made possible by the outpouring of God's own Spirit into our hearts which enables us to be what Jesus was and is, one with the Father in the unity of the Holy Spirit through our unity with him. Or it enables us to be wholehearted lovers of God and one another. Hence, the Christian understanding of moral existence and its vision of life is essentially Trinitarian, as is the Christian understanding of God. If we keep this Trinitarian vision in mind, it will help us to understand why more than the Scriptures need to be consulted in making our moral decisions.

Truth, Freedom, Love

The Trinitarian vision, the mystery of God in Christ, provides the setting or the context in which Christian ethics must be placed. The context itself does not solve particular problems nor does it specify concrete obligations. But it does generate attitudes and convictions, the most basic of which have been traditionally classified as the three theological virtues, faith, hope and love. These in turn lead to a commitment to action and to a special way of life that I shall characterize here as a life of freedom and love. There is a line in the Gospel according to John which has Jesus describe the effect on his disciples of faith in him: "If you make my word your home you will indeed be my disciples; you will learn the truth and the truth shall make you free" (Jn 8:31–32). What we are made free for is to love one another in freedom as he has loved us. A brief reflection on the dynamic relationship of faith to truth, of truth to freedom, and of freedom to love will provide an apt conclusion to this chapter on the relationship of religious faith and moral practice.

There is noticeable in human affairs an interesting progression from faith to truth to freedom to love. There is nothing unique to religious faith about this progression. It is operative in every area of human life. All knowledge, all coming to know the truth of any kind, starts in faith. Faith is not to be equated or identified with knowledge and truth, although there certainly can be true and false faiths. Faith is rather the necessary pre-condition of knowledge and truth. This claim can be supported clearly through some basic illustrations.

Before I seek to know anything at all, before I begin the pursuit of truth, I must first entrust myself to others and believe, or take the chance, if you will, that knowledge is a real human possibility. To learn the truth as a child, I started out trusting my parents, my teachers, my elders. Even when or if I came to learn that such faith in them was often misplaced, that they did not know everything and did not always tell the truth, I learned that I came to know the truth only because I first had faith. To learn whether the love I felt for a particular woman and she, in turn, felt for me was a true love, I had to believe that it was and commit myself to her. In doing this I may come to learn that it is true love; I may come to learn that it is only a counterfeit. But I shall come to know the truth either way only by first entrusting myself to the relationship. One can multiply illustrations, but faith keeps appearing as a necessary pre-condition for coming to know the truth. In the process a particular faith may be confirmed or unconfirmed by what I come to know. But faith remains essential to knowing.

Knowing the truth sets us free. Enhanced freedom is a sign and a consequence of the truth, as is being argued so eloquently today by liberation theologies. Freedom follows the truth because truth has, of its very nature, a liberating and an enabling power. First of all, truth liberates in the sense that it sets us free from the illusions, barriers and obstacles that have falsely limited us and constricted our space for action. Truth frees because it removes limits; it sets us free from something. This removal of limits as an aspect of freedom explains both our experience of freedom as a pleasant and desirable thing, as well as popular and philosophical understandings of freedom as being allowed to do whatever I want to do. This aspect of freedom recognizes that freedom is a matter of being situated in the proper circumstances. To this extent freedom has a passive or receptive dimension; someone else can give this freedom to me.

The capacity of truth to remove limits can also be illustrated by any number of examples, and I have yet to find a single counter-example to refute this claim about truth. Two brief examples will serve the purpose of illustration here. Take an acquaintance whom you mistakenly believe has wronged you. This false belief is a barrier to your relationship. It limits and constrains both of you in your perceptions, feelings and actions in regard to one another. It also constrains the actions of your other acquaintances in their dealings with you. But when you come to know the truth, these constraints are removed. You are set free from the limits that have inhibited a free and easy relationship. Or take a person who lives under the illusion that he is superior to other human beings and so is not bound by the ordinary rules of common decency and social cooperation. While this illusion may produce the additional illusion of being free from all social restraints, such is not in fact the case. The rules of social existence, both written and unwritten, do not disappear. They now coerce and threaten the person, and are experienced as hindrances rather than helps to human living. The person in our example is unable to enter into relationships of freedom and equality with other human beings, and must be on constant guard to preserve the illusion of superiority. This is a person who is not free, but driven. To learn the truth, to have the illusion of superiority destroyed, is to have the barriers removed that have prevented a free and equal social life.

Truth not only has the capacity to liberate or set us free from limits. It also has an enabling power; it sets us free for something new. It places new possibilities before us in the sense that we now *can* do something, not merely that we *may* do it. Where truth does not enable in this strong sense, the prospect of freedom is terrifying and one can be sure that it is not truth which has been grasped but one more illusion. It is possible, and unfortunately a common enough human experience, to exchange one illusion for another illusion, one form of slavery for another. In such cases there is neither truth nor freedom. To use the previous example once again, replacing the illusion of superiority with the illusion of inferiority neither liberates nor enables new relationships of freedom and equality. It merely trades one master for another.

It was Jesus' claim that through faith in him, we come to know the truth about the unconditional love of God for us now and always. This truth sets us free from the enslaving power of sin, guilt, death and the law, and enables us to live in the freedom of God's own children and heirs. That is to say, we are enabled to love one another as he has loved us. That describes the basic structure and dynamics of Christian moral existence. About this structure one final point needs to be made.

The structural progression of faith, truth, freedom and love that has been described is exactly a progression. It involves a process that feeds upon and continuously repeats itself. To grow in truth is to grow more free, is to be able to love more deeply and selflessly, is to have one's faith confirmed. To grow in faith is to entrust oneself still more fully to the mystery of God in Christ, to enter more profoundly into the truth, and the progression continues. The human experience of faith, of truth, of freedom, of love, reveals them to be dynamic, developing, inter-related realities, not fixed, unrelated, once-for-all possessions. Clearly, then, one of the basic attitudes appropriate to Christian faith as it addresses the world is an openness to and acceptance of personal responsibility for one's own growth and development. Joined to this openness and acceptance of personal responsibility will be a respect for the basic structure and limits of human being and becoming. It is, therefore, time to turn our attention to the nature of the human person as a moral agent.

STUDY QUESTIONS

1. What are the major symbols of happiness and success held up to you by society? Do they affect your attitudes toward life?

2. Are there indications in your human experience of how human beings are influenced by these "symbols of success"?

3. What are your favorite images of God? What do they say to you about the character of God?

4. If God loves us no matter what we do, what meaning do the symbols of heaven and hell have?

5. Can you trace the structural progression of faith, truth, freedom and love in one experience in your own life?

6. How deeply does the hope that life is worth living run in you? In what ways does this hope manifest itself?

BIBLIOGRAPHY

Burtchaell, James T., C.S.C. *Philemon's Problem: The Daily Dilemma of the Christian.* Chicago: ACTA, 1973. A brief, highly readable volume relating basic Christian beliefs to basic ethical attitudes and practices.

Greeley, Andrew M. *The New Agenda.* Garden City: Doubleday and Company, Inc., 1973. An excellent work showing how Christian symbols shed light on various aspects of Christian life and experience. The author offers a superb contrast to other less experiential ways of dealing with religious beliefs.

Häring, Bernard. *Free and Faithful in Christ, I.* New York: The Seabury Press, 1978. The first volume of the noted German theologian's trilogy develops at length some of the themes stressed in this chapter. Wordy but rewarding.

Niebuhr, H. Richard. *The Responsible Self.* New York, Evanston and London: Harper & Row, Publishers, 1963. The posthumously published work of one of America's most influential Protestant ethicians, detailing the moral life as a response to God's action. This is a seminal work on the topic of Christian responsibility.

3 The Person as Moral Agent

Human beings are an interesting combination of difference and sameness, possessing characteristics that are at one and the same time unique and yet common. Each one of us is unique, different from all other beings. No one else ever has had or will have precisely the same characteristics, personal history and human experience that is our own. No one else will ever be who I am. The song that has become the theme song of the Marriage Encounter movement has it exactly right: *There Will Never Be Another You.*

Yet even while we acknowledge the joy and the burden of our own unique selves, we also recognize all sorts of common qualities or characteristics in existence which are widely shared by all sorts of beings. There are all kinds of ways in which we function and act that are so similar to the ways other creatures function that we do not appear to be unique at all. This combination of sameness and difference is the basis for an initial distinction that must be made in moral theology. It is the distinction between human acts and the acts of a human.

HUMAN ACTS

If we begin our reflection with what is common to all creatures, the first thing we notice all created reality to have in common is the act of existence. Everything that is, is. To be is to do something—it is to exist. There is nothing uniquely personal or human in the sheer act of existence. To exist is something human beings do in common with chairs and cabbages and cows. To exist is certainly an act of a human, since humans do exist, but it is not a specifically or uniquely human or personal act.

When we begin to notice differences and so to make distinctions in created reality, one of the more obvious bases for these distinctions is the difference we do see in the way creatures function or act. We notice, for example, that some creatures grow, take in nourishment, reproduce themselves, while other existing realities do none of these things. Some creatures are alive, we say, and others are not alive. Accordingly, we distinguish between animate and inanimate reality on the basis of growth or development. The acorn grows into the oak tree, the egg grows into the chicken, the human embryo grows into the adult person. To be alive is to act, indeed it is to perform a whole range of acts, but again there is nothing uniquely personal or human about being alive or doing the actions common to all living things. Growing, for instance, is certainly the act of a human since human beings are alive and do grow, but there need be nothing specifically human about such an act.

Among living beings we also notice differences in the way they act or function. Some living beings are self-moving, react to noise, smells, tastes, reproduce sexually, while others do not do these things. Hence we distinguish between animal and vegetative life, but only the former performs actions involving spatial motility and sensory reaction. Of course, human beings include themselves in the animal category because they, too, move themselves about, react to sensations, and perform all kinds of actions that are also done by birds, beagles and butterflies. These actions must be called acts of a human when they are done by human beings, but there is often nothing uniquely personal or human about merely walking or eating or coming in out of the cold.

Finally, in our focus on common behaviors, we notice one category among the creatures we call animals which performs actions that no other animals perform. The species of animal we have come to call rational has developed languages, written books, organized businesses, created systems of law and religion, established armies and invented elaborate ways of planning for and waging war. Activities like these, and numerous others, lead us to think there is something unique or specific about this category of animals. The members of this category possess some qualities or capabilities that distinguish human beings from all other kinds of created beings. Traditionally we have named these capacities reason and free will.

Acts which involve the use of reason and free will are certainly acts of a human, for they are done by human beings. But
they are also specifically human acts. They have a quality about
them that other acts of a human do not have or may not always
have. It is this quality which marks them as special and leads us
to hold human beings morally responsible for such acts. Human
acts, unlike mere acts of a human, are moral acts, subject to moral
analysis and evaluation or, more simply, to moral praise or blame.

Self-Awareness

If we pause to reflect on this analysis of our differences and
similarities, two important features about human beings emerge.
First, the uniquely human capacities traditionally called reason
and free will are both rooted in a capacity which human beings
evidence to varying degrees but no other material beings do. That
capacity is self-awareness or reflective self-consciousness. It is not
that human beings are aware of reality or conscious of the
demands and complexity of being alive. It is not simply that
human beings know this or that. Animals, at least, give evidence
of such awareness and knowing. Surely my pet dog is aware when
I come into the house and knows that it is I, not a stranger. Cows
know their calves, birds know how to build nests. All animals give
evidence of awareness or knowing.

What is unique about human beings is that their awareness
is a self-awareness. They are aware of being aware of the world.
Their knowing involves a knowing that they know. Their being
conscious includes a self-consciousness, a reflexive awareness of
the self as being conscious of being conscious. My dog knows
me—at least it gives every evidence that it knows me. But it shows
no signs of knowing that it knows, which is why it did not have a
present wrapped and waiting for me on my last birthday. It is
precisely this knowing that we know, this being aware of being
aware that is the unique human quality which confronts human
beings with the need to think rationally, to weigh alternatives, to
make judgments and to act freely rather than instinctively upon
them, and to evaluate the consequences of their acts. We can,
therefore, conclude that a human act, as opposed to a mere act
of a human, is one in which a degree of self-conscious awareness
is involved. Only those acts which are to some degree self-aware

acts are truly human acts. We act in a specifically human way, in a moral way, to the degree that we know what we are doing and why. Moral action, then, requires self-awareness, and growth in self-awareness increases the human capacity for moral action, a most important point to which we will return later.

Freedom

A second important feature about human beings which is revealed in the analysis of our sameness and uniqueness is that not all their acts are free, self-conscious acts for which they are morally responsible. Human freedom is, therefore, a limited freedom, a conditioned freedom or, more accurately, I think, a structured freedom. Much of what we human beings do, we do at the dictate of various necessities or determinisms. These determinisms take many forms: psychological, sociological, biological, chemical, physical. Some of them we may be consciously aware of; others may be hidden from us. But in either case these determinisms structure and limit the range of human freedom and responsibility.

Examples of these determinisms are not hard to find if we recall the difference between human acts and the acts of a human. All acts of a human are determined by something other than the self-awareness of the human agent. Consider some of the most common human actions. We sleep because we must; we eat and drink because we must; we seek pleasure and avoid pain because we must; we try to make sense out of things because we must. We see with our eyes, hear with our ears, reproduce ourselves by using our sexual organs because we must. We are determined by something other than our self-awareness and freedom to act in these ways. It is because of these determinisms that we can speak of having a human nature, imprecise as such a concept is.

These determinisms structure human freedom but do not abolish it. They press upon us, individually and collectively, with different degrees of necessity. All human beings, for example, are under the necessity to sleep. But when we sleep, how much, with whom and under what circumstances are not matters equally determined. All human beings must eat, but this necessity leaves great room for human choice so that what is, of necessity, an act of a human can, if we wish, also be a truly human act. All human beings are under the psychological necessity to seek emotional equilibrium, but the ways in which such equilibrium can be achieved are not equally determined.

Furthermore, as we become consciously aware of these determinisms, as we come to know that we know of these determinisms, the range of our freedom is increased. Knowing that we know of these determinisms does not abolish them but it lessens the degree of necessity with which they press upon us and enables us to turn more and more acts of a human into truly human acts as well. As a person, for instance, comes to understand his or her own sexual nature, its drives and dynamics, he or she is much less at the whim of impulse and instinct and is enabled to act sexually in freer and more responsible ways. Responsible parenthood, for example, becomes a matter for human decision. Or again, as we come to know the necessities under which our physical environment requires us to live and act, both our ability to act wisely and our responsibility to do so is enhanced.

The limited or structured nature of human freedom, then, and human self-awareness are intimately related to one another. Self-awareness is the essential pre-condition of human freedom and morality. Freedom and morality, in turn, invite growth in self-awareness, so that the major moral responsibility of human beings is to act ever more humanly, to add an increasingly human dimension to the acts of a human.

Impediments to Freedom

Recognizing that there are limits to human freedom and responsibility enables the moral theologian to take cognizance of those realities which impede human freedom and so either mitigate or abolish human responsibility. It is possible to construct a general list of such impediments and to describe how they work. Impediments to freedom are basically of two kinds. There are, first, those impediments located in the situation in which we find ourselves. These have been traditionally called actual impediments, because they are either actually present here and now or they are not.

The circumstantial or situational nature of these impediments to human freedom deserves to be underlined. The imped-

iments exist as impediments only because of the particular circumstances or situation. In a different situation the impediment
is either no longer present or is present but is not an impediment.
Among actual impediments are to be counted such things as the
threat of violence, ignorance, and the absence or shortage of
material resources. So, for instance, a sales clerk who is forced at
knife-point to take money out of a cash register is not held
responsible for an act of stealing. Or a doctor who is ignorant of
the fact that the medicine he or she prescribes for a patient will
have a lethal effect is not held responsible for an act of murder.
Of course the degree to which actual impediments lessen moral
responsibility depends upon the circumstances of each case and
can only be assessed in the context of a particular situation. But
it is important to recognize the possibility of such impediments
before accusing ourselves of moral failure.

A second kind of impediments to human freedom is located
not in the situation but in the condition of the moral agent. Traditionally labeled virtual or habitual impediments, they are carried by the person from situation to situation. It is not enough or
even necessary to change the situation to abolish the impediment.
The person would have to change. Among such impediments can
be counted one's psychological personality, one's physical capabilities, one's stage of moral development, and such character
features as prejudice, scrupulosity, or emotional immaturity.
Again the degree to which these impediments lessen or abolish
moral responsibility can only be assessed on a case to case basis,
but one illustration may prove helpful.

Prejudice is a learned but unconscious attitude. Few prejudiced people regard their way of looking at those they are prejudiced against as skewed or biased. It appears to them as natural
or normal, as something taken for granted. Of course, certain
events may conspire to reveal our prejudices to us, at which point
we have the responsibility to try to change our attitudes and at
the least to try to avoid acting on the basis of prejudice. But
unless and until we see prejudice for what it is, we are not fully
responsible morally for our prejudiced acts. That is to say, we
cannot be morally obliged to do what it is beyond our capacity to
do. We cannot fairly be told that we ought to do what we cannot
do.

Now the reason why moral theologians recognize and try to list the impediments to human freedom is not to excuse people or exempt them from their moral responsibilities. Originally the discussion of impediments developed to help confessors evaluate the degree of responsibility their penitents had for their actions and so assign the proper penance. With a less juridical understanding of the sacrament of reconciliation today, this is no longer the primary purpose for discussing impediments, though the discussion may still prove helpful to confessors and penitents. There are two significant reasons for entering into this consideration of impediments, which are worth some attention.

First, in the context of a structured human freedom, it is important neither to under-emphasize nor over-emphasize the range of human freedom and responsibility. To over-emphasize the range of freedom can only lead to frustration, the assuming of unwarranted guilt, and ultimately to despair and an abandonment of moral effort altogether. To ask ourselves or others to do more than we are able to do here and now is to fail in justice. It is also to fall prey to two other equally harmful realities: false guilt and false expectations. To find oneself asked to do what one simply cannot do is to experience constant failure and a lowering of self-esteem. Self-loathing, a persistent sense of worthlessness, is neither psychologically nor spiritually healthy. At the same time, to expect more of ourselves or others than they are capable of is to abolish compassion and mercy from our relationships without which qualities they cannot be sustained.

On the other hand, to under-emphasize the range of freedom and responsibility, to think that impediments simply abolish freedom, is to forfeit what makes us truly human, to succumb to necessity prematurely and without reason. Indeed, it is a form of idolatry, for it grants sovereignty to what is not sovereign, denies our creation in the image and likeness of God and our freedom redeemed in Christ. The discussion on impediments, therefore, is a way to help reason find a way between two false extremes, the better to love our neighbors.

A second important reason for discussing impediments to human freedom is to emphasize once again the importance of self-awareness for moral growth and responsibility. To recognize the possibility of actual or virtual impediments determining my behavior is to push back the walls of necessity, to increase the space available for reasoned choice and free action. Recognizing the existence of impediments to freedom enhances our freedom by giving us an additional choice. We can choose to work to change the situation if we are facing actual impediments, rather than blindly submitting to necessity. Many people, for example, who are committed to working for social justice, are engaged in the effort to remove actual impediments like poverty, threats of violence or practical ignorance from our social circumstances so that all people may have a more fully human life. Other people who devote themselves to helping individuals cope with problems like drug addiction, physical disabilities or emotional immaturity are at work removing virtual impediments to human freedom and responsibility. Both kinds of commitments are to assist in making the acts of humans more fully human acts.

THE CONDITIONS OF FREEDOM

This discussion of impediments to human freedom and the structured nature of that freedom has reached the point where it is now possible to indicate the three necessary and sufficient conditions of human freedom. These three conditions are necessary, for without any one of them we remain under the rule of some form of determinism and necessity. They are sufficient conditions of freedom, for nothing else beyond them is required for freedom. The three conditions I will name space, power, and authority.

Space

In order to act humanly or freely, we human beings need space. We need the room to act, the chance or the opportunity to do what we have a mind to do. The circumstances of our world must be such that action is a real possibility. Without the necessary space we are unable to act. We are not free to do what we would do. The space we need to act, however, is not an empty void or limitless possibility, but a structured space, a defined possibility. Such space is created space, space deliberately constructed to hold off the forces both of chaos and of necessity. The notion of God's creative activity in the Book of Genesis is helpful here. God creates the world by bringing order out of chaos, by putting things in their proper place, by assigning due limits to earth, sky and water. Finally he creates a space for human life in the garden of Eden.

A simple reflection on our own experiences of freedom or the lack thereof further confirms the human need for a structured space. We often experience a lack of freedom because the space available to us is too confined, too constricting. Physically, for instance, the house may be too small for the number of people living in it to do the things they would like to do. Their need is not for no house at all, but for a house with more space. Emotionally, I may be so involved in my problems that I lose control over my actions. I need to achieve some distance from them so as to get my life under control. Economically, my financial burdens may press so heavily upon me that I am driven to work constantly to try to get out from under them, to get some breathing room, as we say. In any area of human life, our freedom can be constrained by a lack of sufficient space, be it physical, emotional, social, economic, political or spiritual space.

Oddly enough, however, too much space can be as inhibiting to free action as too little space. This fact is readily evident to us in the case of young children who find themselves unable to choose when confronted with too many opportunities, or intimidated by large physical spaces with no discernible limits. But more adult experiences are also illustrative of the same fact. Most adults would enjoy a degree of flexibility in how and when they meet the requirements of their job. At the same time they would find a completely unstructured job paralyzing. Without some guidelines as to what they are expected to do, acting becomes impossible. College students may enjoy optional classes and elective assignments, but they also want to have a clear idea of the requirements of the course. Without knowing what is too little and what is enough, that is, without a structured space for action, free rational action is impossible. More simply, houses can be too big, as well as too small. Emotional distance can be too great as well as too little. Having an assigned role in the social order can be inhibiting; having no role of any kind is paralyzing. Truly human acts, human freedom, require a definable space.

Space, then, as a necessary condition of human freedom, may be formally defined as the real, concrete opportunity to act. It exists when a person can truthfully say this action, this way of life is open to me, it is something I really *may* do. There is nothing preventing me from doing it. As a condition of freedom space is something that can be given to me as well as something I can, at times, create for myself. Individually and collectively we human beings are given space by God in his creation of the world with its manifold determinisms and necessities. But we also create space for our family living, our education, our political, economic and religious life by building homes, schools, legal, political and economic systems, churches, and so on. And because we grow and develop, so also must the spaces we create grow and develop, lest what once served human freedom come to inhibit it.

Power

The opportunity to act that I have called space is not all that is required for human freedom. In addition to space, we need power or the ability to act. It is simply not enough to have the opportunity to do something if we lack the ability to do it. Space without power is a cruel or a terrifying joke. Once again we can recognize this most clearly, perhaps, in the case of children. We do not give them certain opportunities, because we know that they lack the ability to take advantage of these opportunities. The need for power as well as space is also reflected clearly in the various liberation movements we can observe in our present world. Once barriers such as segregation laws or colonial rule or even social prejudices are removed, thereby affording people new opportunities for action, the cry immediately arises for power, for the ability to take advantage of these opportunities. Educational opportunities, for instance, are of little use to students who are unable to read. Economic opportunities are empty chances for those with no marketable skills.

Power, as a necessary condition of human freedom, may be formally defined as the real, concrete ability to act to achieve purpose. It exists when a person can truthfully say this action, this way of life is something I really *can* do. I have what it takes to do this. As a condition of human freedom power is not something that can be given by one person to another, except in an incipient or germinal fashion. It is rather something an individual or a group must develop for itself. In this way it is quite different than space which can be given, even against the will of the one receiving the opportunity. We can assist one another to develop power but we simply cannot give our power to another. We can use our power on behalf of others, but our ability to act in whatever way is and remains our ability. Parents, for example, can use their power to enhance the space available to their children and to help the children develop their own power. What they can never do is give their children their own ability, except in the most germinal way as a potential that can be developed.

The two conditions of space and power are plainly manifested in the Christian understanding of redemption, the gift of freedom in Christ. By being set free from the enslaving powers of sin and death, the Christian believer finds that his or her space has been enlarged. New opportunities for acting have been given to him or her. But redemption in Christ involves more than the forgiveness of sin. In baptism, the Christian believer is born again, receives in germinal fashion a new principle and power of life and action, the gift of the Holy Spirit. This gift of God's own Spirit is one that each individual receives as a gift but to which he or she must also respond freely to develop the new life. Christians have been enabled to love one another, but it is they who must do the loving. No one else can do it for them.

Authority

It might now appear that the person with both space and power has all that is needed for human freedom. To be able to say both *I may* and *I can* do this action, however, is not yet sufficient for freedom, albeit necessary. One condition is still lacking, the one I call, for want of a better name, authority. It manifests itself in human experience when to the words *"I may"* and *"I can"* a person adds, "and I ought to" do this action or embrace this way of life. For even if it is the case that I may be a theology teacher and have the ability to be one, there are a whole host of other things I may and can do as well. Until I come to know what I want to do, am called to do, should do, am authorized to do, what is the right thing to do, I either will not act at all, or will act at the dictate of whim, of necessity, or of someone else. Without authorization, my actions will not be fully my own, not determined by my own self-awareness, not fully human acts.

Authority, as a necessary condition of human freedom, is not susceptible to formal definition as were space and power. The chief hallmark of anyone or anything that counts as an "authority" in human life in the sense intended here is that we give authority unhesitating and unquestioning obedience. To many contemporary people this may be a troublesome claim since the language and the practice of obedience to authority has come in for considerable criticism. But such criticism does, in fact, support the claim being made here, for when we question our obedience, we also question the authority of the one claiming our action. We question the right of the one in authority to ask for this course of action, and by implication we question whether the proposed course of action is, indeed, right.

Since authority as a condition of human freedom cannot be formally defined, perhaps it can be explained by way of illustration. Let us try three examples here, and I invite the reader to think up many more of his or her own. In addition to space and power, what is essential to the existence and life of a free people in the political sense of the term? I would suggest that it is a recognized and accepted structure of authority, or more concretely a constitution which charts the rights and the obligations of both the citizens and the government. Without such an authority either tyranny or chaos is the result. About this authority three other points are worth noting briefly. One is that it is authority which structures the social space of the citizens precisely by defining rights, which are nothing but opportunities, affirmations of what they may do, and obligations which limit what they may do. Second, authority is not power, properly speaking, but it is essentially related to power in that it aids people to act together to achieve common purposes. Third, authority can remain authority and still be relative rather than absolute. The Constitution of the United States, for example, contains both limits on what authority itself may ask and a mechanism for changing the Constitution itself.

A second illustration may be drawn from the realm of education. Teachers have two kinds of authority. They are authorized to require assignments, give grades, insist upon order and discipline in class and make life miserable for students in other ways as well. But this authority is secondary and at the service of the other kind of authority they are expected to have. They are expected to be authorities in their field, to know what they are talking about, to understand the problems and unsolved questions in their discipline as well as the accepted facts and prevailing theories. To fail in this task is to lose all authority, and to turn what should be a service to freedom into a form of tyranny. We again might notice the relative nature of the teacher's authority. No teacher knows everything or is beyond questioning, even doubting in some matters. The teacher who admits that he or she doesn't know in response to a question doesn't lose authority. Indeed, such a truthful answer may enhance authority.

A third illustration of the need for authority in human freedom will have a more personal character. Imagine a young woman richly endowed with ability or power and given ample opportunity or space for exercising her power. At the same time she does not know what it is she really wants to do with her life, in what direction or to what purpose she wishes to expend her energies and talents. She has not yet taken charge of her life, despite the required power and space. Such a person can be described as one who has not yet found her calling, or who has not grasped the meaning and truth of her existence, or as one who does not yet know who and what she really is. Whatever the description, she lacks what I here am labeling authority. This is a subject to which we will return in a later chapter on conscience. Suffice it to say, without authority, whim and necessity will continue to prevail in a person's life.

MORAL DEVELOPMENT

Among the characteristics of the moral agent we have seen thus far, one in particular deserves more special attention. That characteristic is the developing nature of the moral agent. Human beings grow into or develop their sense of morality; they are not born with it already fixed. Hence the nature and process of moral development becomes a crucial question for moral theology. Fortunately, a considerable amount of research has been carried out in recent years, investigating the processes of cognitive, psychological and moral development. While there is certainly no definitive word or final theory available on the subject of moral development, some important directions of that development have been mapped out and the process by which development takes place can be roughly described.

The most obvious form of human development, one with which we are all familiar, is the process of physical development. A reflection on this process is a useful entry point into the whole notion of development. It is of the very nature of human beings to develop physically, and to develop according to a pre-determined pattern of growth which can be accurately described in terms of stages of growth. So the infant, having developed programmatically in the womb for nine months, is born, learns to roll over, sit up, crawl, walk, run and so on. Unless something in the child's environment, such as a disease, an accident, or parental abuse, intervenes, physical development takes place according to this invariant yet flexible pattern. The pattern is flexible in that the pace of growth varies from individual to individual. Some children, for instance, learn to walk at an earlier age than others. The age of puberty is different for different individuals. But the pattern is invariant for everyone. No one learns to run before learning to walk. No one enters upon puberty before the body has undergone certain physical developments.

This same invariant but flexible pattern of growth according to stages has been traced in human cognitive and psychological development. It also appears to hold true for human moral development. The eminent Swiss psychologist, Jean Piaget, has described the various stages of cognitive development that children pass through from infancy to early adolescence when they finally develop the capacity for abstract thought. He has further demonstrated how moral development, while different than cognitive development, is dependent upon it. That is to say, until the child has developed the capacity for certain forms of cognitive activity, he or she will not be able to grasp the meaning of certain forms of moral motivation and reasoning. This widely-agreed upon fact of dependency, however, raises the question of just what we mean by moral development and of how such development is to be measured.

The Meaning of Development

At the outset of the discussion of moral development, it is essential to emphasize that moral development is not the same thing as growth in holiness, though it is related to it. Children have a capacity for sanctity before their moral development is complete. Sanctity cannot be measured by psychological or other empirical criteria. What, then, is moral development all about?

In our ordinary, day-to-day talk, when we refer to someone as a good person or as highly moral, we are usually regarding that person's behavior. We make such statements based on our observations of what people do. A person strikes us as patient in dealing with children, or as generous with material goods, or as honest in speech. To develop morally in this sense would be to do more and more of these good actions. For those people who were brought up in a traditional Catholic educational setting, moral development and growth in holiness tended to mean the same thing. They meant, in the first place, that one committed fewer and fewer sins, that one's list for confession grew shorter or at least contained less serious matters. They meant, in the second place, that one grew in the number of virtuous acts performed on a regular basis. One prayed more, did actions to help others, gave money to the needy, volunteered one's time and energy to good causes. Understood in this way, moral development or growth in holiness was measured by action and to a lesser degree by the possession of those virtues or character-strengths related to action.

Students of moral development today do not understand it or measure it in this way for good reasons. They have learned that what people do and what they say about moral practice can be deceptive in providing real clues to the stage of moral development. A six year old child and a sixty-six year old adult can both tell the truth, lend their possessions to a neighbor and be kind to the family dog. They may both perform the same actions without being at the same stage of moral development. Equally, when asked to say what is morally right and wrong, they can recite the same words, e.g., the ten commandments. So neither words nor deeds alone give a clue to the stage of development of a person.

In addition to the above reasons, the importance of human intentionality in morality has once again come clearly to the fore.

It is a person's motivations, the reasons he or she has for thinking an act to be morally right or wrong, the intent behind the act, that is crucial to the moral quality of a person's actions. In more biblical language, "It is what comes out of a man that makes him unclean. For it is from within, from men's hearts, that evil intentions emerge . . . " (Mk 7:21). To study moral development, then, we must attempt to study a person's moral consciousness, the structure of reasoning and motivation in regard to action, the perception of what morality itself means to the person.

The Process of Development

To illuminate this study we may utilize the work of the outstanding American educational psychologist, Lawrence Kohlberg. His theory of moral development is certainly the most widely accepted and influential one available today, though not beyond question. Kohlberg's theory is easily stated, though not so easily explained. He argues that moral development is a process which involves the transformation of cognitive structures which occurs through a person's interaction with the social environment and as a result of experiences of cognitive disequilibrium. The process of development can be traced through three levels and six stages of development. These stages are flexible but invariant. Regression to a previous stage is not possible and an understanding of higher stages than one's own is limited to the stage immediately ahead of one's own. The foundation of this process of development is that the human person is by nature an organism constantly in search of greater equilibrium, an equilibrium which can be achieved in a constantly changing world only by continued growth.

Stated in this way Kohlberg's theory may seem to be hopelessly erudite and impenetrable. But it really is not if we think it out in concrete ways. To begin with the foundational fact, it does appear to be the nature of the human being to seek equilibrium or stability, to find some point of balance. If we stumble while walking, we instinctively reach out to regain our balance. If we experience an emotional upset, we instinctively look for a way to regain our emotional composure. If we encounter something that puzzles us intellectually, we naturally try to make sense of it. The equilibrium we seek may take many different forms and be pursued in a great variety of ways, but we do seek to live life on some kind of even keel.

How well anyone succeeds in achieving greater equilibrium depends to a large degree on one's social environment. It is, for instance, harder to gain our physical balance on an ice-covered hillside than on a dry, flat sidewalk. It is easier to gain our emotional composure in a tranquil atmosphere than in the midst of screaming children. Kohlberg offers a similar picture of the processes of cognitive and moral development. When our way of understanding and evaluating the world proves to be inadequate, we are thrown off balance and instinctively seek for more adequate ways of understanding and evaluating reality. The process of achieving equilibrium at this level is considerably slower and involves a far more complex interaction with the environment. Nor is the process automatic or guaranteed to succeed. Just as some people, for example, never learn to get their balance on ice skates and so fail to develop that physical ability, some people never achieve their moral balance in a way that promotes their moral development. Both the quality of one's social environment and the nature of one's interaction with that environment have a great deal to do with whether development occurs or fails to occur.

As one concrete example of this search for equilibrium and the process involved in it let me cite the college experience of a liberal arts student. The whole thrust of a liberal arts education that has any claim to authenticity is to provide the student with an experience of cognitive disequilibrium. It is deliberately intended to show students the inadequacy of their ways of understanding and evaluating reality. The experience is disorienting and can even be painful, alienating the students from traditional values and family ties. But the purpose of the education does not stop there. An authentic liberal arts education also challenges and helps students to develop more adequate ways of understanding reality, to regain equilibrium on a more truthful and more useful basis. The experience is afforded in the interest of students' development, which is why college teachers look upon it as a beginning of development that goes on through life and not as an end or a product to be possessed once for all.

The Stages of Development

The actual process of moral development Kohlberg has described in three levels, each of which has two stages. The levels of moral development are distinguished from one another on the basis that the person uses for making moral judgments, or on where one perceives moral value to be located. The stages of development have to do with the attitudes and motivations of the person making moral judgments. What develops in this process is the person's moral consciousness. The direction of growth or development is away from heteronomy toward autonomy, and toward an increased rationality in one's moral perceptions. While there are serious questions that can be raised about Kohlberg's theory of moral development, for our purposes here let us sketch this development in its basic and most agreed upon form.

There is a point in human life when we are simply unaware of any moral demands upon us at all. Until we reach approximately the age of two, we lack any awareness of moral rules, any sense of authority, any basis for moral judgments. Our lives are largely centered around our own needs and the experiences of pleasure and pain. During this stage zero, we lack any capacity for moral reasoning. Sooner or later, however, under the impact of our social environment, that is to say, our family, we do become aware of the existence of rules, that some acts are called good, others are called bad, some acts are rewarded, some are punished and some are simply ignored. Hence we start making moral judgments and have entered upon the process of moral development.

At the first level of development the basis of moral judgments is the physical consequences of an act. Moral value is located in external happenings or in physical needs and satisfactions. The intentions of the moral agent are of no account in assessing moral value. So, for example, to break ten dishes is a bigger moral fault than to break three. To speak a falsehood to six people is worse than to speak it to one. To strike an adult (a big person) is morally worse than striking a person of one's own size. A gift is better if it is bigger or more expensive. Moral value is perceived as if it were a thing independent of the will and purpose of moral agents. Hence it makes no real difference whether

one has done the act on purpose or not. The physical consequences are determinative of moral value.

Corresponding to this level are two distinctive stages of
moral development. The first stage can be characterized as an orientation to reward and punishment. An action, whatever it may
be, is wrong if it is punished, right if it is rewarded. This stage
reflects the altogether irrational belief that it is the punishment
which makes the action wrong and the reward which makes it
right. The focus of the person at this stage of moral development
is naively egocentric. All actions are judged in terms of how they
affect the self and so how they affect authority figures. The primary motivation for doing what is right is fear of punishment, a
punishment which is conceived of as magically connected to the
forbidden action.

A second stage of development is discernible at level one. A
greater degree of rationality enters in as the person begins to be
able to grasp that different people have different needs and
desires. Right action is now understood to be whatever satisfies
one's own needs and desires, and occasionally the desires of others. Human relationships take on the aspect of strict reciprocity.
I'll do this for you and you'll do that for me. The major motivation for doing the right thing is that it is the means for getting
what I want. And if I do the right thing, then I have a strict right
to get what I want. Anyone who has ever watched two little children hitting each other while yelling, "You hit me first," has a
clear example of stage two's mode of moral reasoning.

The second level of moral development finds its basis for
moral judgment to be certain social roles or expectations. Moral
value is located in conformity to these roles or expectations.
Again we can distinguish two stages at this level. Stage three may
be characterized as the good boy, nice girl orientation, an orientation marked by the desire to please others by living up to their
expectations. Right action is understood to be action that con-
forms to these expectations, though now the intentions of the
agent are often the decisive consideration in what counts as good
or bad. "I tried" and "I didn't mean it" are often heard at this
stage of moral reasoning. To have meant well is often held to be
sufficient, or even not to have meant to hurt or displease. This
stage of moral reasoning represents an advance in rationality in

that it takes into account the interests and intentions of others as having equal or greater weight than one's own.

The fourth stage of development takes into account a still broader perspective. It recognizes the need for social order and for maintaining this order, and so for general rules as a framework for everyone in society. This mode of reasoning is often referred to as a law and order mentality. It is seen to be essential that everyone do his or her duty. One important and distinctive feature of this stage of development is the concern for the earned approval of others. It is no longer enough to have meant well. It is important also to have done well, that is, to have fulfilled one's duty.

If we pause briefly to reflect on these first four stages, several points are of interest. First, what changes or develops in this process is not the substantive content of morality but the form of moral reasoning. Individuals at stage one and stage four may both agree that it is wrong to steal, but the reasons they would give for why it is wrong will differ. Second, the development toward greater rationality does not mean that the reasons given at an earlier stage were simply wrong. They were rather inadequate. It might well be true that I'll be punished if I steal your money, as a stage one person would tell me. What a stage three or four form of moral reasoning has grasped is that such an action is still wrong, even if I am not punished. Third, the process of development through the stages does not take place by leaving the old stage behind but by taking it up and incorporating it in the light of the new stage. That is why we can understand and still be partially motivated by the reasoning appropriate to earlier stages of development.

The most important aspect, however, about the stages of moral development to this point is that they all involve a heteronomic view of morality. The law *(nomos)*, the sense of obligation or authority, comes from without, from another *(hetero)*, not from the self. Why I should do something, my understanding of the "ought to do" in my experience, refers to someone other than myself or ourselves. The words "I ought to do" would more accurately be rendered as "I had better do" or "I must do" or "It is the only way or the best way to get along." Consequently, the content of one's morality is given from without by others and is not yet seriously questioned. A brief example can clarify this. Take an American soldier and a German soldier who fought for their respective countries during World War II. If they both gave as a reason why they should fight and kill that it was their duty to support and obey their government, they are both at a stage four level of moral reasoning and there is nothing to choose between them. They are unable to raise the question of whether justice is more on one side than the other, or even whether a just war is a meaningful term. It is only with the advance to level three and stages five and six of moral reasoning that such a question can be raised and the content of one's morality critically appropriated in self-awareness.

At the third level of moral development the basis of moral judgment is now taken to be shared and shareable standards or principles, and moral value is located in the conformity of oneself and one's behavior to these standards. Again two stages of development can be briefly distinguished. Stage five reasoning may be described as contractual. It recognizes that there is an arbitrary starting point in many of our rules, a starting point which has been chosen simply for the sake of agreement and is morally binding only because of that agreement. The decision to drive cars on the right or left side of the road is an example of such an arbitrary starting point. So, we ought to do certain things because we have agreed to do them. And, further, the rights and obligations we have as a result of such agreements can change if we agree to a new starting point. Contracts can be renegotiated when circumstances change. Agreements lose their binding force when the terms of agreement no longer exist. Moral obligation is seen to have its origin in mutual consent, and the primary reason for living up to one's moral obligations is that one gave one's word. At last, moral obligation is self-imposed or autonomous.

Finally, a sixth stage of moral development reflects a form of moral reasoning that is marked by an appeal to principles of logical universality and consistency. What is morally right is seen to be a decision of conscience in accord with universal ethical principles that respect the dignity and equality of all human beings. The major reason for doing what is morally right and good is precisely that it is the morally right thing to do, the fully human act most in accord with one's and others' human dignity as free, self-aware beings.

This sketch of moral development, which certainly, needs to be supplemented and amplified, leads us to three important conclusions about the human person as a moral agent. Once we recognize that our sense of and understanding of morality develops over time, we also recognize that we have at least a partial responsibility for fostering our own moral growth. Just as we assume some responsibility for our own physical growth and well-being, so also we have a responsibility for ourselves as moral beings. For this task a spirituality is essential, a conscious effort to learn how to interact with our social environment in ways that will promote growth or strengthen our lives of freedom and love. The spiritual practices and disciplines that some human beings make part of their lives, practices such as daily meditation, fasting, spiritual reading and so forth, do not find their meaning and value as ways to win God's favor or earn some reward. Such practices are ways to assume responsibility for one's own growth as a moral agent. More specifically they are a means to become more aware of the impact of our social environment upon us and to become more deliberate and purposeful in our response to that environment. Without such conscious attention, how will one discern or recognize the call of God's Spirit, how will one grow in moral awareness?

A second important conclusion to be drawn from the fact and the process of moral development is that human beings are, by their very nature, dynamically ordered to self-transcendence. Such technical language can, perhaps, be more clearly explained if we acknowledge our unrestricted desire to know and to love. No answers, no amount of understanding, ever satisfies our desire to know, at least in this life. No value, no experience ever fully satisfies the desires of our hearts to love and be loved. Like it or not, we have the capacity to go continually beyond ourselves, to know more widely, to love more deeply and universally. We can, of course, try to stifle this desire, refuse the capacity, prefer a closed attitude toward reality rather than an open one. Just as we can refuse our own physical development in a radical way by committing suicide, so also can we refuse moral development by a premature closure of our minds and hearts. We can blunt our self-awareness and turn our attention away from the demands of the real world. But we pay a very high price for such a choice. Once again, this dynamic drive toward self-transcendence argues for the need of a spirituality.

The third conclusion to be drawn from the phenomenon of moral development confirms the central moral message of Jesus, the demand for conversion as both the initial and the continuous center of the Christian life. Upon meeting the Lord and hearing his message, the question arises: What are we to do? The answer is always the same. "Repent and believe in the good news" (Mk 1:15). We may, then, conclude this chapter with a brief discussion of the meaning and importance of conversion in the Christian life.

CONVERSION

In the New Testament two Greek words are used to refer to conversion. One word, *metanoia,* means literally to have a change of mind and heart. If taken seriously, this means that we are called to think differently, to understand life in all its complexity in a new way, to put on the mind of Christ. It does not ask us to be blind to what we already see or to falsify what we know, but to see more deeply and more truthfully what is there to be seen, the grace and glory of God at work among us, as well as the power of sin to mar and distort reality. It asks us to evaluate and love life differently, to embrace what before we found distasteful, or to reorder our priorities so that what was once of small importance becomes of greater importance.

The second word for conversion, *epistrephein,* means literally to turn oneself around physically, to turn away from this and toward that. In the New Testament context, to turn away, for example, from the fishing boats and, leaving them behind, to turn toward and follow Jesus. When one turns oneself around physically, what happens is that one sees the world from a new perspective, one directs one's attention and interest in a new direction. It is this turning, this new way of attending to and intending that is the beginning of, and an ongoing need in, the Christian life.

Conversion, then, is crucial to our moral life precisely because it turns us toward wanting to love our neighbor, to the desire to love one another as Jesus has loved us. Conversion does not tell us concretely how to love the neighbor. It does not supply the content of our morality. It does, however, structure the form of our moral consciousness. It means that we come to understand all moral claims, all moral obligations as the demand of love, as the way we acknowledge and respond to the One who has first loved us. Conversion means that we want to know and love the good, that we want to be morally good and loving persons and are willing to accept the responsibility for trying to be that kind of person.

It is sometimes thought and taught that conversion is a dramatic, once for all or once in a lifetime experience. Occasionally this appears to be the case in the lives of some people. St. Paul and St. Augustine would seem to be examples of such dramatic and thoroughgoing conversion experiences. But even their life-stories indicate that appearances can be deceiving. For conversion is not simply an act of the will nor a permanent possession, however dramatic the initial experience of turning toward Christ may be. We are called to conversion by the events or experiences of our lives, by our interaction with our social environment, if you will. And that call is a repeated and continuous call. We grow into discipleship, we learn to walk in faith and hope, we develop in our desire to love one another. The example of Peter might serve us well here. Even after leaving his boat and following Jesus, Peter had to learn what such following entailed, had to repent on more than one occasion and believe again. God's grace, in short, is neither magical nor coercive. It is effective and powerful, but it works only in and through human freedom, a freedom which we have already seen is a concretely structured and developing freedom.

In discussing moral development, I have repeatedly mentioned our social environment. That points to another aspect of the human person as a moral agent—he or she lives in community, lives with other human beings, has a social nature as well as a personal nature that needs to be understood. So we turn next to a consideration of what society means for our efforts to love one another.

STUDY QUESTIONS

1. What are some examples of acts of a human which are not also human acts?

2. What are some actual impediments in your world which limit and structure your freedom? What are some virtual impediments?

3. Can you give some specific examples of how the lack of space, power or authority restricts your freedom?

4. Apply the stages of moral development to the practice of lying. What reasons would a person at each stage give for why lying is morally wrong?

5. Why is a spirituality necessary to foster the experience of conversion?

BIBLIOGRAPHY

Curran, Charles E. "Conversion: The Central Moral Message of Jesus," *A New Look at Christian Morality*. Notre Dame: Fides, 1970, pp. 25–71. A comprehensive essay on conversion which explores the many dimensions of the experiènce and shows the need for continuous conversion.

Duska, Ronald and Mariellen Whelan. *Moral Development: A Guide to Piaget and Kohlberg*. New York: Paulist Press, 1975. An easily accessible and readable introduction to the theories of Piaget and Kohlberg with useful applications to the practice of Christian education.

Dykstra, Craig R. *Vision and Character: A Christian Educator's Alternative to Kohlberg*. New York; Paulist Press, 1981. A useful corrective to Kohlberg's excessive rationalism by a Protestant theologian.

Hanigan, James P. "Conversion and Ethics," *Theology Today* XL, 1 (April 1983), pp. 25–35. A brief essay on the nature and process of conversion using biblical examples to indicate both the dimensions and the implications of conversion.

Monden, Louis, S.J. *Sin. Liberty and Law.* New York: Sheed and Ward, 1965. An old but still useful book dealing with some of the themes of this chapter; pp. 3–17 have a superb description of a person's response to moral obligation at the three levels of moral development.

4 The Moral Agent in Community

Philosophers, since the time of the ancient Greeks, have been fond of pointing out that human beings are by nature social animals. We live together in groups from the time of our birth until we embark on the solitary journey that is death. We are not, of course, the only animals that live together in groups or who are dependent upon others for our early training and socialization. But in keeping with what is distinctively human, we live self-consciously in groups and construct and order our social groupings deliberately in accord with our freely chosen intentions and purposes. Human beings, therefore, are more properly called political animals, as Aristotle noted, because they construct their social organizations in accord with some notion of the common good in order to realize consciously and freely chosen goals, not simply for biological survival.

SOCIAL NATURE—ITS MEANING
Despite the obvious fact of human sociality, it is not always so easy to say what having a social nature means and what the implications of it are for our moral existence. For in encountering society, we once again encounter one of the ambiguities of human experience. Marriage, for example, a fundamental social institution, can be embraced as a source of happiness and fulfillment or feared as a trap putting an end to growth and new experience. The family, the most basic of all social groups, can be both a blessing and a bane, a source of comfort and grief, a welcome protector and an inhibiting burden on our personal freedom. Other social institutions and groups show the same ambiguous face. Hence, it is important to try to come to grips with our social nature and its implications for our lives as moral agents.

76

To say that human beings are social by nature is to say a great deal more than that there are many of us inhabiting the same planet and that we therefore have to learn how to get along with one another. More than one philosopher in history has regarded the existence of and need for society and social organizations to involve a regrettable yet necessary loss of human freedom, so that the less one had to do with society the better. Such a view, I suggest, is badly mistaken and profoundly alien to Christian faith. To say that human beings are social by nature is also to say a good deal more than that it is enjoyable to have other people around with whom to share experiences, to collaborate on tasks too large for any one of us, and to assuage our loneliness. As welcome as all these opportunities for human interaction may be, our fellow human beings are not mere means to our own pleasure and satisfaction.

To recognize the social nature of the human person is to recognize that human beings need one another in order to be what they are—human. Human life is not possible in isolation; human development cannot take place apart from a human community. The second creation story in the Book of Genesis has a graphic way of expressing this truth. In looking at his creation, God saw that it was good, except for one thing. "It is not good that the man should be alone" (Gn 2:18). Human life needs other human lives in order to be human.

The extent of our essential inter-dependence on one another shows itself in numerous ways: in our conception and birth and early nurture, in our use of language, in the houses we inhabit, the food we put on our tables, the education we receive, the entertainment we enjoy, even the clothes we wear. We are made, nourished, protected, instructed and entertained by society even as we ourselves contribute to society's ability to do all these things. We are also imperiled, misinformed, disfigured and enraged by society even as we ourselves contribute to the deformation of society. The time and the place in which we live, our social environment, are not unimportant accidents of our personal being but constitutive elements of who and what we are. To ignore the social dimension of human life, to turn our backs on society, to contemn the social order, is to ignore, turn away from and contemn ourselves. Little wonder that St. Augustine advised his fellow Christians that "it is a wickedness to abandon society."

If such language seems too strong or to overstate the case, consider the example of individuals who do, in fact, attempt to turn away from sociality and seek the meaning of life in something other than divine and human fellowship. Take the miser who lives only for the accumulation of possessions, or the addict who lives only for the next high and the oblivion that drugs will bring. The twistedness of such human lives is clear for all but the most blind eyes to see. Consider the person who has rejected all ties to family, friends, church and country, all sense of inter-personal and social loyalty, and in the process has lost all human warmth and sensitivity. Reflect on the individual who claims to be a "self-made man" and in living out this illusion loses any semblance of gratitude and humility. Such a person forgets all that has been given to him, including his indebtedness for the very fact of his existence. While there is, to be sure, a healthy individualism appropriate to human life, an individualism that has lost sight of its social rootedness and continual social indebtedness is an individualism that has lost touch with the truth of its own existence.

Ambiguity

The traditional Christian symbols of heaven and hell help to throw light on the ambiguity of our social existence. Human life as we know it and experience it is neither a heaven nor a hell on earth. It is rather an ambiguous mixture of laughter and tears, pleasure and pain, understanding and ignorance, love and loneliness, life and death. We are, individually and socially, often the cause of both joy and grief to one another. The natural human striving is for life and light, love and laughter, yet the striving is often discouraged or deformed by the power of sin in the world. Jesus' promise is that our human striving has a final fulfillment, and the fulfillment requires others with whom to live and love and laugh. The symbol of heaven points to the fellowship with God and one another for which our restless hearts yearn. The symbol of hell, on the other hand, points to the void, to the utter emptiness, loneliness and darkness of a human life bereft of all relationships. There is and can be no passage to life and light, no sharing of love and laughter, except in the company of one another. Jesus' command to love one another as I have loved you is both the way toward and the definitive description of what the symbol of heaven represents.

THE FUNCTIONS OF SOCIETY

Our social nature finds its expression, not by living in some abstraction called society, but by its concrete rootedness in specific communities or social groups. We live in concrete families, occupy defined neighborhoods, are citizens of a definite state and country, attend a specific school, work for identifiable companies, belong to determinate organizations, are members of a particular church. These various communities to which we belong have great moral significance, a significance which we often overlook because we take them so much for granted. This moral significance of community can be elaborated under four main functions: the community is a transmitter of values, a shaper of personal identity, a teacher of skills, and a giver of mission.

Transmission of Values

Let us start with the community as a transmitter of values. Every social group holds certain convictions as to what is important to it. To join the group is quickly to be made aware of its values. If one is at all at home in the group, one will soon come to share these values to some degree at least. It is not necessary here to examine the dynamics by which the process of transmitting values occurs. It will be sufficient to notice the fact that all social groups transmit values to their members and to reflect upon some examples of the fact. The family will serve as the most obvious example. By the time a child has reached the traditional age of reason, seven, he or she is aware of what is and is not important to the family, what occasions are celebrated, which relatives are welcome, which foods are considered special and which ordinary, which achievements are praised and which ignored or condemned. The more cohesive and stable the family is, the more strongly are these values transmitted and the more definitively shaped are the attitudes and convictions of the individual family members.

Among the values the family passes on, one set of values is
particularly of interest here—the religious and ethical values the
family has. If religious belief and practice are ignored or given
little importance or emphasis, children will see little worth in religious values. The content of children's moral perceptions and the
importance they place on ethical values will reflect fairly accurately the moral practice of their parents and older siblings.
(Note: the reference is to the moral *practice* of parents, not to
what they teach or say.) Of course, as children grow, they become
members of other social groups besides the family: the class in
school, the playmates in the neighborhood, the girl scout troop,
the little league team and so on. These groups also transmit values, values which may in some instances be in sharp conflict with
the values of the family. Hence, social belonging leads to the process of weighing and choosing among competing values. But without social groups, the process would never begin at all.

This process of transmitting values is neither automatic nor
magical, though it is highly complex and even dialectical. Each
one of us contributes to the shaping of the values of the groups
to which we belong, even while we ourselves are being shaped by
those values. The process of transmission is initially one of which
we are largely unaware. But to the degree we develop our self-
awareness, our critical faculties come into play. We begin to recognize both a plurality of social groups and a plurality of competing values. We are faced with significant moral choices as to
which social groups we will support and which we will hold at a
distance. While our personal appropriation of values often
becomes self-critical at first in a way that distances us from social
groups, as reflected in the common remark, "I don't know what
I want to do and be, but I don't want to be like them," the appropriation of values always has this social referent.

However self-critically aware we become, the personal
appropriation of values does not and cannot take place apart
from community. It is the illusion of nihilism, anarchism and clas-
sical liberalism that the individual self is sufficient unto itself and
that the pursuit of self-interest or self-realization can be a sufficiently meaningful and trustworthy goal of human existence. For
such individualistic pursuits lead not to continual self-transcendence but to a closure of the self upon the self, and finally to

alienation and loneliness. In this context it is, perhaps, easier to understand the words which the Gospel of Matthew attributes to Jesus. "Anyone who finds his life will lose it, and anyone who loses his life for my sake will find it" (Mt 10:30).

The important role that social groups play in the transmission and personal appropriation of values argues for the moral importance of the choices we make to join particular social groups or to withdraw from them. Whom we take as colleagues or friends or co-workers, whom we reject as such, the systems and structures we develop to order our lives together, are not morally indifferent or insignificant matters. For the concrete form we give to our social natures will be one of the structural determinants of our freedom. More simply put, the communities to which we belong will serve either to enhance or to impede our freedom to love one another as we have been loved.

Shaping Identity

The second importance of the community for the moral agent is as a shaper of personal identity, a function closely related to the first function of the transmission of values. We come to know who and what we are and ought to do precisely in terms of the social groups with which we identify. I am, for example, both son and husband, indicating my identity with two different families. I am a theology teacher which reflects my identity with the university community of which I am part, as well as with the wider academic community of scholars. I am a citizen of the city of Pittsburgh, the state of Pennsylvania and the United States of America. I am also a member of the Roman Catholic Church. No one of these identities exhausts who and what I am, but all of them are intrinsic to who and what I understand myself to be. All claim my devotion and loyalty to a greater or lesser degree. They all tell me, in part, where I belong in the world and what I am about. Without some kind of rootedness in community, I would be nowhere and would not know what I should be doing.

On the other hand, as we come to know who and what we are in community, we also come to understand what the various social groups to which we belong may and may not rightly ask of us. One advantage of belonging to multiple social groups is the clarity we gain about their limits. No one social group is all-sufficient to human needs. No one social group, certainly not the state and not even the Church, may claim our absolute loyalty and obedience which belong to God alone. For all social groups exist not for their own sake but for the well-being of individual persons. Human beings do not exist for the sake of the social group.

There is a basic principle of Catholic social thought called the principle of subsidiarity which casts a clear light on the relationship of the individual to social groups. It was first formulated by Pope Pius XI in his encyclical letter *Quadragesimo Anno* in 1931 and has been used repeatedly by later Popes in their social teaching. Pope Pius XI expressed the principle this way:

> It is a fundamental principle of social philosophy, fixed and unchangeable, that one should not withdraw from individuals and commit to the community what they can accomplish by their own enterprise and industry. So, too, it is an injustice and at the same time a grave evil and a disturbance of right order, to transfer to the higher and larger collectivity functions which can be performed and provided for by lesser and subordinate bodies. Inasmuch as every social activity should, by its very nature, prove a help to members of the body social, it should never destroy or absorb them (QA 79).

If we examine this principle for a moment in regard to its practical implications, we notice that it establishes a complex set of inter-related mutual rights and obligations between the individual and his or her social groups, as well as between smaller and larger social entities. The individual has both the right and the obligation to do what he or she can do on one's own to fulfill basic needs and satisfy the demands of human dignity. The social group has the obligation to honor and to protect individual initiative. But it also has the right and the obligation to do what individuals alone are unable to do to meet their needs and honor their dignity. The individual, for example, has both the right to an education and the obligation to seek it with diligence. But his or her community has the obligation to provide the means by which an education may be gained, e.g., a school system, libraries, teachers. It also has the corresponding right to tax individuals to support the system and to require students to attend school.

More specifically, teachers should not do for students what students are able to do for themselves, but teachers may and should provide the structured setting and discipline that education requires when individuals are unable to do this.

The key word in the principle is help, the Latin *subsidium*—hence the name of the principle. A *subsidium* is a support or undergirding of the individual. There are things essential to human life and dignity which human beings cannot do alone, for which they need to and ought to band together in common action. It is, therefore, a fundamental feature of our love for one another that we join together to create and to care for social bodies, social structures and social systems which help us to be more fully human. Or, as the Second International Synod of Catholic Bishops expressed it in 1971, "Action on behalf of justice and participation in the transformation of the world fully appear to us as a constitutive dimension of the preaching of the Gospel, or, in other words, of the Church's mission for the redemption of the human race and its liberation from every oppressive situation" (*Justice in the World* 6). To know ourselves as social beings summoned to love one another is, then, to know ourselves called to the tasks of social justice guided by the principle of subsidiarity. It is to understand the words of Jesus on social authority as an essential component of loving one another as he loved us. "You know that among the pagans the rulers lord it over them, and their great men make their authority felt. This is not to happen among you. No, anyone who wants to be great among you must be your servant, and anyone who wants to be first among you must be your slave, just as the Son of Man came not to be served but to serve, and to give his life as a ransom for many" (Mt 20:25–28).

Teaching Skills

The third important function of social groups for moral agency is as a teacher of skills. Real love for others is not sentimental well-wishing or pious exhortation, but is expressed in action to meet concrete needs. To love one another demands that we develop skills, the personal strengths necessary to help others. These skills are received, developed, refined and employed in community. Some skills are learned in the family, some in school, some on the job, some in solitude, but all learning of skills is dependent upon the contribution and guidance of others who first mastered them. The learning of skills also depends upon our interaction with the people for whose sake we learn and exercise these skills. Parenting skills, for example, are learned in the family as we live out the roles of child and then parent. Teaching skills are learned in the classroom, first in the experience of being taught and then in the experience of teaching. Nursing skills are learned in the interaction with both experienced nurses and patients. Business skills are learned both in the classroom and in the marketplace. Even the skill of interpersonal sexual loving is learned in the community called marriage, which skill is not, of course, to be identified with the ability to induce orgasm in oneself or one's partner. The latter ability can be learned in isolation, and machines can be fashioned to do it just as well as humans.

The deprivation of community also entails the deprivation of skills, by which we love and serve others. How often does one hear the lament from a lonely, isolated individual: "I'm no good for anything; no one needs me anymore." While we might wish to reply to this lament, with some justification, that everyone is good for something, apart from a sense of social belonging, a perception of having some place in the community, such a reply will fall on deaf ears. If it appears to the individual that he or she has nothing to offer the community, no contribution to make to the well-being of others, no skill of value to the social group, he or she will feel isolated, rejected by the community, and so will perceive the self to be of no human worth. The unwanted orphan, the unemployed worker, the unappreciated artist, the friendless misfit, all resonate to the cry, "Nobody wants me, nobody loves me." And they do so resonate precisely because they lack skills— or appear to lack skills—which would put them in a relationship of service to and love for others. While it is true, from the perspective of Christian faith, that every individual is of infinite worth in the eyes of God and is to be loved for what he or she is rather than for one's social usefulness, loving, unlike being loved, is active and always entails a practical dimension. It seems clear, then, that if we are to follow Jesus' command to love one another, the formation of communities and the teaching and learning of personal and social skills is essential.

Giving a Mission

There is a fourth important function of community for the moral agent, a function I have earlier called the giving of a mission. Literally, a mission is a being sent forth. The human person who has a mission has been called in one way or another, tested and trained, and then sent forth to perform a task, deliver a message, or exercise an office. This calling, testing and sending forth is done, not by the individual person on his or her own initiative, but by the community to which he or she belongs. The individual goes forth, not in his or her own name, but in the name of the one who has called, and the mission of the individual finds its significance in relation to the mission of the community. As individuals in community, as members of a social body, we find ourselves involved in something larger and more significant than our own private interests and personal survival. Only in community do our lives take on a significance that reaches beyond the temporal and spatial limits of individual existence to realize a transcendent meaning.

The biblical stories in the Old Testament concerning such figures as Abraham, Moses, David, the judges, and the prophets, and in the New Testament in regard to Jesus and the apostles, clearly illustrate the meaning of mission. The call by God is a call mediated through the community, calling the individual from the community so as to serve the community. It is Israel who has been called to be a holy people, and it is that calling, that mission which gives meaning to the mission of a Moses, a David, a Jeremiah. It is the Church which has been established and sent forth to proclaim the good news of salvation in Christ, and it is that mission which gives meaning to the mission of Paul and Peter and John and their many successors.

Unfortunately, we too often restrict the notion of mission to those individuals who claim some dramatic religious experience, or who have received a solemn ordination or consecration from the Church, or who hold some highly visible office in public life. In doing this we fail to take seriously the meaning of the sacraments we receive, as well as the significance of the social functions we perform. In baptism, all Christians receive the call to a life of holiness and service in the Church for the world, as the Second Vatican Council so strongly reminded us (*Apostolicam Actuosita-*

tem, 3). This call to holiness is heightened in a more personal and adult manner in the sacraments of confirmation and the Eucharist. Couples who enter into the sacrament of matrimony are charged with a mission of love and service no less than those who receive the sacrament of holy orders. Furthermore, all worthy work in the world, however little praised or publicly noted, has the capacity to be no less a mission of love and service to others than more visible public responsibilities or celebrated roles. The garbage collector, the secretary, the farmer, the nurse, all can serve the community as lovingly and as vitally as the mayor, the company president, or the celebrated athlete.

The importance of a sense of mission for the moral agent can be illustrated by an experience which I recall from my years in graduate school. In a course I was taking in Protestant systematic theology, the professor assigned a brief paper to the twelve students in the class. We were to answer the question, "Who Am I in History?" After the usual grumbling about such an ambiguous topic and some discussion about how we might approach it, we were each given a week to prepare the paper for presentation in class. On the appointed day for the presentations, it turned out that only two of us had been able to make even a start on the paper, because only two of us had any sense of social identity and location. One student who had succeeded in answering the question was a young black minister who identified deeply with the black struggle for civil rights and human dignity. My own answer was rooted in my identification with the renewal efforts of Roman Catholicism as a result of the Second Vatican Council to be a Church both faithful to its tradition and of service to the modern world. Both of us had a clear sense of the significant values of our communities, a clear social identity, a knowledge of how the skills we were developing in graduate school could be of service to our communities, and so an experience of our academic work as being a fundamental aspect of our mission to love and serve others. The other students in the class did not have a clue as to who they were in history. They confessed to an uncertainty as to what they were about in graduate school and why they were about it. Indeed, they confessed their hopes that graduate school, a place for learning skills, would somehow also give them a sense of social location, identity and purpose, something it could do only on a very temporary basis. Until they could find a community in which to be at home, they had no clear sense of the meaning of their labors.

THE LIMITS OF SOCIETY

At the same time that we recognize the necessity and significance of social groups for our moral existence, it is equally important to acknowledge both the limits and the problems that social groups pose for us. For if social groups, with their structures and systems, their laws and processes, are essential servants of human well-being and necessary instruments in and through which we love one another, they are also continually tempted to, and often do, become not our servants but our masters. Life in community can deform as well as form individuals; it can alienate persons as well as liberate them; it can stifle human growth just as well as promote it. Just as we can expect too little from our communities and esteem them too lightly, so also can we expect too much of them and esteem them too highly. The family, the school, the athletic team, the business organization, the nation, can all become objects of an idolatrous love, claiming from us and receiving from us the absolute love and loyalty that is owed to God alone.

Family

The possibilities, the limits and the problems of social existence for the moral agent can be illuminated by considering our membership in three distinct, if related communities: the family, the nation, the Church. The family, that most basic of all social institutions, is the initial protector, nurturer and guide of individual human existence. While the family is based on ties of blood, that is to say, on natural, biological relationships, it also develops deep psychological and spiritual bonds between family members. Parents and children are tied to one another throughout life by bonds of love or hate, joy or anger, responsibility or guilt, frequently by all of these at the same time. The family is the place where we learn to consider the needs of others even while asserting our own needs and finding them satisfied or frustrated. The family is the place where we are sheltered and encouraged and made to feel at home in the world. It is also the place where we are molded to a pattern of life, restricted, possibly even smothered by demands to conform to the expectations of others. In the family we learn to love and be loved, to forgive and be forgiven; we also learn to hurt and be hurt, to manipulate and be manipulated. Family membership may be more or less a joyful experience, but it is never a perfect one. It can ask too little of us or too much, but whatever the case, it is the necessary springboard and foil for our developing personality. We cannot develop humanly at all without it. And just as the family shapes us in our fundamental attitudes and convictions, so in turn do we shape the family by our moral choices and deeds.

Membership in a family, then, reveals in microcosm all the ambiguity of our moral journey in society. It needs and demands our love and loyalty, our obedience and service, even while the family shows itself to be both deserving and undeserving of what it demands. More ironic still is the fact that we contribute to the strengths and weaknesses of the family by our own attitudes and action. If there is security, warmth, intimacy and emotional satisfaction to be found in family life, it is because the family members create those happy characteristics. If the family is a place of frustration, hostility, misunderstanding and personal alienation, it is again because of the attitudes and actions of the family members. Life in the family, as in any social group, makes clear that for any social institution to serve its members two things are needed: a continual reformation of the interior attitudes of the individual members and the intelligent reformation of the structural relationships by which the members relate to one another and the larger world.

This last point is of special importance and deserves some additional attention. In seeking to love one another as Jesus loved them, all family members are confronted with a double challenge. One side of the challenge may be described as the struggle with one's own selfishness or egocentrism. As a family member I am tempted to want my very real needs and desires to come first, to want my way of doing things and arranging things to prevail. I would prefer family life to be structured around my work, my recreation, my tastes, my habits. I might even think it is only right that things should work that way. On reflection, one can recognize that there is a lack of wisdom and generosity in such an attitude, and so one can acknowledge the need for a change of heart, a conversion to a more generous, less self-centered attitude. If family membership is to be a happy, healthy and helpful experience, there is this basic need for the continuous, progressive interior conversion for all the members, a conversion to which they are summoned by the daily events of family life.

But interior conversion alone, important as it is, will not suffice. The structural relationships in the family will also have to undergo reformation. With all the good will in the world and the best of intentions, family life will not promote human well-being if the structures and processes of family life do not afford the individual members the space to grow as persons. To offer but a few examples of the kinds of structural change intended here, false stereotypes of male and female roles may have to be challenged and altered. Father may have to take up some of the responsibilities of cooking and cleaning and child care. Mother may have to assume work or financial responsibilities. Teenagers, along with greater freedom to discipline themselves and express their feelings and opinions, need to take on greater responsibility for the physical maintenance of the home. Adjustments must be made in family relationships as friends, teachers, and employers enter the picture. Loving one another will call for the continuous and intelligent alteration of relationships and responsibilities. It is in this process of continuous reformation that we come to love one another more truthfully and realize our dignity as free and responsible moral agents. The family structure can make this growth in freedom and love more or less difficult for the individual, but it remains the essential context for such growth and, short of barbaric abuse, can never destroy the possibility of such growth entirely.

Nation

Membership in a nation poses the same sort of ambiguity to the individual and reveals the same need for continual reformation if the structured systems of the larger society are to serve individual well-being. While the ties that bind citizens together are generally less personal and intimate than family ties, they are no less real and no less important to our moral existence. They also have the additional merit of inviting us into a wider circle of concern and a more universal love. Our nation, like our family, needs and demands our love and loyalty, our obedience and service. The nation can show itself to be both worthy and unworthy of what it asks of us; again like the family, it may ask too much or too little of us. The nation, too, can become an object of idolatrous worship as in the case of excessive nationalism, or it can become an object of demonic derision as in the case of mindless rebellion. The nation can foster and provide opportunities for human growth; it can fail to provide such opportunities; it can actually limit and suppress such opportunities.

Citizenship is, of course, a more complex reality than family membership, and the love and service we give to our fellow citizens is usually more impersonal and less emotionally involving. But the same need for interior conversion and structural reform is manifest if we are genuinely to love one another as Jesus loved us. I may find, for example, that I have to wrestle with my own ethnic, racial, regional or sexual prejudice. I may discover a distaste for the poor, or the uneducated, or the handicapped that wants them hidden from public view. The plurality and inequality in society will challenge my sense of justice, tempting me to seek more for myself at the expense of others. My own social and economic status in society will inevitably color my perceptions of how well the social system works, tempting me to judge others on the basis of my own opportunities and gifts. Life in society is rife with temptations to the seven deadly sins of pride, envy, anger, sloth, lust, greed, and gluttony. A loving citizenship which is concerned with more than national pride and obedience to law, which seeks the well-being of one's fellow citizens, demands a continual interior reformation of mind and heart.

More obviously even than in the family, interior conversion in one's social attitudes and convictions, crucial as it is, will not suffice to promote human well-being. The systems and structures, the laws and customs which order political, economic and cultural existence will also require reformation from time to time. Segregation laws, for example, will have to be abolished; affirmative action programs will have to be instituted to achieve real dignity and opportunity for victims of past discrimination. The tax structure may be a candidate for alteration to achieve greater fairness.

Unions may have to be opened to protect the rights of all workers, not just an established elite. Educational systems may have to be expanded to teach new skills to people. All these structural reforms are demands of justice, but they are also the works of love, of a love that has grown more self-aware and self-critical. As the author of the Epistle of James pointed out long ago, "If one of the brothers or one of the sisters is in need of clothes and has not enough food to live on, and one of you says to them, 'I wish you well, keep yourself warm and eat plenty,' without giving them these bare necessities of life, then what good is that?" (Jas 2:15–16).

Changes in public attitudes and social structures are, of course, notoriously more complex and more difficult to achieve than reforms in the family. But if we take Jesus' admonition to love our neighbors seriously, we discover that much of our daily work and public participation can indeed be occasions for loving others and so for experiencing the presence and call of God. The ordinary civil courtesies and respect we show to one another—what we once referred to as good manners before becoming snobbish—the conscientious and effective performance of our jobs, the learning and teaching of new skills, the responsibilities we assume for the effective operation of a union, a day care center, an academic department, can all be ways of exercising neighbor-love and responding to the call of God. As we grow in self-critical awareness about who we are and what we do as a people, the possibilities for loving one another continue to expand and the works of justice are seen to be one of the chief vehicles for the expression of love. The passion for justice in the interest of love expands until it takes in a concern for justice in the world, justice for the entire human family.

Church

Finally, let us consider our membership in the Church. From a sociological perspective, Church membership is considerably different than family membership or citizenship. We are born into a family: we live in a country by birth or choice. But we voluntarily join a Church. Sociologically speaking, a Church is a voluntary association, little different in the social form it assumes from any other voluntary group like the Elks, the 4H clubs, the local bridge club, or a political party. But from a theological perspective, the Church's own self-understanding is considerably different. The Church is a moral community charged with a mission and a way of life to which its members have been called. While membership in the Church is, to be sure, freely chosen, it is chosen as something I ought to do and be, as the only true and right response to the call of God in Christ. Church membership is not optional for the Christian, but morally mandatory.

Furthermore, the basic tenets of faith and the basic moral demands that Church membership entails are not the products of a popular vote or of a majority will that can be changed as it suits the membership. The Church is ruled by the word of God as that word is read and interpreted through history under the guidance of the Holy Spirit. The Church, therefore, is a normative community, living under a transcendent ideal that is not of its own making or choosing. The Church lives under and awaits the kingdom of God which serves as the eschatological norm and judge of all human efforts and achievements. Nor is the existence of the Church dependent upon ties of blood or geography or law. While membership in the Church has many sociological similarities with membership in any social group and confronts the individual with the same ambiguity, it also has unique features which affect moral existence in significant ways. I want to discuss here one important way that Church membership affects our moral lives.

RITUAL AND MORALITY

Active Church membership involves the obligation to attend religious services or to engage in the practice of public worship. In a specifically Roman Catholic context, one might refer to the serious moral obligation to attend Mass on all Sundays and holydays of obligation. This is both a religious and a moral obligation, but one which is often badly misunderstood, with the result that, even when the obligation is technically fulfilled, no positive meaning is found in the practice. The experience of meaningless Church attendance soon leads to indifference and non-attendance. Participation in religious rituals becomes radically divorced from one's moral existence. How often we hear the claim that I can be a good person, love and serve my neighbor without going to Church. Of course, such a claim is abstractly true; in some cases it may even be existentially true for a time, but it certainly misunderstands the nature and significance of religious ritual and its relationship to morality.

Definition of Ritual

A ritual may be defined as any ceremonial observance or formal, solemn act or procedure carried out in accordance with prescribed rules or customs. Defined in this way there is nothing specifically religious about rituals or ritual behavior. Ritual activitiy pertains to and grows out of our social nature. Most of us are quite familiar with ritual activity, even though we may not think about or speak about such activity as ritual. One may point, for example, to family rituals like Thanksgiving or Christmas dinners which are carried on in traditional ways according to largely unwritten customs. As citizens we are familiar with the patriotic rituals which accompany national holidays like the Fourth of July or Memorial Day. Most people throw parties to celebrate birthdays, anniversaries, promotions or departures. Such parties are forms of ritual behavior. We also witness ritual acts upon the inauguration of presidents and governors, upon the graduation of students, on the occasion of athletic triumphs as in the case of the Olympic games, the World Series and the Super Bowl. And the list could go on.

Dangers of Ritual

While ritual activity may often appear to be an unnecessary luxury or a frivolous, if welcome, distraction from more important matters, it is, in fact, vitally important to human life. This is no less true for our religious life than for our political, social and family life. Religious rituals and our participation in them have great significance for our moral existence precisely because they remind us of who we ultimately are, help us focus on the ultimate meaning of all our human activities, and actually strengthen our faith for the future.

There is some reason for Christians to hesitate in the face of religious rituals. For one thing Jesus is portrayed at times in the Gospels as having curious reservations about public prayer and worship. He rebukes the Pharisees for their public displays of piety and urges his followers to pray to their Father in heaven in the secrecy of a closed room (Mt 6:5–6). He favorably contrasts the quiet publican in the rear corner of the temple to the ostentatious Pharisee standing proudly in the front (Lk 18:9–14). He seemed to be indifferent to the place, time and manner of worship, stressing that it was worship in spirit and in truth that really mattered (Jn 4:19–24). Such reservations alert us to the fact that ritual behavior has certain dangers attendant upon it, against which it is imperative to guard. Yet these very dangers also enable us to see the positive importance of ritual in our lives.

The first danger to which religious ritual is consistently prone is the danger of hypocrisy. Religious worship is directed toward God, but because it is done in the presence of other human beings, we are always tempted to engage in it in order to be noticed by others. Whether we wish to make a public display of our piety, or to show off our new wardrobe, or to have our talents at singing, reading or preaching admired by others, there is always the risk of engaging in public worship simply to show off. The intentionality that informs our participation in religious ritual can easily corrupt the meaning of the ritual and leave us with a sour taste for the whole business. Whether I attend to my own hypocrisy in the ritual, as for instance the college student who attends church simply to placate his or her parents, or whether I attend to the hypocrisy of others, the pious eucharistic minister for instance who discriminates in his business against racial minorities, the awareness of hypocrisy leads to a perception of religious ritual as an empty show and a fraud. Indeed, for the morally conscientious person, to participate in such a sham is not merely a morally indifferent matter; it is morally corrupting. It is the height of inauthenticity, so morality demands that I not participate, and certainly that I do not pretend to participate.

A second persistent danger which besets religious ritual is boredom which arises from either of two causes. Ritual is by its very nature repetitive and somewhat formal. While it may be possible to make room for novelty and spontaneity in the conduct of ritual, it is essentially carried out time after time according to the prescribed rules or customs of the social group. In the Roman Catholic context, for example, the eucharistic celebration is basically the same day after day, Sunday after Sunday. It is easy to grow tired of the repetition, bored with the same old thing, and to turn to something new and more exciting. Ritual can also become boring and distasteful when it is done badly or inappropriately. If the hymns are atrocious, the singing abominable, the readings unintelligible, the prayers mumbled, and the sermon vacuous, we are tempted to close our eyes, grit our teeth, and turn in on ourselves while we wait impatiently for it all to end. All the while we endure, we ask ourselves, "Who needs this?" Surely there are better, more profitable, and certainly more interesting ways to expend one's time and energy. Again moral conscientiousness seems to foreclose participation in religious ritual.

The final danger plaguing religious rituals is what I call the danger of magic. This danger again can have either of two causes. In participating in religious worship which is directed toward God, we can easily come to think that the ritual in some way changes God or affects his attitudes toward us. By saying the right words, by performing the proper actions and gestures, we think that God's favor is won or his anger is diverted. Perhaps if we sing a bit louder, pray a bit longer and with more fervor, or participate more frequently, God will hear us and grant us our desires. It is as if we think consciously or unconsciously, that our participation in the ritual gives us some claim upon God, assures us of his favor, guarantees an answer to our prayers. Expressed in this way, religious ritual is purely and simply a form of magic, an expression not of living faith but of superstition and fear. A self-critically aware conscience can have nothing to do with such superstitious practices.

The second way in which religious rituals can assume a magical form is to think that religious worship is or can be a substitute for responsible and loving service to the neighbor. We do not become loving persons or serve our neighbors simply by going to church or by participating in religious worship. To think that we do is again to reduce ritual to a form of magic. Our neighbor's need always takes precedence over participation in religious rituals, as Jesus made vividly clear in the parable of the good Samaritan, and as the Church has always taught. While it is both proper and good to pray for our neighbors, to commend them and their needs to the Lord, such prayer is no substitute for responsible action on their behalf. If, then, a person expects participation in

Sunday worship to change God or to solve people's problems, it is little wonder that in time such a person will cease to participate in religious worship on the utilitarian grounds that it seems to be a waste of time. "I don't get anything out of it." "It doesn't seem to make things any better."

Reflecting upon these dangers, to which religious rituals of any kind are always prone, helps us to realize that ritual activity in and of itself can neither supply meaning nor substitute for the lack of meaning in human life. Ritual activity is not a substantive activity we do for its own sake. It is rather a celebratory activity, an activity we do to celebrate something else we have experienced. Where there is no prior meaning, no occasion to celebrate, nothing to ritualize, the ritual will inevitably be empty and inauthentic. It would be like a party which was thrown to celebrate a job promotion when, in point of fact, I was actually fired.

Benefits of Ritual

Granting that ritual always runs these dangers we have mentioned and cannot supply meaning where meaning is absent, the clue to the positive significance of ritual is to be found in the very dangers themselves. For although hypocrisy is always a possibility because of the public character of ritual, nevertheless religious faith and life are inescapably public, social realities. They are not and cannot be a private affair and still remain alive. Religious rituals are the way we give social form and social expression to our beliefs and convictions. Ritual reminds us that we are a people called to be one body in Christ, and such memory is essential if we are to continue to be a people. More, the public gathering to celebrate our oneness in Christ gives present social form and reality to that which we remember.

We might briefly illustrate the above claim by considering the rituals surrounding the celebration of Christmas. That the Word became flesh and dwelt among us, that the Lord of the universe was born of a woman, that upon entering human history he was welcomed only among the poor and the humble of the world, these are not private beliefs unshared by others and of no social meaning or consequence for our lives together. They are convictions about public, historical events, convictions which have given birth to a people who have continued to celebrate and pass on the good news of salvation. They are the convictions of a people who know that they would lose themselves and cease to be a people if they did not gather together and continue to recall the good news from the past, to celebrate it in the present, and to transmit it to the future. The public celebration of the good news of salvation is not an optional act for the Church but an essential practice of who we are and what we are called to be.

The fact that ritual activity has a formal, repetitive character means that it is always subject to the danger of being boring. Yet it is the very formality and routine character of ritual that is the antidote to the daily routine of our lives. Religious ritual is the occasion on which the daily routine is interrupted and brought temporarily to a halt so that we may focus on and celebrate the deeper, lasting meaning of our lives. Ritual is necessary to human beings precisely so that they do not lose sight of the significance of their daily activities and relationships and become worn down by the daily burdens and humdrum tasks they carry. Participation in religious ritual is the opportunity to glimpse anew the divine meaning of the world and our activity in it. It is the chance to remember and celebrate again that our lives are lived in the presence of a loving, saving God. Participation in religious ritual is not the occasion to shut out the world or to forget our human cares and responsibilities in it and for it. We go on vacation for that purpose. It is the occasion to see these cares and responsibilities in their divine meaning. The formal, repetitive character of religious ritual is essential to the break with the daily routine, as well as to give form and continuity to our life as a people. It invites our faith and our participation. It cannot supply either. The responsibility for the quality of our participation is our own, and that responsibility is part of the moral responsibility we have to love one another so that we may recognize one another as the people of God.

Finally, while ritual acts run the danger of magic, they are not in fact magical. They are not events in and through which we earn God's favor or gain our salvation. Nor are they the acts by which we emerge from our sins and are transformed into loving human beings at the service of others. God's favor and our salvation are freely given gifts offered by God in Christ. The emergence from sin and our transformation in love takes place in our daily activity. Ritual activity celebrates the fact of God's gift, celebrates that there is a saving God at work transforming us by his love, and so reminds us that there is more involved in our daily activity than meets the eye.

Yet it is also true that ritual, as a symbolic expression of a prior meaning, has a powerful shaping effect on human beings. Not only does ritual focus and celebrate the meaning of our lives in particular ways, but in so doing it actually reinforces and enhances the meaning. That is why Catholicism has called its central ritual acts sacraments, symbolic acts that actually effect what they symbolize. There are many possible illustrations of the power of religious rituals to reinforce and enhance meaning, but I would share with the reader one particular example from my own past.

A number of years ago I had occasion to visit Taiwan for two days, during which I went alone to a Sunday liturgy. The Mass was said in Chinese, all the people in church were Chinese, the liturgy was inescapably conducted in a Chinese mode. I found it all very strange, and yet also very Catholic and familiar. Vividly I became aware of the universal Church. These strangers, too, were my brothers and sisters in Christ, and we recognized this and expressed it in our presence and celebration together, in the kiss of peace, and most emphatically in our reception of the eucharistic bread, the body of Christ given for us. Only the formal character of the ritual enabled me to participate since I could not speak, read or understand a single word. But participate I did, and I left with a faith renewed, deepened and glad.

Not all participation in religious rituals will prove to be so vividly striking or memorable. But the shaping power of ritual activity for those who bring to their participation a living faith is undeniable. The price we pay for no ritual is forgetfulness, a loss of meaning, aloneness. If the Church did not celebrate the Eucharist, it would cease to be the Church. If as individuals we refuse to participate in public worship, we deny our rootedness in Christ, our ties to one another and our membership in God's people. It is, then, not surprising that such participation in the Sunday Eucharist has long been regarded as a serious moral obligation, since it expresses and reinforces who we are in history. This understanding of the importance of ritual participation for our moral existence might also help us be more patient and more tolerant with young people who are struggling to find their identity and are not yet sure what is and is not worth celebration. I would only add that patience and toleration are not the same as indifference to a practice of great moral significance.

It is in part because we are blind or indifferent to some of our moral obligations that we need the Church body to point them out to us and urge them upon us. It is in this context that we become concerned with the significance of our moral failures. What difference, if any, do they make? What importance do they have, either for ourselves or for others? For this reason we next turn to a consideration of the reality we call sin in order to understand the obstacle that sin is to our efforts to love one another.

STUDY QUESTIONS

1. Specify some of the ambiguity you experience in your life as a member of a family, as a citizen. How do you deal with this ambiguity?

2. Can you identify some ways in which the social groups to which you belong have transmitted their values to you, conferred an identity upon you, taught you skills, given you a mission?

3. Is the call to holiness received at baptism real to you? If not, why not? How could it become so?

4. Apply the principle of subsidiarity to your own life. What social groups do you need to help you? Which overstep their bounds? What do you properly expect from government and Church in the person of officials? Do you sometimes expect too much, asking groups to do what you can do yourself?

5. In your Church attendance do you experience any of the dangers of ritual participation? How do you deal with them?

6. Does ritual participation help you remember your roots in Christ, your unity with his body in the present, and the signi-

ficance of your daily activity? How could you participate in ritual more meaningfully?

BIBLIOGRAPHY

Barta, Russell, ed. *Challenge to the Laity.* Huntington: Our Sunday Visitor, 1980. A short collection of essays exploring the rights and responsibilities of the laity in the Church in light of the call to holiness and mission.

Gremillion, Joseph. *The Gospel of Peace and Justice: Catholic Social Teaching Since Pope John.* Maryknoll: Orbis Books, 1975. A collection of the significant papal and episcopal statements on the major social issues, with an excellent introduction and discussion of the issues by the compiler.

Hollenbach, David, S.J. *Claims in Conflict: Retrieving and Renewing the Catholic Human Rights Tradition.* New York: Paulist Press, 1979. Contains a full discussion of the principles of Catholic social thought, including the principle of subsidiarity, and their implications for today's world. An excellent introduction to social morality.

Niebuhr, Reinhold. *Moral Man and Immoral Society.* New York: Charles Scribner's Sons, 1932, 1960. A classic work by one of America's most able Protestant theologians, indicating the limits and the possibilities, the resources and the difficulties for living together. A challenging but rewarding book.

Vanier, Jean. *Community and Growth: Our Pilgrimage Together.* New York: Paulist Press, 1979, A down-to-earth book of practical and proven suggestions for successful family and community life.

Worgul, George S., Jr. *From Magic to Metaphor.* New York: Paulist Press, 1980. A careful and scholarly development of Christian sacraments, which incorporates the conclusions of the human sciences on the importance and necessity of ritual for social life.

5 The Reality of Sin

There are two sentences in St. Paul's Letter to the Romans which are frequently cited, even by non-Christians, because they so accurately capture a very common feature of our human experience. Wrote Paul, "I cannot understand my own behavior. I fail to carry out the things I want to do, and I find myself doing the very things I hate" (Rom 7:16). All human beings, at one time or another, could make these words their own as they experience an inner division in themselves. It is a division in the self that results in their feeling and acting in ways that are contrary to their own more considered and detached desires and purposes. We might, for example, find ourselves growing impatient and acting rudely toward an elderly parent or a sick child, even while we recognize the unfairness and folly of such a reaction. We might find ourselves eating or drinking more than is good for us even while we experience shame for breaking promises we made to ourselves to exercise greater moderation. We might want to take a bold and courageous stand on an issue of justice, even while we remain immobilized for fear of the consequences to our reputation and fortune.

SALVATION AND SIN

These experiences of inner division or self-alienation are manifestations of the reality which Christian theology has traditionally called sin. This is a reality which manifests itself empirically not only in self-alienation but also in the obvious alienation which exists between individual persons, human social groups, and the human and animal worlds. Ultimately, of course, it points to and finds its deepest meaning in the alienation between the human and the divine. While these perceived experiences of alienation and the evil consequences attendant upon them provide strong experiential confirmation for the doctrine of sin, they are not the appropriate theological starting point for a reflection on the reality of sin. Nor is the appropriate starting point the biblical story of the fall of Adam and Eve (Gn 3:1–24), or more comprehensively the stories of the progressive character of human sinning in the Genesis account of our pre-history (Gn 4–11), though these texts are important. The starting point is not even the famous text of Paul in Romans (5:12–21) from which a doctrine of original sin was developed by later theologians, nor his more extended discussion of sin, law, liberty and the Spirit in Romans 5–8.

The primary theological consideration, the initial affirmation for thinking about sin, the whole reason why Christians concern themselves with the reality of sin at all, is the confession that Jesus is Lord, Christ and Savior. "For us human beings and for the sake of our salvation he came down from heaven," the Apostolic Creeds proclaim. "For of all the names in the world given to men, this is the only one by which we can be saved," is the confession put on the lips of Peter by the author of the Acts of the Apostles (Acts 4:12). "Though the law was given through Moses, grace and truth have come through Jesus Christ," we read in the prologue of the Gospel according to John (Jn 1:17). "Just as sin reigned wherever there was death, so grace will reign to bring eternal life thanks to the righteousness that comes through Jesus Christ our Lord," Paul joyfully proclaimed to the Romans (Rom 5:21b).

Christian believers confess Jesus to be the Savior of all humankind, and the simple corollary of the confessional claim is that all human beings stand in need of salvation. Why do they need salvation? What do they need to be saved from? Why can they not save themselves? The simple answer to those questions is sin. It is, therefore, the Christian doctrine of redemption in Christ which makes all talk about sin both necessary and intelligible. It is because there is such good news to proclaim that the bad news of sin can be faced and discussed.

There is a second theological affirmation associated with the central doctrine of redemption which also bears heavily on the need to talk about and understand the reality of sin. That is the doctrine of *creatio ex nihilo*, the claim that everything that exists comes from the loving hands of the all-good God, was created by him out of nothing and is accordingly very good. But if that is the case, how are we to account for the existence in the world of so much misery and evil? Are we forced into the position of denying either that God is indeed the author of all reality or that evil really exists? To deny the first—the divine origin of all reality—is to surrender the faith. To deny the second—the reality of evil—is experientially untenable and ultimately self-contradictory. It involves a surrender of reason. Again the simple answer to this dilemma by which Christian theology accounts for both God's omnipotent goodness and the presence of evil in the world is sin. It is, therefore, because of the good news of God's loving creation and our redemption in Christ that Christian theologians find it necessary to talk about sin, not because they are joyless, puritanical moralists.

TO MISS THE MARK

The Greek word most often used in the Bible to refer to sin is extremely helpful in trying to understand the reality of sin. The word is *harmartia* in its noun form or *harmartano* in its verb form. Literally it means to miss the mark, an image taken from hunting or archery. When used in an ethical context, it means to do wrong or commit a moral fault. The notion of sin as a missing of the mark deserves to be taken seriously and so merits some development here.

In order to miss the mark, there must first of all be some mark to hit, some target or object outside the self at which one is aiming. There is something present in the world to be hit, and to miss it brings dire consequences. If, for instance, we take the image of the hunter stalking his or her prey, the hunter is aiming at an animal which will provide food for the people. Should the hunter miss the mark, disaster will befall the people in the form of starvation. If we reflect upon the sporting image, to miss the mark will entail the loss of the game. In a specifically religious context, the mark to be hit is God's will. Should one miss the mark, the inescapable result is alienation from the mind and heart of God. To sin, then, is to be out of union with God.

What this image of missing the mark to explain sin helps to make clear is that moral activity has both a subjective and an objective dimension. It always involves our wanting or intending to hit the mark—what I shall call human intentionality—and the actual execution of our intentionality, our ability to hit the mark in fact. Sin, then, is not merely a matter of having bad intentions, of wanting to miss the mark or hit the wrong mark, or of being indifferent to whether we hit or miss it. Morally important as this subjective intentionality is, we may well intend to hit the mark but for various reasons fail to do so. The same serious consequences ensue as if we had had bad intentions. Our good intentions do not avert the unhappy, objective consequences of our failure to be on target. The hunter in search of food for the tribe may desperately want to hit the animal he tracks, but if he misses despite his good intentionality, the tribe will be without food and face starvation. By the same token, I may fully intend to do God's will, but if I miss the mark, I am not in union with God's mind and heart.

This objective, external dimension of sin enables us to understand Israel's joy, even exultation, in the revelation of the law to them through Moses (Ps 119:12–16; 147:19–20). It seemed to them that they were especially blessed as a people because they knew the marks to be hit. It also enables us to understand the importance that the Roman Catholic tradition has placed on the official teaching office of the Church (the *magisterium*) in the person of the Pope and the bishops. The people are blessed because these officials are graced to serve them by teaching the objective norms of morality, thus indicating the marks to be aimed at in the social, sexual, economic and other dimensions of human life. In a similar way fundamentalist Christians rejoice in a literal reading of the biblical text because they believe that it enables them to know the mark that is God's will. However adequate or inadequate these ways of knowing the mark may be in various situations, at least they all take seriously the existence of a mark to be hit. They all recognize that God's will is not to be identified simply with the desires, aspirations and plans of any human individual or group.

The objective dimension of sin also explains why it is not enough, morally, to mean well or to have good intentions. It makes sense out of the popular saying, "The road to hell is paved with good intentions." Hitting the mark requires execution of one's intentions. It therefore requires training and practice and the development of the abilities or virtues essential to carrying out what one intends. The basketball player, for instance, who is faced with the challenge of making the winning basket, may well intend at the moment of the shot to hit the mark. But if he did not practice faithfully, work hard to attain good physical condition and to learn the team's strategies and patterns, we are inclined to think that he did not want or intend to hit the mark all that passionately. Apart from the execution that intentionality seeks and the discipline that execution requires, human intentionality is suspect and surely flawed.

Finally, the objective dimension of missing the mark sheds light on why sin was perceived in the biblical tradition to be such a terrible evil. The outcome of hitting the mark is that human life and well-being are served and flourish, proper human relationships are established, and God is glorified. But when the mark is missed the opposite occurs: human lives are marred and twisted, relationships are broken and people become estranged from one another, and false gods are given honor. Hence all missing the mark, all sin, puts people into false and idolatrous relationships with the result that, knowingly or unknowingly, the whole divine point and purpose of human life is missed. Sin causes human beings to be lost, alienated from their own good, incapable of hitting the mark. Hence they need to be redeemed and saved.

Sin as Slavery

There is another image in the biblical vision of sin which further emphasizes the objective dimensions of sin and its consequences. The image of missing the mark focuses more on the individual acts of a person or the individual relationships in that life. If I use such an image to evaluate my life, I recognize that sometimes I hit the mark while at other times I may miss it. I may, for instance, hit the mark in my business relationships and miss it in my marital relationship. Or I hit the mark on six days of the week but miss it on the seventh day when I take a moral holiday. On balance I find that I hit the mark more often than I miss it, so that I judge that sin does not have an overwhelming hold on my life. True as such an evaluation may be, it fails to plumb the depths of the biblical vision of sin and trivializes both sin and grace.

Once we realize that hitting the mark involves more than the proper intentionality, that it also requires ability, strength, power to execute one's intentions and hit the mark consistently, we also begin to realize that the formation of a proper intentionality is also an ability not easily developed. We may say we are intent on hitting the mark, but not really be so. The fact that we miss the mark, often or even only on occasion, manifests a radical inability in the human person, an inability to love God above all things and our neighbor as ourself always and everywhere. Hence we arrive at an understanding of sin not primarily as an action we do but as a condition of the self we are. Sin is not simply a missing of the mark on this or that occasion but is a deforming, disabling, enslaving power that makes hitting the mark of my total life radically impossible.

To comprehend sin as a disabling power that deforms and enslaves human life, it may be helpful to consider first some analogous powers in human existence to which we no longer attach personal fault or moral odium. Chemical addiction is one such power. The person addicted to drugs or alcohol has become a slave. The addiction has become the ruling force in his or her life, dictating the person's actions, deforming the person's personality, blocking all personal potential and development; rendering the individual incapable of even helping himself or herself. Putting aside all judgments about who may be responsible for the person's condition of enslavement to a drug, clearly the person in the grip of an addiction is a slave in need of salvation from a power hostile to human life. A similar situation befalls the individual who becomes an unwitting victim of such disabling powers as prejudice, superstition or neurosis. These powers exert an unhealthy, unholy control over the individual's life. Again putting aside all moral judgments about personal responsibility for the situation, one is here in the presence of a manifestation of the power of sin, a power which disables human beings from love and laughter and the fullness of life.

SIN AND SINS

One difficulty we may have in speaking about and understanding sin as a power which enslaves human life is our learned propensity to associate sin with a deliberately chosen moral fault. Surely no one chooses chemical addiction, or a prejudiced or superstitious mental outlook, or an emotional sickness. Does not sin, as many of us were taught in our catechisms, require sufficient knowledge and reflection as well as free consent of the will? And does it not also require serious matter if the sin is to be truly deadly or mortal? That traditional teaching on the three conditions necessary for mortal sin is not without important merits and admirably served a useful purpose, but it can be misleading. It can cause us to trivialize sin and grace and human freedom, to miss the deeper biblical sense of the virulence of sin, and can cloud our own human experience of good and evil. In order to clarify the issue further, let me suggest a distinction between sin and sins. Sin is a condition and a power in human life, while sins are individual acts which are the manifestation and consequence of sin. In making this distinction I would remind the reader that Jesus forgives our sins, which is good news, but the even better news is that he saves us from sin.

The distinction between sin and sins can be briefly illustrated by a reflection upon some of the so-called deadly sins mentioned in the previous chapter. These traditional capital or deadly sins are, of course, not sins but sin. Pride and greed and envy are not actions but interior tendencies or attitudes. Lust and gluttony are not deeds but disabling dimensions of our character. I do not do a deed of envy; I am envious. Let us, then, take anger and sloth as examples here, since a later chapter will have something to say about pride, envy, greed and lust.

Anger

Anger is a common human emotion felt by almost everyone at some time or other. It is an important emotion, for it often provides the necessary energy to mobilize us for action. As such, it can be an altogether appropriate response to certain events or conditions in the world. Personal outrage, intense indignation in the face of an event like the Nazi holocaust or a practice like racial discrimination is not only emotionally healthy and fully appropriate to human life; it is also not sinful, or, more accurately, may very well not be sinful. Indeed the inability to feel outrage in the face of such events or experiences is both psychologically aberrant and a likely sign of the power of sloth.

But anger is a tricky business, for it so easily gets out of hand or is misdirected. Rather than serving our freedom and intelligence, our anger begins to rule us and to control our choices and behavior. We lose our tempers, act wildly and irrationally, strike out at the nearest person or object to no useful end. Our anger is readily turned away from the conditions or events which triggered it and turned toward people, be they the creators and sustainers of those conditions or events, or merely the unwitting victims of them. Anger, which has the potential to move us to work for a greater measure of justice in the world, so easily moves us instead to seek revenge, to inflict new and additional harm on people rather than seeking the relief of sin's victims.

We may also note that anger, like the other deadly sins, is not initially a freely chosen attitude or feeling, but a reaction welling up within us from the unconscious depths of our being. For that reason it often takes us by surprise, in regard to both its presence and its power. We are amazed to discover how deeply and passionately we feel about this insult or that slight. As a reaction, anger may at times be appropriate, but it is most often unruly. It is rarely, if ever, fully under the control of our rationality and freedom, rarely, if ever, fully integrated into our life projects and purposes. Upon experiencing anger, we may not always lose our tempers, but the control of one's temper is always a struggle. And our anger is also deceitful. It leads us to believe we have rights where we have none—hence the rationalizations of our righteous anger. It convinces us that we are serving the cause of justice when we are merely seeking relief for our own guilts and frustrations. It blinds us to our own failures in loving others by giving us the excuse of the other's unlovableness.

In all these ways, and many others, anger shows its true colors as a deforming, disabling power in human life, one which, if left untamed and uncontrolled, will lead us to death both physically and spiritually. Thus, the traditional claim that it is a deadly sin is well-founded. If this were not the case, if anger were not a deadly sin, we would not trouble to instruct people that they must learn to acknowledge their anger, to control their temper, and to find constructive outlets for their anger-fueled energies.

To feel anger, to be angry, is not in itself a sin. It does not fall under the category of free actions which include sins for which we must duly repent. But it is a manifestation of the power of sin in human life as well as a consequence of the broken condition of human relationships in the world. My anger at myself, at others, and even at God reveals the alienation that is part of all these relationships. To be angry is not something it is appropriate to feel guilt about, even if one's anger is directed at God. But it is a sign of the still unfinished liberation from sin in my life, a reminder, if you will, that I have not yet realized the perfect freedom of the sons and daughters of God. Being angry is a comment not on my behavior but on my character and a good clue to what I really do and do not love as Jesus loved.

Sloth

A similar analysis may be made, in briefer compass, of the deadly sin of sloth. Sloth is no longer a word in common English usage, at least in the American form of English. We are more familiar with sloth in such manifestations as laziness, as the inability to feel or care about anything, as the reluctance to commit oneself to any lasting relationship or course of action. Sloth reveals itself as a lassitude of spirit, a weariness of the soul which also infects the body. Its psychological manifestation is depression; its social manifestation is the inability to assume responsibility; its interpersonal manifestation is the absence of friends; its physical manifestation is simple inactivity expressed as boredom; its spiritual manifestation is the experience of meaninglessness in life.

To be or to feel slothful is also more or less a common human experience. Like anger, it is not initially freely chosen nor can it be simply willed away. We may have to wait it out or seek professional help to break its hold upon us. Like anger, sloth is not an act, not a sin, but a manifestation of the power of sin to deform and disable human life. Sloth robs life of its zest, its joy, its meaning, so that finally life seems empty and not worth living. Sloth would move us all to suicide if it had its way, except that for the slothful person even suicide is too much trouble.

To find oneself under the power of sloth is not a matter for guilt and repentance. It is, however, a sign that all is not well with me, that I have, consciously or unconsciously, closed myself off from the wellsprings of God's healing, liberating grace. Very possibly a period of rest and renewal, a retreat of some sort, is called for. This indicates a further difference between sin and sins. Sins are actions, the remedy for which is repentance, confession and a firm resolution to stop doing such actions. Sin as a disabling power, as an enslaving force, also requires recognition and acknowledgement, but the remedy lies at a deeper level of experience than a mere act of the will. Just as liberation from an addiction to heroin, for example, calls for new patterns of life and relationships, so liberation from the power of sin may also call for new patterns of prayer, life-style and relationship. Above all it calls for an openness to the varied vehicles of the one remedy for sin, the grace of God, the source of all new life.

It should be clear at this point that the disabling power of sin which causes us to miss the mark has many and varied manifestations. Just as there are a variety of diseases that threaten our physical well-being, so there are a variety of powers that impede our spiritual and moral health. The Bible has a story to account for the origins of this tragic situation (Gn 3:1–24), and theological thought has developed the notions of original sin and the sin of the world to illuminate the full extent of the human dilemma. In popular language the dilemma may be put like this. You are going to die someday, and no matter how much you love life, no matter to what lengths you go to take care of your health, you will die and there is nothing you can do about it. But even worse than that, you are a sinner, deserving the eternal pains of hell. You are damned for all eternity, and there is nothing that you can do about that either, try as you may.

ORIGINAL SIN

To be quite sure, it is no longer fashionable to express the human dilemma in this way. Many people, not a few Christians among them, no longer take hell seriously and regard death as the natural outcome of human existence to be accepted with either a resigned equanimity or fatalistic regret. That death, so understood, renders all human hopes and strivings ultimately meaningless is a fact faced only by some courageous existentialists whose moral integrity insists that we face facts, however unpleasant they may be. And the fact to be faced is that death means we can only make the best of a bad situation. Either we eat, drink and be merry now for tomorrow we die, or we live in perpetual but hopeless rebellion against our unhappy fate.

Hell is more easily dismissed—by non-believers since there is no empirical or rational evidence for its existence, by believers since it appears to be incompatible with a God of everlasting love. Besides, few of us really believe that we are so bad that hell is our just desert, that children, especially infants, are capable of mortal sin, or that even conspicuously malevolent people are fully responsible for their choices and actions. Such an understanding of the symbol of hell, and its correlative symbol, original sin, seems to me to misunderstand the very thing toward which the symbols point.

Original Sin in History

Theologians have traditionally discussed original sin under two aspects, using the handy Latin expressions, *peccatum originale originans,* and *peccatum originale originatum,* to indicate the two aspects or dimensions of original sin. The first expression focuses on the source of sin, on its historical roots, if you will. The story of Adam and Eve eating the forbidden fruit in the garden of Eden has served the Christian tradition so picturesquely to express the origins of sin and evil. Hard as it may be for us to accept, the story, and the doctrine of original sin, both point squarely to the party responsible for human misery and suffering in all its forms. It is our own fault. It is we who have turned away, in the course of the human journey, from our true good to seek illusory and deceitful goals. We have nobody else to blame for the human condition but ourselves. How, when, where or why this turning away first occurred are all matters of speculation and story. That it did occur, as a matter of historical fact, is a theological conclusion drawn from our belief in an all-good God and the very evident signs of human alienation and misery.

The *peccatum orginale originans,* then, does not find its significance in an event from some mythical past, but in its affirmation of a human freedom and responsibility that have in fact lost their way and have nobody to blame but themselves. The theological diagnosis of the human condition is clear. It is not our finitude, nor our bodiliness, nor our stars, nor angels, nor devils that are to blame for our sorry state. It is we ourselves, in the misuse of our freedom to pervert our loves, who bear the guilt and the responsibility for the broken state of the world. It is as if we were children whose parents gave us a marvelous and fragile toy which we, in our foolish arrogance, shattered, thinking to make it still better. And the secret of its restoration is beyond us.

Original Sin in Us

The second expression, *peccatum originale originatum,* focuses upon the consequences of this turning away, this fall, this shattering act, for all who enter human history after it has occurred. The consequences are both personal and social, affecting everyone in their mutually reciprocal interaction. The social consequences are often spoken of as the sin of the world, referring to the harmful, often deadly influence that the social environment has on individuals. Such manifestations as life in an anger-filled home, or in a racist or sexist culture, or in a totalitarian political system, or in a polluted city are instances of the sin of the world. Recent theology has taken to speaking of sinful social structures to capture this same reality. By this term it points to those familial, legal, political, educational and economic systems and processes which impede or distort human being and becoming. All of us are affected by these systems, and since there are no perfect systems, we are affected adversely to one degree or another.

But it is the personal consequences of the fall with which the *peccatum originale originatum* is most concerned, for it is primarily persons who need salvation and it is persons who are the recipients of God's healing, liberating grace. And it is precisely here where we begin to run into trouble and so much misunderstanding. For while it is easy enough to see how we are socially affected by someone else's sin, it is extremely hard to understand how or why we are personally affected to the degree that we are born in original sin, are in fact sinners at birth and in need of being born again of water and the Holy Spirit (Jn 3:5), if we are to enter into the kingdom of God. How can we be held responsible for something we did not do and to which we in no way contributed? If it is fair to say that we do not deserve heaven at birth, why is it not also fair to say that we do not deserve hell either?

As long as we continue to think of the symbols of heaven and hell as pointing to places which are the external reward or punishment for our actions in this life, we will not be able to make any sense out of *peccatum originale originatum.* Nor will we understand what is at stake in our choices and behaviors which the coming of the kingdom of God insists is urgent and all-important. If, however, we recall that we are made for eternal communion with God the Father in Christ the Son through the Holy Spirit, that this communion involves a fellowship of love, a union of mind and heart, that, in Augustine's phrase, our restless hearts will remain restless until they rest in God, then we begin to have some understanding of what the symbol of heaven points toward. We also see why heaven, or, more accurately, a share in God's own life, is never something we earn or deserve but can only receive as gift. We have no right to what is not ours, nor can we ever earn what belongs to the very essence of another. Life, both temporal and eternal, can only be gratefully welcomed as a gift or rejected as a burden.

If the symbol of heaven points to our eternal communion in the life of the Trinity and to the rest that our restless hearts seek, the symbol of hell speaks to the very real possibility that we will refuse God's offer of life and love. It says that we can and may choose to say no to God, that in the folly and perversity of our knowing and loving we may prefer death to life, darkness to light, self to God. Furthermore, the doctrine of original sin, in its dimension of *peccatum originale originatum,* says that each one of us is unable to say yes to God without the healing, liberating gift of God's grace, a gift which is symbolized and effectively received in baptism.

FUNDAMENTAL OPTION

The significance of our moral choices and actions, then, is to be seen in this yes or no response to God's offer of life in Christ, an offer which is repeatedly renewed to us as the horizon of all our moral experiences. Contemporary moral theologians have developed the notion of a fundamental option to conceptualize this basic yes or no situation. This fundamental option is the orientation of the self to or away from God that may be present within every moral choice. We might try here, however, to explicate the notion in more concrete, metaphorical terms.

Picture yourself standing at a fork in a road, facing the choice to turn right or left. You do not know what lies ahead on either the right or the left path. To enter the path on the right it is necessary that you agree to help all those you meet along the way, starting with the poor crippled beggar sitting at the entrance to the path. To enter the path to the left it is not necessary to agree to anything at all. The two additional bits of information you have that will help you with your choice are that, first, you can expect the same challenges, problems, joys and sorrows to be present on both paths. Each road has roughly the same number of pitfalls and possible helps. Second, both paths will lead you to the same place, but from different directions, so that on your arrival at the end, you will see the end from a different perspective. The choice of paths is yours. What you do not know, but what can now be told, is that at the end of the left path you will arrive at the impenetrable darkness of the back of God who is turned facing the right path. Those who have chosen the right path will arrive to see the face of God and live.

The choice to be made at the fork in the road is a fundamental option in that it sets a basic life direction or orientation. In making the choice one enters upon the path to life or one enters upon the path to darkness and death. The latter choice captures the literal meaning of a mortal sin, a deadly, death-dealing choice or action. As I have painted the picture, it is a choice for self or for others, a choice to respond to the dignity and the needs of one's fellow human beings or to ignore their dignity and need except when it suits one's own convenience or purposes. If we extend the picture to follow people along the paths they have chosen, we discover that this fundamental option is challenged, confirmed or denied, and even sometimes reversed in the multitude of choices that face each individual along the road. On the left path I continue to encounter the claims of human dignity and need. I may continue to ignore these claims, growing more callous and indifferent to them as I go, taking advantage of human need only when it makes my journey easier or more pleasant. I may find myself occasionally challenged by the claims of human dignity and need. I encounter others who have turned back from the path ahead to walk the right path. I may regard them as fools; I may be altogether indifferent to them; or they may even give me pause to reconsider and repent of my original choice. For the grace of God in the compelling call of the Spirit is not absent on the left path, though often unrecognized or wrongly named "chance" or "luck" or some unknown god. But as long as I con-tinue along the left path, I live in sin, I grow more selfish, and the closer I come to eternal darkness.

The journey along the right path is similar in its challenges and problems. The claims of human dignity and need which I have agreed to honor and help are constantly present. My good will is challenged; I sometimes grow weary of the effort. I fail at times to help; I even refuse to help. I pause, unsure whether I wish to go on or turn back. Such actions, which manifest the con-tinuing power of sin in my life, are properly called sins, tradition-ally venial sins. They are departures from my fundamental option, actions in which I fail to hit the mark, actions in which I fail to love my neighbor as Jesus loves us. They weaken the vigor and the passion of my fundamental choice; they may even incline me to turn back, to reverse the choice. But if they do not, they are not deadly sins, setting me on the path to death. Yet they are not to be taken lightly, for if they are, I may soon find myself marking time on the road and more and more inclined or tempted to go back the way I came toward darkness.

Four Implications

The theory of fundamental option, then, illuminates several important facets of our moral existence which can be summarized here by way of a conclusion to our consideration of the reality of sin. In the first place, it makes clear that the terminus or end of all our moral choices is our relationship to God. In choosing to be for the neighbor, we also choose to say yes to God's offer of love and life. In choosing either to be against or to ignore the neighbor, we choose to say no to God. Second, fundamental option theory makes clear that the most significant aspect of our moral existence is not the actions we perform but the persons we choose to be and become in and through our actions. The malice of sin, therefore, is not to be found only, or even primarily, in the external consequences of our actions, but in their effect upon our characters, on the kinds of persons we are as a result of what we do. Third, the theory of fundamental option distinguishes mortal and venial sin, not on the basis of the matter of the act itself—what was traditionally called grave or serious matter—but on the basis of how those acts, be they acts of commission or omission, affect our fundamental orientation to and for God. This is not to suggest that the content or matter of our actions is of no importance, for it certainly is. But it is not of decisive importance. That honor belongs to the intentionality which informs the action. Finally, the theory indicates that our fundamental orientation or choice for the good is not a once and for all determination of the self. We can turn away from the good; we can fail to give accurate expression to our orientation and so miss the mark. Hence there is the need in every moral life for repentance and for renewing, deepening and solidifying our orientation toward God. That is to say, the Christian moral life requires continuous and ever more profound conversion.

Sin, quite simply, is bad news; indeed, it is the worst possible news. It is, therefore, no surprise that we do not enjoy hearing about it, or thinking about it, or, most painful of all, examining ourselves and discovering its presence in our lives. One of the clearest manifestations of sin's power can be seen in the human refusal to face sin, to acknowledge it for what it is, to call it by its right name. Sin does not like the light of day; it flourishes in the darkness of night. Sin produces and, in turn, is nourished by hardened hearts, deaf ears, blind eyes, stiff necks and closed minds, to use some scriptural metaphors. It is really only in the light of God's grace, in the light of the good news which Jesus proclaims and is, that we dare to face the reality of sin and are able to see it for what it is. For sin and our own sinfulness cannot be measured or understood through comparisons between ourselves and our fellow human beings. Its true nature and extent are revealed only when measured against the awesome holiness of God. It is little wonder, then, that so many prophets and saints, who knew themselves well and had caught a glimpse of the holiness of God, have taught us that the fear of the Lord is the beginning of wisdom and that we all, every one of us, live continually at the mercy of God. The good news which makes the bad news of sin bearable is that God is a God of infinite mercy and compassion. There is simply no better place for human beings to be than at his mercy.

It is the reality of the human conscience that alerts us to the existence of sin in our lives. As conscience grows more sensitive, so also does our sense of sin. As conscience grows lax, the sense of sin fades. We, therefore, turn next to a consideration of the reality that is conscience.

STUDY QUESTIONS

1. If sin involves missing the mark, what are the marks you are missing when you accuse yourself of sin?

2. What is the difference between sin and sins? Does an examination of conscience concern itself with both? Which is more important for the sacrament of reconciliation?

3. Why is it not sufficient morally to have good intentions? What else do we need? Do you trust your own or another's intentions when they are not carried out?

4. Can you detect signs of the sin of the world in your own social environment? What are some of the signs?

5. How would you assess your own fundamental option? Do you think it possible to know the fundamental option of another person?

BIBLIOGRAPHY

Basch, William. *It Is the Lord: Sin and Confession Revisited.* Notre Dame: Fides, 1970. Has a very good chapter on sin and its effects in community; also a very good treatment of sin and the reconciliation process.

Fairlie, Henry. *The Seven Deadly Sins Today*. Notre Dame: University of Notre Dame Press, 1979. An excellent treatment of the seven deadly sins in both their individual and social aspects in relation to contemporary culture.

Kerans, Patrick. *Sinful Social Structures*. New York: Paulist Press, 1974. A brief but good introduction to the idea of social sin and to the concept of a sinful structure.

Maly, Eugene H. *Sin: Biblical Perspectives*. Dayton: Pflaum/Standard, 1973. A fine study of the concept of sin in the Bible by an excellent biblical scholar.

Menninger, Karl. M.D. *Whatever Became of Sin?* New York: Hawthorn Books, 1973. An eminent American psychologist diagnoses the disappearance of a sense of sin from the American psyche and stresses the importance of its return for a renewed sense of personal and social responsibility.

Schoonenberg, Piet. *Man and Sin: A Theological View*. Notre Dame: University of Notre Dame Press, 1965. A scholarly, somewhat speculative work, but highly suggestive and stimulating. It stresses that the great human sin was the crucifixion of Jesus, the human effort to expel the holy one from our midst.

6 The Reality of Conscience

In making moral judgments about a particular action, as good and so to be done, or as evil and so to be avoided, it is necessary for human beings to have some kind of standard or yardstick, as it were, by which to measure the action and so pass judgment. If I am asked, for example, whether it is morally right or wrong for an individual to participate in war, I will have to have some standard or norm against which I can measure the action of participating in war. Without a norm by which to measure, no judgment of right or wrong will be possible.

Moral judgments are not unique in the need for a norm of some kind. All evaluative judgments require some standard or norm by which to measure whatever is being evaluated. If I am asked whether a student is smart or stupid, I will need some criterion by which to measure his or her intelligence. Or again, in order to decide whether an athlete is a good basketball player, I will need to know whether to judge this on the basis of high school standards, or small college standards, or major college or even professional standards. Until I know what the norm is, I simply cannot pass any meaningful judgment.

In considering norms, it seems that we can put two distinct questions at the outset. We may ask *what* norms are to be used in making judgments. In this case we are concerned with some kind of objective norms, that is to say, with norms which exist outside of and independently of the judging person. Objective norms could be used by any number of different persons to arrive at similar or even identical judgments. Once it is clear, for instance, that the judgment about a student's intelligence is to be made on the basis of an IQ score, any number of people can make the same judgment. But we may also ask about *whose* norms are to be used in making our judgments and *who* will be doing the measuring. In that case we are concerned with subjective norms of judgment. Subjective norms are those which do not exist independently of the judging person or subject and are accessible only to that subject. The most obvious example of a subjective norm of judgment is a person's taste for food and drink. If, for instance, an individual judges that pizza tastes good and hot dogs taste awful, he or she is using personal taste as the norm of that judgment. No one can dispute the judgment or say it is wrong because no one else has access to how the food actually tastes to the person making the judgment.

THE FUNCTION OF CONSCIENCE

Whether or not there are objective norms of morality is a question that we will address in later chapters. It is a difficult and much disputed question. What is not a matter of dispute is that there are subjective norms of morality, and that among these subjective norms, the reality called conscience has pride of place. Conscience may simply be defined as the ultimate, subjective norm of morality.

To define conscience as the ultimate, subjective norm of morality is, of course, to give a functional definition of conscience. It is to say what conscience does, what its job is in human life. A functional definition does not yet identify the reality that conscience is. To offer a comparison by way of illustration, you might know that there is a person arriving at your home today to offer you an enjoyable job at an excellent salary. You know that there is a person who will do this. But you do not know the identity of the person. You want to listen to and follow the advice of the person offering the job, but who is it you are to follow? Similarly, while there is widespread agreement that human beings ought to follow their consciences in order to find their way morally, there is much less clarity and consensus as to what it is one is following when one follows one's conscience.

In discussing conscience, therefore, it is helpful to start with its function and the extent of its authority in the moral life. Once these matters are clarified, it will be time to go in search of a likely candidate to fulfill the required role. We have already defined conscience functionally as the ultimate subjective norm of morality. A word about each of the elements in that definition will be in order.

The Final Authority

To affirm that conscience is the *ultimate* norm is not to suggest that it is the only norm, or even necessarily the best norm. There may well be other norms of morality which we should employ, and certainly from the viewpoint of religious faith God's will is the best and highest norm of morality. Unfortunately, we human beings have no direct, unobstructed access to God's will. We have to judge for ourselves what God's will is or demands; that is to say, we have to make our own moral judgments, even as we may hope that they correspond to God's will. In making our moral judgments there is no higher authority than conscience. Conscience is the final arbiter, the court of last resort; conscience should always get the final say. For all practical purposes there is simply no authority in moral matters that can over-ride the personal judgment of an individual's conscience. So much so is this the case that to be conscientious, to follow one's conscience, to act in accord with the judgment of conscience is what it means, by definition, to be a moral person.

Lest there be any misunderstanding about what is being said here, or that someone think that this is novel teaching for a Roman Catholic theologian to propose, some additional comments are called for. The primacy of the authority of conscience in the moral life means that no other authority has the right or even the ability to usurp the place of conscience—not the Pope, not the Bible, not the bishop, not the Church as a whole, not one's parents, not the state, not anyone, not even a trusted confidant or counselor. We might be well advised to consult some or all of these authorities in the process of making a moral decision, but, when all is said and done, the decision is one's own. Even if, for example, I make my decision on the basis of the Church's teaching or by following the lead of some biblical text or story, it is I who have made the judgment that this is what I should do, and it is I who am responsible for that decision. It is never an exemption from personal responsibility to say that I only did what the Pope said or the Bible said or the state said. For it is I who decided that obedience to this or that authority was the right course of action or the way to follow my conscience. The fact that this has long been standard Roman Catholic teaching is reflected in the fact that it is only the penitent who can accuse himself or herself of sin in the sacrament of reconciliation. For only the penitent knows whether conscience has been violated.

This understanding of the authority of conscience as the *ultimate* norm of morality could be shown to be traditionally Catholic, even if it has not always been clearly taught or sufficiently emphasized. Let it suffice here, however, to turn to the words of the Second Vatican Council for confirmation of its Catholic character. In speaking of the dignity of conscience, the council fathers wrote the following.

> Deep within his conscience man discovers a law which he has not laid upon himself, but which he must obey. Its voice, ever calling him to love and do what is good and to avoid evil, tells him inwardly at the right moment: do this, shun that. For man has in his heart a law inscribed by God. His dignity lies in observing this law, and by it he will be judged.

> His conscience is man's most secret core, and his sanctuary. There he is alone with God whose voice echoes in his depths. By conscience, in a wonderful way, that law is made known which is fulfilled in the love of God and of one's neighbor. Through loyalty to conscience Christians are joined to other men in the search for truth and for the right solution to many moral problems which arise both in the life of individuals and from social relationships. Hence, the more a correct conscience prevails, the more do persons and groups turn aside from blind choice and try to be guided by the objective standards of moral conduct.

> Yet it often happens that conscience goes astray through ignorance which it is unable to avoid, without thereby losing its dignity. This cannot be said of the man who takes little trouble to find out what is true and good, or when conscience is by degree almost blinded through the habit of committing sin (GS 16).

There are many important points in the above passage which deserve to be emphasized and to which we will shortly return. For the moment I only wish to note that the council fathers insist that human beings can discover in the depths of their being the voice of conscience urging them to do good and to avoid evil. They further claim that human dignity, that is to say, the worth that is unique and proper to human beings as human, lies in following this voice, so much so that it becomes the criterion, the norm by which they are adjudged to be good or evil persons. Finally, the council speaks of conscience as the innermost sanctuary of the human person where each one of us is alone with God. Conscience is impenetrable and inviolable by any other human being. It is each individual and only each individual who must listen to the voice of God echoing in the depths of personal conscience and respond appropriately.

For all practical purposes, then, the Council teaches that conscience has the authority of the voice of God in the individual's life. While conscience cannot simply be identified with the voice of God since it can go astray through unavoidable ignorance and other limitations of our human finitude, it does not thereby lose its dignity or authority. Conscience still remains the ultimate subjective norm of morality. It is, therefore, always certainly a sin to violate one's own conscience or to urge another person to violate his or her conscience. About no other human action can such a thing be said. Love of neighbor demands above all else that we respect the freedom and the integrity of the neighbor's conscience.

A Subjective Authority

In addition to defining conscience as the ultimate norm, we have also called it a *subjective* norm. Conscience does not exist apart from the person, nor is it accessible to anyone but the person whose conscience it is. Each human being is the exclusive authority on what his or her conscience commands. No other person has the right or the ability to judge accurately and certainly about the integrity of the individual's judgment of conscience. We have every right, of course, even the obligation, to say that we think a judgment of conscience is wrong, and so to ask the person to reconsider the judgment, to take additional factors into

account and so on. But in the face of the person's claim to be
following conscience, we have no grounds for disagreement.
Conscience is the secret core of the person where one is alone,
and only the Lord may enter. Hence we come to see the truth
and the wisdom in the instruction of the Sermon on the Mount:
"Do not judge and you will not be judged" (Mt 7:1).

A Moral Authority

Finally, we have defined conscience as the *norm of morality*.
This means that conscience is the yardstick, the criterion we use
to measure the moral goodness or badness of our attitudes, intentions and actions. If they accord with our conscience, we judge
them to be morally good and so to be cultivated, pursued and
acted upon. If they appear to be in conflict with conscience, we
judge them to be evil and so to be avoided or changed. For example, if I am faced with the decision whether to suppress some
important facts about my work, as my boss wishes, or to make
them known at the risk of losing my job, there are many things to
be taken into account. I may seek advice and counsel from my
wife, my pastor, my fellow workers, and any number of other people. But finally, ultimately, in the silence of prayer before God, I
make the decision and I alone, except for God, know whether or
not it was a decision in accord with or in conflict with my conscience. Conscience, then, functions as the ultimate, subjective
norm of morality.

THE NATURE OF CONSCIENCE

However, only to stress this primacy of the individual conscience, to say simply that people should follow their consciences,
is hardly adequate or even useful moral teaching. Nor is it entirely
fair to the Catholic tradition of moral theology. For while it
clearly highlights the function of conscience in human moral
experience, it leaves unclear exactly what conscience is, makes no
mention of the dynamics or processes involved in conscientious
reflection, nor does it clarify the relationship of conscience to
other norms of morality. No one can truthfully follow his or her
conscience without knowing what conscience is, what it is that he
or she is following. Nor can a person follow conscience without

some idea of how conscience works, of its capabilities and limits, and of how it relates to other normative sources of morality like the Bible and Church teaching.

Some False Candidates

To begin a discussion of the nature of conscience it is helpful, first, to dismiss some false candidates for the role of conscience. So let us start by saying what conscience is not. Conscience is not to be identified with guilt feelings nor equated with those gnawing, unsought and often unwelcome feelings of anxiety or of impending doom if I do this action or fail to do that action. Nor is conscience to be confused with feelings of elation and self-esteem because I helped this person in need, or with feelings of shame and self-disgust because I neglected to meet a neighbor's need. We reject all such feelings for the role of conscience, not because they are unrelated to or unimportant for our moral existence. They are often useful clues for discerning our moral condition, for examining the strengths and weaknesses of our moral character. But these feelings are simply not qualified for the role of conscience, and it is not too difficult to understand why they fail to qualify.

Whatever conscience is, it functions as the guide for the actions of a human person whose dignity consists in freedom and rationality. Human beings are moral beings, as we have seen, precisely because they enjoy the capacity for reflective self-awareness. This capacity means that they can make choices and have reasons for those choices. But the feelings we have mentioned are not freely chosen; they are blind and often irrational. They well up unlooked-for out of the depths of the human unconscious; their presence in our lives is simply not the result of rational calculation and free choice. Because they are not the consequence of free choice, feelings are not subject to a moral analysis that would declare them to be morally good or morally evil. To tell people that they should not feel as they do is as silly as telling them that they should feel what they do not feel. Feelings, in the whole range of their possibilities, may well be useful clues to one's own psychological and spiritual condition, but they are treacherous guides of moral action. They provide helpful insight into our characters, but tell us precious little about the truth of the world in which we act.

To illustrate the above argument briefly, let us reflect on two simple examples. A man who has been raised to put high moral importance on weekly church attendance will almost certainly feel twinges of guilt and remorse for missing church on Sunday, even if he had the best reasons in the world for not attending. Priests who hear confessions regularly are more than familiar with the confession that one missed Mass on Sunday becaue he was sick in bed. When pressed, the penitent will acknowledge that he knows this it not a sin, but he feels guilty about it and confessing it will make him feel better. Or again, consider a woman who has always emphasized and valued patient understanding and non-violent responses to situations of conflict and injustice. She will very likely feel devastated the first time her young son comes home with a bloody nose from a schoolyard fight, especially when she learns he started it. She begins to feel that she has done something wrong, is failing in her responsibilities as a parent. In both examples, the feelings, while humanly understandable, clearly manifest themselves as irrational and unfree. Hence, they are hardly suitable guides for the conduct of free and rational human beings. Conscience cannot be equated with our feelings, and the popular song which tells us that "this can't be wrong because it feels so right" does not embody a judgment of conscience.

Neither is conscience to be understood as some kind of psychological or biological mechanism, innate to human nature, that works automatically in response to certain stimuli. Although we often refer to conscience metaphorically as an inner voice or as an internal judge that seems to pass judgment independently of our wishes, we need to recognize the metaphorical character of such language. What the great pioneer in psychoanalysis, Sigmund Freud, called the super-ego is, indeed, a psychological mechanism of the human unconscious. It does have some resemblance to and a relationship to conscience. It might even be called a primitive conscience or the seed-bed of conscience. But it is not the reality of conscience itself, nor does it rightly lay claim to the authority of conscience. Conscience must be a dimension of the free, rational self, a dimension of what Freud called the ego, not the super-ego.

That conscience is not a mechanism of human nature, as opposed to a characteristic of human personhood, is further confirmed when we consider human beings who manifest no signs of having any sense of morality, any idea of moral right and wrong. Such persons, often called sociopaths, personally testify to and reveal in their behavior a complete lack of moral awareness and moral sensitivity. Experience also shows that individuals differ greatly in both the intensity and the range of their consciences. Some people have consciences that are rigid to the point of scrupulosity; others have consciences that are lax almost to the point of moral indifference. Some people have consciences that seem restricted to matters of sex and personal honesty. Others have consciences that extend to the whole spectrum of human behavior, being sensitive to matters of both personal and social morality. Whatever we affirm conscience to be, therefore, must be compatible with the diversity and complexity of conscience as evidenced in human experience.

Conscience and Scripture

In determining just what conscience is, the biblical text is of only limited help. The books of the Bible evidence a complete awareness of the phenomenon of conscience, but generally refer to the phenomenon in functional and metaphorical terms. One especially useful clue to the reality of conscience which Scripture affords us, and which we will try to develop later in this chapter, is to locate the human sensitivity to good and evil in the heart of the human person. (Psalm 95:7, Jeremiah 11:20, Ecclesiastes 7:22, 1 Samuel 24:6, Job 27:6, Matthew 15:11–17, and 1 John 3:19–21 are but a few of many examples.) This location suggests that conscience is an aspect of human knowing and loving and is rooted in the very core of our personal being—the "secret core and sanctuary" of the self which Vatican II referred to in the passage quoted above.

The word conscience itself points us in the same direction. The English word comes from two Latin words: *cum* (con) which means with, along or together with, in company with, and *scientia* from which we get the English word science. Literally, it means a knowing, a knowledge of, and then what is known, a body of knowledge. Put together, then, *conscientia* or conscience means a knowing of something along with something else. More simply put, it involves evaluative knowlege, the knowledge of some reality along with a knowledge of its worth or value as good or bad. We may define conscience, therefore, in fairly traditional terms, as the practical judgment of human reason about an individual act as good and so to be done or as evil and so to be avoided.

Conscience as Practical Reason

This definition of conscience, however, is not quite as simple as it may appear at first glance. As one reflects upon the definition, it emerges that there are three distinct, yet inter-related aspects to conscience, all of which need to be carefully distinguished and understood in their relationship to one another, if we are going to grasp what conscience is. Conscience is, first, the human mind considered from the aspect of its practical ability to evaluate, judge and decide. Conscience refers, in the second place, to the process of reasoning the mind goes through in order to arrive at its judgments. This involves whatever it is a person does when advised to consult one's conscience. Third, conscience refers to the actual judgment itself which is the purpose and end of the reasoning process. I should do this; I should not do that. Each of the three aspects of conscience requires some further consideration.

That human beings do, in fact, often think about, talk about, and argue about right and wrong, good and evil, seems almost too obvious to mention. What is equally true but not quite as obvious is that we really cannot help ourselves in this regard. It is as if we must do this; we are driven to try to understand what is good and evil, to find reasons that will justify our decisions and behaviors or, perhaps, excuse them. The human mind in its practical aspect is by nature oriented to this pursuit. The quest for justification or excuse is natural to us as human. Whether or not the human mind in its aspect of practical reason is capable of attaining true and accurate knowledge of what is good and evil, whether or not there is even such knowledge to attain, we cannot escape the effort to do so, even if we finally conclude that the effort is vain and pointless.

Furthermore, human beings cannot help but acknowledge that what appears to them as good should be done and what appears as evil should be avoided. While they may and do disagree passionately over what is, in fact, good and evil, why it is what it is and why anyone should care about the difference, nevertheless, what commends itself to them as good commends itself as something to be done. What they take to be evil, they take as something that should not be done. One might say, then, that human beings in the aspect of practical reason have a dynamic and settled natural orientation toward the good as something which commands their free loyalty and obedience. (Religious believers may well attribute this natural disposition or orientation to God's creative providence.) The existence of this dynamic inclination to the good may be confirmed in human experience by simply reflecting on the persistent, pervasive human need to give justifying reasons or excuses for even the most morally barbaric conduct. We simply cannot escape the ethical horizons of our existence.

Three important consequences for conscience follow from practical reason's dynamic orientation to the good. Since conscience involves this cognitive or intellectual aspect, it appears that human moral development is dependent upon cognitive development. We have good reason not to expect the conscience of a ten year old to be as sensitive as the conscience of a forty year old. So we must understand conscience to be a developing or dynamic reality rather than a fixed or static thing. There is growth in conscience, growth which can be made more or less difficult or even stifled altogether. For conscience to develop, conscious and careful nurture is required. It does not just happen. It is not simply a matter of luck or fate or destiny. Like physical development, the development of conscience can be retarded by personal choice or neglect, by physical, chemical and biological deficiencies in one's own body, and by factors in the social environment.

A second important consequence that follows from practical reason's dynamic orientation to the good is that the human judgment that good is to be done and evil avoided is a certain and infallible judgment. About this judgment it is impossible to be mistaken. This fact helps to account for the authority of conscience in the moral life. It is important not to misunderstand what is being said here. I have not claimed that the particular judgment of an individual's conscience is certain and infallible.

Only the most basic moral principles and truths, of which the most fundamental is do good and avoid evil, have the characteristics of absolute certainty and infallibility. Nor have I suggested that any of us are infallible in the reasons we might give for why we should do the good and avoid evil. I have said that we know with infallible certainty that we should do the good, and, what is more, we know that we know we should, even if we do not know why we should or how we know we should. Indeed, we know we should do the good even when we do not know concretely and specifically what the good thing to do is, or whether there is any good thing to do. That is the extent of the infallibility of conscience which has been claimed here.

The dynamic orientation of practical reason to the good is often denied or misunderstood because of an incorrect understanding of original sin or a misinterpretation of human experience. That original sin and its consequences have darkened our minds and so made coming to a knowledge of the good difficult, if not impossible, is quite true. That the consequences of sin lead some people to the conviction that the good is an illusion, that morality is just a cloak for self-interest, is also quite true. The indifference toward what is morally good which we may encounter in other people—or even in ourselves at times—may well lead us to reject the idea of practical reason's dynamic orientation to the good. But neither the human inability to know what we should do nor human indifference to moral right and obligation gives lie to practical reason's orientation. Rather, they both confirm this orientation inasmuch as they are both excuses, justifying reasons for why we do not do what we know we should do. Try as it might, the human mind cannot escape its own demand to know, evaluate and judge, even when it expresses that demand in rationalizations and justifying excuses.

A third important consequence of practical reason's dynamic orientation to the good is that God, the supreme Good, is seen to be the horizon and term of the human drive toward the good. Practical reason's orientation to the good does not afford a philosophical proof of God's existence, but it does enlighten the person of religious faith to detect in the demands of conscience the presence and the power of God. For the religious believer, then, the moral experience is also and more profoundly a religious experience. God, the Creator, Sustainer and Lover of life, is also the holy, jealous God who summons us to be holy even as he is holy (Mt 5:48). For Christian faith, morality always has this transcendent dimension; conscience most fundamentally urges us to make a fundamental option, to say yes to God in and through saying yes to the good we know we should do in its various, concrete forms.

THE PROCESS OF CONSCIENCE

The second aspect to be considered in our definition of conscience as the practical judgment of reason about an action as good and so to be done or as evil and so to be avoided sees conscience as the process of reasoning any person goes through in order to arrive at a particular judgment. It refers simply to what it is we do when we consult our consciences or try to be conscientious in our decision-making. It is not to the point here to try to describe this process of reasoning in any detail, even if it might be possible to do so. Rather I wish to notice two things that are true about any process of human reasoning, including that of conscience.

First of all, some ways or processes of reasoning are better than other ways for coming to know the truth. We do not simply know by some instinct what the better ways are. We learn, either by trial and error or by formal training, what these ways are, their limits and their possibilities. As is the case with many other things, processes of reasoning are learned and in the learning some people prove to be more adept than others. Second, as a human process, the reasoning process is fallible, easily prone to mistakes for a variety of reasons. Who, however expert in a form of reasoning, would want to claim that he or she never makes a mistake? From these two observations about the reasoning process, some important conclusions for conscience may be drawn.

Fallible Conscience

If conscience involves a learned process of reasoning, then once again we must understand conscience as a processive or developmental reality, as dynamic rather than static. And we must recognize that the very first demand conscience makes upon us all is not simply to follow conscience but to form it correctly. For conscience to be conscientious, practical reason must learn to reason properly, to adopt true principles, to be consistent and coherent, to attend to facts, to develop a measure of self-critical objectivity in its evaluations. While conscience is a subjective norm of morality, it has within itself the demand for objectivity, the demand that it pay careful and truthful attention to the world it inhabits. It is conscience itself which requires that we be able and willing to give reasons for our evaluations and judgments, and to test our judgments against the reasoning of others. Conscience is, to be quite sure, radically private and personal, but it is not closed off to reality for all its inaccessibility to others.

The fallibility of the human reasoning process also argues for the objective need of human moral reasoning to be open to the views of other people. Once we recognize that the process of reasoning that conscience pursues may possibly go wrong and result in a wrong judgment, we lose all possibility of absolute certitude in regard to any of our personal moral judgments. There is always the chance that I could be wrong for any number of reasons. And so we also begin to recognize the need for and the importance of other moral authorities in our life, most especially the Church in its graced role of teacher of faith and morals. A conscience that is true to its own dynamics will give high regard, even presumptive regard, to the accumulated moral wisdom of the Church and the insights of fellow believers. A conscience that is true to itself will seek its own formation in and through the stories and symbols of the Christian faith as well as the official teaching office of the Church. This teaching authority does not and cannot take the place of personal conscience, but it can become a central feature in the formation of conscience. To ignore this authority or to fail to give it due regard is already to fail in conscientiousness, as would also be the case if one gave it excessive or exclusive regard. Conscience, it needs constantly to be recalled, is answerable to God alone, not to the Church.

The loss of absolute certitude in our moral judgment which comes with the recognition of conscience's fallible reasoning process poses two problems for us. The first problem arises because of the apparent contradiction between the infallibility of conscience in its first aspect as practical reason's dynamic orientation to the good and the fallibility of conscience in its second aspect as a process of reasoning. This problem will be addressed when we consider the third aspect of conscience, the particular judgment that I should or should not do this specific action. The second problem arises because of moral uncertainty. If we recognize the possibility of error in our most conscientious decisions, the question comes as to how certain we have to be in order to act in good conscience. The answer is simple. It is enough to be morally certain about the correctness of one's judgment. But what, then, is it to be morally certain? What are the conditions of moral certitude?

Moral Certitude

In many of our moral judgments we have no serious doubts about what is the morally correct thing to do. While we might be willing to admit the theoretical possibility that we could be wrong, for all practical purposes we are reasonably sure about what we ought to do here and now. That is the experience of moral certitude. At times, however, we lack this sort of confidence in our moral judgments. For any number of reasons we have doubts about the right course of action to pursue. What do we do in such cases in order to act in a way that honors the integrity and authority of conscience? To act in the face of serious doubts of conscience about the rightness of the act would surely not be to follow conscience.

Two general guidelines exist to help us in our quest for a degree of moral certitude, and there is a third guideline for situations in which serious doubts still persist, but a decision to act is inescapable. These guidelines will not assure the correctness of one's decision. Nothing can do that. They are intended to aid us in the conscientiousness of the decision-making process, so that when we do act, we can reasonably claim the authority of conscience for our decision.

The first guideline is to do what we can to remove serious doubt. Are one's doubts well-founded or are they, perhaps, only childish and irrational fears? Are they doubts about matters of fact or matters of opinion? Are they doubts about what my own responsibilities are, or are they doubts about what someone else is responsible for? The second, related guideline is to make every reasonable effort to learn what the right course of action is. "Reasonable effort" may sound somewhat imprecise and elusive. It is. But the point of the guideline is to assist us in excluding laziness, indifference to facts and the wisdom of others, from our moral existence. Positively, it points to such things as discussing the situation with other people, reading something on the subject matter of the decision, and a careful, personal weighing of the pros and cons of any choice. Certainly a believing Christian would attempt to seek insight into the situation from the Scriptures and the teaching of the Church.

It may well happen that after all such efforts have been made as one's time and situation permit—the meaning of "reasonable effort"—serious doubts still remain. Yet circumstances force the person to make some sort of a decision to act in one way or another. A doctor, for example, may need to know whether heroic measures should be made to revive one's sick and senile parent. Or a person may have to decide whether to keep a confidence and let harm come to others or tell what she knows here and now to those who can prevent the harm, but in so doing violate a trust. In situations like these, the moral certainty essential to conscientious decision requires that we choose that action which promises the least moral harm, a calculation which is not an easy one to make. To illustrate this third guideline briefly in the case of the senile parent, one ought to say yes to heroic measures if in doubt. The calculation would go something like this. If I say no to heroic measures, my parent is likely to die without the effort. I will be unable to reverse this result if I resolve my doubts tomorrow and judge in conscience that I should have said yes to heroic measures. If, however, I say yes now, and my conscience becomes clear that the correct decision should be no, I can reverse course. My conscience will not accuse me of contributing to my parent's death by a doubt-filled neglect.

This problem of moral certitude reveals two interesting things about human moral existence. It clearly dispels any notion of conscience as mechanically or instinctively knowing the right thing to do. None of our personal moral choices, none of our conscientious decisions, have infallible guarantees. After we have made the best, the most conscientious decision we are capable of, we still live in hope at the mercy of God. To want more certitude in moral matters than it is possible to have is a frequent, if understandable, temptation. But it is a temptation, and so to be resisted, for it will lead us into smug self-righteousness or callow indifference to moral truth. The moral life, if taken seriously for what it is, has the capacity to teach us both humility and compassion. It can bring to life for us the words Luke attributed to Jesus: "When you have done all you have been told to do, say, 'We are merely servants: we have done no more than our duty'" (Lk 17:10).

The problem of moral certitude also confirms that our moral decisions, however conscientious and certain they may appear to us to be, are our own decisions for which we must own responsibility. Our moral judgments are never purely and simply the dictates of God to us. We may sincerely want to do God's will; we may be reasonably confident that we are doing God's will to the best of our ability; but our judgments and actions are our own, the products of our freedom. We bear the responsibility for them, not God. For they are our response, our free response to the goodness and the grace of God, and in making our response we are and always remain free, autonomous subjects.

The Judgment of Conscience

There is the third and final aspect of conscience to be considered, the actual judgment of conscience to do this or avoid that. It is evident that, if the reasoning process by which we reach this judgment can be faulty, then the judgment of conscience itself can be wrong. Nevertheless, if all the conditions for conscientious decision-making and moral certitude have been met, then one ought to do whatever conscience bids him or her to do. It is only at this point that we can properly speak of the primacy of the individual conscience. And while we insist on this primacy, it is also important to recognize that a person can act in good conscience and still be wrong, but without sin. Yet no one can act in good conscience, if he or she does not care about being right.

The reason why primacy of authority must be given to the judgment of conscience, even as we acknowledge its fallibility, can be found in the twofold nature of that judgment. When a person judges in conscience that "I ought to give a larger share of my income to charity," that judgment is really a double one. It has

both a subjective and an objective focus. It is a judgment both
about the self and about the world.

To clarify the objective focus first, every judgment of conscience says something about the objective worth of the proposed
action. In the context of the present example, there is the judgment that giving money to charity is a morally good practice, not
just for me but for anyone who does it. It is a worthy object of
our intentionality. True, the moral quality of such an action may
be altered by either the intentionality of the agent (e.g., reasons
of pride or hyprocrisy), or by the circumstances of one's life (e.g.,
other people are owed the money). But the action itself has objective worth. It can be commended to anyone as a good thing to
do, given the proper intention and circumstances. The same
objective focus is present in our negative judgments. If, for example, I judge that "I ought not to commit adultery," that judgment
includes a judgment about the negative worth of marital infidelity
as a practice, a negative worth that may or may not be able to be
altered by the intentionality of the agent and the circumstances
of life.

Our judgments of conscience in their objective focus are
clearly fallible, precisely because we may misinterpret or fail to
consider the relevant circumstances of our proposed action, or
because we are not attentive to the objective worth of the action.
If the reader recalls the earlier discussion on the impediments to
moral freedom, he or she will find some of the reasons we go
astray in the objective aspect of the particular judgments of conscience. If the objective focus were all that there was to our moral
judgments, conscience could not claim the authority attributed
to it in the moral life. But there is the subjective aspect of the
judgment of conscience to consider as well.

When we make judgments of conscience, we say something
not only about the world but also about ourselves. We affirm in
these judgments something about our own identity and integrity
as human beings. When, for example, I say that *I* should not commit adultery, I say something about how I understand myself, my
marriage, and my own integrity as a human being. I speak the
truth about myself. In regard to the subjective aspect of the judgment of conscience, the individual person is the absolute and
infallible expert. An individual's judgment about his or her own

sincerity, about what personal identity and integrity demand, cannot be mistaken. Consequently, the individual ought to act on that judgment though all the world stands opposed to it. It is for this reason that conscience can err, yet not lose its dignity and worth as conscience, for it remains conscientious. I would like to re-emphasize, however, that such is not the case where conscience refuses to recognize its own objective demands for social and ecclesial formation and moral certainty. Personal sincerity that takes no trouble to inform itself or that remains indifferent to the claims of moral truth cannot lay claim to moral integrity.

CONSCIENCE AS SELF-AWARENESS

Throughout this discussion of conscience I have emphasized that conscience involves the exercise of practical reason. It is now time to take more serious notice of Scripture's location of conscience in the heart of the human person with its overtones of affectivity and emotion influencing the judgment of conscience. I do this to deepen our understanding of just what conscience is. To assist in this task, I wish to employ a distinction between two kinds of human knowledge, thematic and pre-thematic knowledge.

Two Kinds of Knowledge

Thematic knowledge refers to explicit, abstract, conceptual, reflexive knowledge. It is the kind of knowledge we are capable of expressing in words and concepts. We can write it down in books, teach it in classrooms, test it out and refine it through scientific experiments. Pre-thematic knowledge, on the other hand, refers to that knowledge we have that is real but which either we have not yet learned to express in thematic form or is incapable of being given thematic expression. To give but two brief examples: there are people who know how to do certain things very well, but are unable to say how they know and cannot teach what they know to others. Their knowledge is pre-thematic. Many athletes, actors and actresses could illustrate this type of knowledge. Or again, there are instructive human experiences from which we truly gain knowledge, but the knowledge cannot be reduced to words and concepts. That is one reason we paint pictures, play music, throw parties, and hug each other.

These two forms of knowledge are both real in that both of them really know something. Thematic knowlege is plainly a derived and secondary form of knowledge, dependent entirely upon the prior pre-thematic knowledge, or at least dependent to a large degree. Pre-thematic knowledge is not to be equated with, reduced to, or considered inferior to thematic knowledge. The two forms of knowledge are simply two different ways human beings have of knowing the world and themselves. Nor are the two forms of knowledge necessarily at war with one another, though at times they may come into conflict individually or socially. Rather, they are, or can be and should be, mutually corrective and expansive of one another. Individually, what I call my intuitive knowledge can be corrected and expanded by my book learning; but my book learning also needs and can receive correction and expansion from my pre-thematic knowledge. Socially, we need to listen seriously to the words of technical experts in various fields, but we also need to hear the more intuitive, felt claims of people living life.

When applied to our moral existence, there is no reason not to give both forms of knowledge a place in the reflections of conscience, or, more accurately, in the reflections of the conscientious person. Conscience, then, must be understood to precede any analytic division of the human person into the various capabilities of reasoning, feeling and deciding. The reality that is conscience may quite simply be said to be a person's deepest, most authentic self-consciousness or self-awareness. And the judgment of conscience is a judgment that a proposed action is or is not compatible with the person's origin and destiny, with what one understands the self to be and to be called to become. For the Christian believer, self-awareness will include such identifying traits as a person created in God's image, fallen and redeemed in Christ, given new life in the Spirit through baptism, united to the member's of Christ's body and called to holiness expressed in loving one another as Jesus has loved them. Conscience, understood as the person's deepest self-awareness, is clearly a processive, developmental reality, and a call to a continuous self-transcendence. It is conscience that will be restless until it rests, finally and fully, in the Supreme Good, God.

External Moral Authority

This way of understanding conscience does not, of course, resolve all conflicts of conscience. No understanding of conscience could be expected to do that. But it does answer one important question, the question of the relationship of conscience to all other moral authorities. No external authority, be it the Bible, the Pope, the local Church, the state, or whoever, can replace or usurp the authority of personal conscience. No external authority should be preferred to the judgment of one's own conscience. Not only do human beings have the moral right to follow their own consciences; it is also their most fundamental and solemn moral obligation to do so. To force or attempt to force another person to violate his or her conscience is a major sin, a major failure to love the other, for it is, quite simply and inescapably, to ask that person to sin, to turn against God and betray his or her very own self.

Confusion about the relationship of conscience to external moral authority often arises because people fail to distinguish the subjective and objective aspects of the particular judgment of conscience. In failing to make this distinction they confuse personal sincerity with truth. As we have seen, it is the dynamic orientation of practical reason to the good which grounds the most basic of all moral principles, do good and avoid evil. That I should do the good is a judgment about myself in relation to the world. It is also a true judgment about which I cannot be mistaken. But if I should do the good, then I should also seek to know what is good. I must engage in the process of moral reasoning, seeking as best I can to know the truth about what is and is not good. Hence, the loyalty of conscience in its second aspect is to the truth, not to personal sincerity. It is only to the truth that conscience should submit.

Now in our quest for the truth about what is and is not good, it seems important that Christian believers acknowledge three significant theological facts. The first is that the Holy Spirit, the Spirit of truth (Jn 16:13), has been poured out upon the entire body of Christ, not simply on one lone individual, me. Further, this Spirit is a Spirit of unity, not division (1 Cor 12:4–11). For Catholic Christians there is the added conviction that the official teaching office of the Church in the person of the Pope and the bishops receives special help from the Spirit in interpreting the divine and natural moral law, even to the point of sometimes being able to teach infallibly in matters of faith and morals. (Whether they have ever done so and to what degree they can do so are entirely different questions which we bypass here.) Given this theological truth, the presumption of any individual conscience must be that the whole Church, and the teaching office in particular, is more likely to be correct in its perceptions of what is morally good and evil than any one individual conscience. I ask the reader to note that this is only a presumption, not a certainty or a guarantee and not to be treated as if it were. The presumption in favor of the teaching office does not rule out disagreement or dissent. It merely puts the burden of proof on the one who disagrees or dissents. In any case a Catholic Christian conscience that did not give serious, presumptive attention to the official teaching of the Church has little claim to being either conscientious or Catholic.

The second theological fact to be acknowledged in conscience's quest for the truth is our own sinfulness, our own propensity to rationalize, to call attention to ourselves, to see things as we would like them to be rather than as they really are. This demand to acknowledge our own sinfulness is not an invitation to doubt our own sincerity or to question our own integrity or, still less, to blindly obey those in authority. It is a reminder to recognize our own fallibility and so to be sure we have met the requirements for moral certainty. It is love for the truth about what is good, and so ultimately love for God and neighbor, which impels conscience to recognize its own limitations in the quest for the truth.

The third theological fact to be acknowledged as we pursue the truth about the good is that it is divine love that impels us to love our neighbor as we have been loved. This love seeks not an aspect of the good, not a good that is partial or discriminatory, but an integral and a common good. It is a love that seeks human well-being, that seeks the well-being of the whole person and the well-being of the whole human family. It is a love for all and forever. One test we can apply to our judgments of conscience to see if they have grasped a good that is both integral and common is to ask if the proposed action will lead to future possibilities of growth and relationship. Evil often manifests itself in its inability to sustain a future. For example, a relationship that is built upon a lie cannot sustain itself. It will collapse sooner or later. If we do not attend to this concern of the divine lover for an integral and common good, we may well miss the moral worth or disvalue of a proposed action.

Conscientious Dissent

These three theological truths seem to me to be the essential elements surrounding the question of conscientious dissent from the teaching of all external moral authorities, and, in the case of Roman Catholics, from official Church teaching on morality. Together they point to the fact that in the actual process of moral discernment and judgment, dissent is never sufficiently warranted or grounded simply because an individual fails to see the objective worth or evil in a proposed action. The mere fact that I do not see why a certain practice is wrong or why a specific practice is obligatory, or the fact that I am not persuaded by any reasons that authority gives for its position, does not give me a basis for conscientious diagreement and dissent. The fact that I do not recognize the moral worth in a law or in the dictates of authority does not mean that I have no obligation to obey authority. It is quite true, of course, that there is no moral worth in obeying law simply because it is law or in submitting to authority just because it is authority. There is moral worth in obedience only insofar as law and authority mediate the good or God's will to us. But my failure to discover or see the good in what authority proposes is not sufficient ground for refusing obedience. Others may, in fact and in all probability, see the good and they may be reasonably expected to have done so when my limited and sinful eyes remain blind.

But this does not mean that there are no grounds for conscientious dissent from law or authoritative moral teaching. It can and it does happen that an individual—correctly or incorrectly— becomes convinced that he or she has positive reasons for thinking that the law or the official teaching is wrong, that the truth about what is good lies elsewhere and truth summons him or her to act in a different way. Love for the neighbor may well have reasons for action that law cannot comprehend. Love may well recognize values demanding to be served in a situation which law or external authority cannot see. Consequently, while it is not enough not to see what is wrong or right about a practice in order to have grounds for a conscientious dissent, for the individual who sees—or is sincerely convinced that he or she sees—that the truth about the good lies elsewhere than authority proclaims, conscientious dissent is not only a possibility; it is an obligation.

By way of summary, we have seen in this chapter that conscience, as the ultimate, subjective norm of morality, is the particular judgment of practical reason upon an action as good and so to be done or evil and so to be avoided. In clarifying the three aspects of conscience contained in that definition, we came to an understanding of conscience as the deepest, most authentic self-awareness of the person, a self-awareness that is in constant development, dynamically inviting the self to transcend what is, in order to be and become what God has made us to be, the holy lovers of God and neighbor. We stressed the primacy of conscience's authority in the moral life, but only as it takes seriously its own objective demands for formation, critical objectivity and moral certainty. In this context we raised the question of the possibility of conscientious dissent from official Church teaching.

The discussion of the relationship between conscience and external moral authorities has raised the question of objective norms of morality. More specifically, it has raised the question of love's relationship to law. Consequently, we will turn to these questions in the next two chapters, beginning with the important matter of how love and law are to be understood in relation to one another in our moral existence.

STUDY QUESTIONS

1. Why is it a mistake to identify conscience with our feelings of guilt or elation after we have done something? What value do such feelings have?

2. What sort of infallibility does conscience have? In what ways is conscience fallible?

3. Why is the formation of conscience such a fundamental moral obligation? What are some of the things that contribute to the formation of conscience?

4. Can you give some concrete ways you could use the guidelines for moral certainty? Why can we not expect to have anything more than moral certainty in regard to our moral decisions?

5. Do you find yourself disagreeing with any of the moral teaching of the Church? Using the guidelines suggested in the chapter, is this disagreement a conscientious one?

BIBLIOGRAPHY

Curran, Charles E. and Richard A. McCormick, S. J. (eds.). *Readings in Moral Theology, No. 3: The Magisterium and Morality.* New York: Paulist Press, 1981. A series of essays offering different perspectives on the role of the magisterium and of conscience in making moral decisions.

Miller, Donald E. *The Wing-Footed Wanderer: Conscience and Transcendence.* Nashville: Abingdon Press, 1977. A difficult but rewarding work by a liberal Protestant theologian, integrating psychological and spiritual development around the growing sensitivity of conscience.

Nelson, C. Ellis (ed.). *Conscience: Theological and Psychological Perspectives.* New York: Newman Press, 1973. An excellent collection of articles on conscience written from a variety of theological and psychological perspectives. The essays are often technical, but almost always readable.

O'Connell, Timothy, M. *Principles for a Catholic Morality.* New York: The Seabury Press, 1978. Chapter eight has an excellent discussion of the idea of conscience to which the present chapter is deeply indebted. This chapter may be the single best treatment of the subject presently available to the general reader.

Regan, George M. *New Trends in Moral Theology.* New York: New-
    man Press, 1971. Chapter ten surveys the fundamental
    themes of contemporary theologians in regard to consci-
    ence. It is particularly helpful in relating conscience to fun-
    damental option and in clarifying conscience as the deepest
    form of self-consciousness.

7 Love and Moral Rules

Among the many biblical passages that are cited again and again for their wisdom and inspiration, St. Paul's hymn to love (1 Cor 13:1–13) is surely one of the best known. Love, as Paul writes of it in this letter, would seem to be a summary or compendium of all the human virtues. "Love is always patient and kind; it is never jealous; love is never boastful or conceited; it is never rude or selfish; it does not take offense, and is not resentful" (1 Cor 13:4–5). Love delights in truth; it also trusts, hopes and endures. Best of all, it lasts forever and is the greatest of all the things that do last. It is little wonder that, at the conclusion of the hymn to love, Paul exhorted his readers, "You must want love more than anything else" (1 Cor 14:1).

If, however, we try to assess our experiences of love in the light of Paul's description of love, it seems that many of the experiences we call love do not measure up to Paul's claims about love. Indeed, they sometimes flagrantly contradict his claims. Human experiences of loving and being loved are often marked by jealousy, possessiveness and resentment. Human loves not infrequently wither and die. Human beings often conceal the truth from loved ones rather than delighting in it. Human love often despairs. In short, the human experience of loving and being loved is but one more of those ambiguities of human existence which both attract and repel us.

THE VARIETIES OF LOVE

Surely one of the reasons why our human experience of love comes up short when measured against Paul's description of love is because human loving takes on a variety of forms. The word love itself in the English language is used to refer to a wide range of different human experiences and relationships. So diverse are the experiences we call love that it appears love has no precise content, no definite shape or structure. It is not surprising that people often remark that love cannot be defined or explained; it can only be experienced.

True as this commonplace of human wisdom may be in some senses, it is also the case that Christians are commanded to love God with their whole heart and mind and strength and will, and their neighbors as themselves (Mk 12:28–34). John's Gospel, as we have seen, urges Christians to love one another as Jesus loved them. What is it they are being asked to do when such exhortations are made? Unless we can say something more precise about the nature and meaning of love, and about the experience to which the word points, how are we to know what we have now been commanded to do?

Fortunately, the language in which the New Testament was written, Greek, had more than one word for our English word love. The Greek language was sensitive to the different forms and experiences of human affectivity, and so it can help us in trying to understand the central ethical imperative of the Christian faith, "to love one another as I have loved you."

Philia

One form of human love, for which the Greek language used the word *philia,* is the love that is appropriate to friendship. Americans are familiar with the word *philia* in reference to one of their major cities, Philadelphia, the city of brotherly love. *Philia,* the love that exists between friends, is a love that is based upon shared or mutual interests. There is some thing, event, or experience that brings friends together, that provides them with a shared focus of attention and concern, that mediates the personal relationship they develop with one another. Friends are often described as standing shoulder to shoulder with both focused on some common interest or purpose outside themselves. This description is in contrast to lovers who stand face to face gazing into one another's eyes, their focus exclusively on one another.

Almost anything can serve as the basis of friendship. A common job, a mutual interest in stamp collecting or football, a shared delight in square dancing or growing roses, a common vocational or educational experience, are but a few examples of what can unite two people in a bond of friendship. It is, however, both the nature of the shared interest and the intensity of that interest which determines the length and the strength of the friendship. College students, for example, often become friends during their college years only to find that the friendship withers and dies when the college experience ends. The shared experience is over and they no longer have anything in common to sustain the relationship. Some college friendships, however, do endure because other, longer-lasting and deeper common interests were also shared, until the friendship itself became the bond that the two friends had in common.

Because *philia* is based on mutual interests, and because there are many interests, and because it is possible to share interests with any number of people, *philia,* or the love proper to friendship, is by its very nature a non-exclusive love. It is both possible and healthy for human beings to have more than one friend, albeit the intensity and degree of intimacy in plural friendships will differ. Nevertheless, because friendship takes time and energy and a common attention to the shared interest, *philia* of its very nature cannot be universal. Nor can it be simply willed into existence by a free choice or decision. I may want to be interested in the cycles of the stock market, or the beauties of the ballet, or the fortunes of the Pittsburgh Steelers; I may even pretend to be interested. But if I am not really interested, I cannot simply will myself to be so.

Philia, therefore, is not the sort of love we can be commanded to have for others or to enact in our lives, nor is it the form of love that Jesus or Paul and the other New Testament authors bid Christians have for one another. This is not to say that *philia* is unimportant or irrelevant to our moral existence or to our relationship with God. Quite the contrary is true. True friendships, or, more accurately, true friends, are a great gift and support in the human journey, and they are certainly among the clearest mediators of God's love to us. But the command to love one another as Jesus has loved us does not urge us to form a relationship of personal friendship with every neighbor we encounter. That would be a simple human impossibility.

Eros

A second form of human love for which the Greeks had a distinctive word is that form of love they called *eros*. The word itself has passed into the English language in the adjective erotic and related words. The English word erotic suggests that there are strong overtones of sexual attraction and desire in this form of love, which is, indeed, the case. For *eros* refers to that form of love which reveals itself as the passionate desire to possess and be possessed, the desire to become one with the beloved. This desire has its most obvious human expression in the longing for sexual union and possession, and its clearest symbolic realization in the act of sexual intercourse.

But sexual desire is not the exclusive domain of *eros*. The longing, the desire that is at the heart of *eros* is not a mere desire for sexual pleasure or sexual gratification. Such a desire, divorced from or unrelated to the longing for personal intimacy and union with the beloved, is not a form of love. It is plainly and simply lust. Rather, the desire of *eros* is precisely for a union with the other that is personal, exclusive, and forever. This desire may be explicitly sexual in content, but it need not be so. The classic picture of *eros* is two lovers staring into one another's eyes, oblivious to everyone and everything else, yet perfectly content. In the grip of the power of *eros*, lovers have no need or desire for anything but one another. The desire that sparks the quest for mystical union with God in prayer is *eros* at work, which is one reason why mystics are fond of sexual imagery to describe their mystical experience. Artists in pursuit of beauty and intellectuals in hot pursuit of truth are also moved by *eros*.

As a form of love, erotic desire is marked by passion, intense and exclusive focus on the object of passion, and instability in human experience. While some degree of erotic desire is essential to the marital relationship, for example, it is hardly a sufficient basis for a long-lasting relationship. It is simply too unstable, despite the fact that eros' own longing is for permanent union. Two lovers at the height of their erotic longing for one another cannot imagine that their love is not forever.

As the Greeks well knew, *eros* has a demonic dimension or aspect to it; it wants what it wants imperiously, immediately, often blindly, and in total indifference to the consequences of getting what it wants. Unrestrained, undisciplined *eros* is compulsive and obsessive; it is the root of jealousy, possessiveness and the violence that often accompanies unrequited or frustrated sexual passion. Unrestrained *eros* disrupts not only personal existence but social existence as well. The ancient Greeks had the story of the twenty year Trojan War, started by Paris' erotic desire for Helen whose face launched a thousand ships, to remind them of the disruptive, demonic power of *eros*.

While *eros* longs for exclusive and permanent union with the beloved, it is neither universal in scope nor capable of being willed as a matter of free choice. It is, therefore, not a form of love that can be commended to people as a moral stance toward the neighbor. It is not the form of love that Christians are urged to have for others. Again this is not to say that *eros* is unimportant or irrelevant to human moral existence or to one's relationship with God. It is likely that most human lives could well do with more, not less, erotic passion. Without *eros* we will not eagerly pursue truth and beauty and goodness. We will not be staunch in the pursuit of justice and peace. But, as a matter of fact, Christians are not called upon to enter into erotic love relationships with everyone they meet, not even with all other believers. That would be a human impossibility, contradicting the very nature of *eros* itself.

Agape

The form of love which the New Testament commends to us it calls *agape*. Theologically, *agape* is understood first of all to refer to God's love for us as that love is revealed in the life, death and resurrection of Jesus of Nazareth, the Christ. It is at work in human beings insofar as God has poured out his Holy Spirit into their hearts, enabling them to love one another with his own love. Agapaic love, therefore, is an enabling, transforming power in the life of the individual person; it is a power which enables one to act freely and deliberately, and not merely to feel a certain way.

Since *agape* is God's love revealed in Christ, it is from the paradigmatic story of Jesus of Nazareth that the characteristics of agapaic love are drawn. The first characteristic of *agape* is that it is free, a gift, or, in the language of theology, a grace. Like the other forms of love we have discussed, it is not a self-willed or self-adopted attitude. It can only be received humbly and grate-fully as a gift and a challenge, and given freely in the same spirit. Human beings are capable of this form of love only because God has first loved them and redeemed them in Christ, only because something has first been done to them and for them.

The second characteristic of *agape* is that it is unmotivated by any quality or function in the object of love. This way of expressing the matter, however, has the potential for being seri-ously misleading, especially if it suggests that agapaic love is arbi-trary and irrational or entirely independent of reason. In its pri-mary meaning of God's love for us, it is quite true that *agape* is not motivated or called forth in God by any attractiveness in or activity of human beings. God does not find something in us which is lovable and to which he responds with love. God does not love in response to the beauty or the goodness of his crea-tures. Instead, God creates that beauty and goodness by loving his creatures into being. God's reasons for loving are to be found in himself, not in the objects of his love.

We human beings, however, do not and cannot love in this way. We do not initiate or create *ex nihilo* truth or beauty or goodness; we find it and respond to it. An unmotivated love, a love that does not have an already existing basis in reality, a love that is not intent upon some good already real, is humanly incon-ceivable. Human beings always have reasons for their loves, how-ever bizarre and inarticulate those reasons may be. It would also be misleading to understand *agape* as disinterested love and so contrast it too sharply with *eros*. Even God, in his loving creation of the universe and his calling of Israel to be his people, and Jesus in his loving, sacrificial death on the cross, were not disinterested lovers. They wanted something. In the most general terms, they wanted the well-being of creation, the abundance and the fullness of life for all of humankind (1 Tim 2:4; Jn 10:10). The biblical witness testifies that the divine wanting is both passionate and powerful.

The characteristic of *agape* under discussion here might best be described as other-directed love. The good on which agapaic love is intent is the good not of self but of the neighbor. *Agape* is a love motivated or called forth by no need of the self, by no desire of the self for the self. It is called forth by the need of the

other. Agapaic love is a love of the other in his or her own interest. It is a love that seeks nothing for itself, but which affirms and
delights in the being and in the well-being of the other. *Agape,*
therefore, is a love both universal in scope and particular in practice. It is universal in scope because it is not dependent upon
some quality or some activity of the other to call it forth. It
requires only the decision of the lover to love, the decision to
rejoice in and serve the well-being of others for the simple reason
of who and what they are, children of God made in his own image
and redeemed in the blood of Christ. It is particular in practice
because it loves this neighbor here and now in specific ways
responding to specific needs. *Agape* is not that vague sort of sen-
timentalized good will which loves all of humankind but loves no
human beings in particular. It is rather a love exemplifed perfectly in the parable of the good Samaritan (Lk 10:29–37).

The third distinctive characteristic of *agape* is that it is a forgiving, redeeming love. This should not be misinterpreted to
mean a sloppy, sentimental tolerance which takes offense at nothing because it has no convictions of its own. Such a misunderstanding would rob *agape* of its substance and strength. Dorothy
Day, the co-founder of the Catholic Worker Movement, once
described God's love as harsh and dreadful. That description of
agape is much closer to the reality than a placid tolerance. For
implicit in a forgiving, redeeming love is the truth that there is
something to forgive, something that needs redemption, someone who needs salvation from being lost forever. Agapaic love is,
indeed, a demanding form of love, for it calls us to repentance
and conversion and new life. It summons us to live up to the very
best within us, to be holy as the divine love is holy. *Agape* is truly
a free love freely given with no strings attached and not dependent upon the response it seeks. But it is also a tough love, so
tough, in fact, that it cannot be turned back or overcome, no matter what the response of the person toward whom it is directed.
As St. Paul wrote to the Romans, "Nothing therefore can come
between us and the love of Christ, even if we are troubled or wor-
ried, or being persecuted, or lacking food or clothes, or being
threatened or even attacked. . . . For I am certain of this: neither
death nor life, no angel, no prince, nothing that exists, nothing
still to come, not any power, or height or depth, not any created

thing, can ever come between us and the love of God made visible in Christ Jesus our Lord" (Rom 8:35, 38–39).

While, then, it is *agape* that the New Testament commends to us as the love with which we are to love one another, in many of our personal relationships all three forms of love may well be present to some degree. The three forms of love are not, or at least need not be, competitors or rivals one with another. A married couple, for instance, may happily find *philia, eros,* and *agape* all giving form to their relationship, mutually supporting and enhancing their two in one flesh unity. But *agape* has the primacy of place morally in all our relationships precisely because it is love, as a theological virtue, which is the inner shaping force of all other virtues. This will become clear if we reflect briefly on the virtues and see why love has the primacy in moral theology and Christian life among all the virtues.

LOVE AND VIRTUE

A virtue is a character strength, a settled attitude or disposition of the self which inclines the person to act in a certain fashion. The person, for example, who has the virtue of patience, has the habit or stable inclination of acting with controlled calm in situations of hectic anxiety or stress. Such a person may not, in fact, always act patiently, but at such times he or she will surprise those who know the person well. "That is not like you—it is out of character," they will say.

Virtues, of course, are learned; they develop only over time through the exercise of acts of the virtue. They gradually give shape to our personal character, establishing a certain predictablity or trustworthiness to our personal responses to life's varied situations and unpredictability. We can count on the person who has the virtue of honesty to deal honestly with us even in the midst of temptation. And the more deeply rooted and developed the virtue, the more trust we extend to the person. While virtues have been defined classically as habits of the soul, it is important to emphasize that they are not static or mechanical reactions of the self to external stimuli. Virtues are strengths, enablements, enhancers of human freedom, making it possible for the person who possesses them to act in ways of his or her own conscious and deliberate choosing.

Among the many human virtues, three can be singled out as the theological virtues—faith, hope and love. They are called theological virtues because their term or object is God. God is the good or the goal toward which these virtues incline the virtuous person. Hence, among all the virtues these three have the primacy because they incline the person to the Supreme and Universal Good. And among the three theological virtues the greatest is love.

The reason why love has the primacy among all the virtues is because love alone is universal in its range and is present as the inner core or form of all other virtues. Love opens up human beings to the whole of reality and is an appropriate human response in all situations. There is nothing in reality that cannot and should not be or become an object of our love, no time or situation in which we ought not to be loving people. Some of our life experiences call for one virtue; other life experiences require a different virtue. Concretely, sometimes we are called upon to be generous with our worldly goods, sometimes to be chaste, sometimes to be truthful, sometimes to be patient. But always we are called upon to be loving. Unlike the other virtues, love is not for this or that occasion; it is for all occasions.

Furthermore, the theological virtue of love, *agape* in us, is the inner core of all other virtues, giving them their moral character or form as virtue. While such abstract language may be difficult to grasp, the concept can be readily illustrated from common human experiences. It is, for instance, quite possible to practice truthfulness in a non-loving way. One can tell the truth to wound, to scandalize, to embarrass others. Such behavior certainly has the external appearance of the virtue of truthfulness, but the absence of love means that it does not have the form of moral goodness. It is simply not a virtuous act. Or again, it is quite possible to abstain from immoral sexual actions and thoughts because one finds sex dirty, disgusting or unpleasant. Such behavior has the external appearance of the virtue of chastity, but in the absence of love it fails to have the moral form of virtue. It is love, then, that is the inner core which gives a virtue its form as virtue. So chastity is a virtue, a human strength; prudery is a vice, a human weakness. And it is love which makes the difference, not the external content of the activity.

The Limits of Love

Given this primacy of love, it is understandable why many Christians think and say that love is all one needs to live a Christian moral existence. In St. Augustine's words, "Love and do what you will." If we were perfect lovers, this would be quite true, and there are times in our lives in which our love for another human being unerringly leads us to do or say exactly the right thing without any need for reflection, reasons or explanation. We just know what action fits love's demands here and now and we do it with ease and spontaneity.

But, at other times and in other situations, we just do not know what to do. We are in a quandary as to what love demands. So we often fall back upon the moral rules or commandments we have been taught to guide our behavior. Yet even then, it may well appear that love inclines us to act in one way, while the moral rules we have learned impel us to act in another way. We experience an apparent conflict between love and law. The Gospels present us with an exemplary case of this conflict between love and law. Jesus, in his healing people on the Sabbath, violated one of Judaism's strictest and most sacred moral rules (Mk 3:1–6; Jn 9:1–41). It is in the context of such an example that the question necessarily arises as to the relationship of love to law or to moral rules.

LOVE AND LAW

The question of love's relationship to law is a critical one for the Christian faith for a number of reasons. In the first place, it is a question of very long standing in the Church, going all the way back to New Testament times when Jesus' first followers had to wrestle with the obligations that faith in Jesus imposed upon Gentile converts. Were they or were they not required to observe the Mosaic law? (Acts 15:1–29). The decision that the Mosaic law was no longer binding on the new Christians gave the new faith a universal appeal, but it did not put an end to confusion and controversy about love's relationship to law (Gal 3:1–5:26; Jas 1:19–25; 2 Pet 3:14–18).

Second, the same question has continued to resurface again and again in Christian history. It was one of the central points of controversy in the Protestant Reformation where it was wrongly argued as a faith-works controversy. The Reformers rightly insisted that salvation was God's free gift offered in Christ and received in faith, not something earned by our good works or by our observance of the law. They misinterpreted the Roman Catholic insistence on works of love being essential to faith to mean that we earn salvation by observing the laws of God and the Church. The Catholic Counter-Reformation rightly insisted on the Christian obligation of faith to respond to God's free gift of salvation in both word and deed, and wrongly interpreted the Reformers to say that good works were not an integral and constitutive aspect of the Christian life. With the benefit of historical hindsight we can now see that there were, and continue to be, substantial theological differences between the Protestant and Catholic understanding of faith, but how human beings are saved is not one of them. The relationship of love to law, however, is one such difference in many cases.

Third, the love-law question has important bearing both on the motivations we bring to our moral activity and on the method we use for knowing what love of neighbor requires or forbids in various situations. This third reason often has practical import in the way people understand the relationship of justice and love. If, for example, one is the victim of a criminal act, does love require that you forgive the criminal and forego prosecution and punishment? And does justice require that we insist upon restitution and retribution? To use another case, does justice require that we stand up for our own rights and insist upon them no matter what the cost to self or others, while love urges us to forego our own rights in the interest of others and for the sake of unity within the community of the faithful? (Rom 14:13–21; 1 Cor 6:1–8). Do love and justice point us in the same direction or in different, even opposite directions? In sum, are justice and love identical, complementary, or contradictory?

The Function of Moral Rules

In order to speak to the question of love's relationship to law, it is helpful to begin by reflecting upon the function of moral rules in human life. One clear purpose that the formulation and transmission of moral rules serve is to pass on to present and future generations the accumulated moral wisdom of the past. We humans living in the last quarter of the twentieth century are not the first people to wrestle with questions of moral good and evil. Others before us have wondered how best and most nobly to conduct themselves sexually, how to use their possessions most justly, how to protect and care for human life, and so on. To ignore the wisdom gained from their experience and handed on to us in moral rules, proverbs, sayings, and stories would be the height of folly and arrogance. It would be neither loving nor conscientious. Nor does each one of us have the leisure and the genius to be another Augustine, Aquinas, Calvin or Kant. But we can benefit from their genius and their efforts and we would be foolish not to do so.

On the other hand, we do face new problems, new situations and new possibilities in our time. To treat the moral wisdom of the past as absolute, final, complete and unchangeable would also be a grave folly. We are all too aware that previous generations have been relatively blind to moral problems like slavery, parental and political tyranny, racial and sexual exploitation, and so on. We certainly can and should learn from the wisdom of our ancestors, and moral rules can help us to do so. But it would be a mistake to absolutize their wisdom and hold their rules and their ways as sacred.

A second important function of moral rules in human life is that they afford us a needed degree of psychological and social security. There is a degree of security in knowing as clearly as possible what is and is not expected of us, what we will and will not be held accountable for, what will be tolerated in our behavior and what is simply unacceptable. Psychologically, such security is helpful in the formation of one's sense of personal identity and in the organization of one's psychic and physical energies. Socially, moral rules help a people order the common life against the forces of chaos and anarchy. Again, the longing for a secure existence can be overdone, leading to a rigidity of personality and to a society incapable of cultural and historical adaptation. But for both personal and social life, some structure of meaning and value is necessary and moral rules help to provide this needed structure.

Moral rules have a third purpose in human life. They help to prevent present indecision and moral paralysis. It is sometimes necessary for us to decide and to act before we have had the personal opportunity to weigh everything involved in a decision. Moral rules can help us to be ready to meet such occasions, by forewarning and forearming us on the basis of the previous experience of others. If every situation we encountered in life were completely unique and unlike anything else, we would be overwhelmed at the randomness of things and paralyzed. Moral rules help us to order experience by grouping similarities together, enabling us to face the new situation in relation to the past.

A fourth contribution that moral rules make to our moral existence is to serve as a prod and a corrective. Moral rules help us recognize our shortcomings and failures, and so they prod us to correct and improve ourselves. Without moral ideals we would become complacent. Without moral rules which concretize our ideals, we would become abstract and vague about what our ideals require. The traditional Roman Catholic practice, traditional since the Council of Trent in the sixteenth century, of requiring penitents to confess their sins according to their specific kind and number had the merit of concreteness, whatever other faults it might have had. Everyone is perfectly willing to admit in general terms to being a sinner or to being somewhat less than perfect. But that kind of generality has no cutting edge. It blunts the impact of self-examination as well as the criticism of others. It dulls the impetus to growth and silences the self-transcending call of conscience and the Holy Spirit. Moral rules have the merit of correcting us and prodding us in concrete and specific ways.

Finally, moral rules are one way that people have of sharing experience in order to create a common world with a common authority. To be a people, to sustain a degree of social unity and social purpose, requires a shared set of values articulated in law under a commonly accepted authority. Moral rules which guide both personal and social behavior aid in achieving and sustaining this unity and purpose. They would seem to be essential requirements for both love and community to exist.

These five functions of moral rules in human life suggest that love and law are not altogether antithetical to one another. To disregard moral rules as either useless or, even worse, positively harmful to the quest for moral truth and loving action seems shortsighted, to say the least. Any view of the Christian life and the virtue of love which ignores or rejects the usefulness of law must be judged to be inadequate. It remains blind to the social nature of human persons as well as to the enclosed character of the self which needs other selves to call it out of itself into a variety of relationships. Freedom from the law is not freedom to ignore or reject the law; it is rather freedom from the bondage of law, a freedom based on the recognition that law is an essential servant of human well-being, but not the master of our decisions and actions. Or as Jesus is portrayed as having said, "The sabbath was made for man, not man for the sabbath; so the Son of Man is master even of the sabbath" (Mk 2:27–28).

Moral rules, then, may be said to be at the service of love, to be subordinate to love, to be a help in guiding love toward what is authentically good. But can anything more than that be said about the relationship of love and law? Take the ten commandments, for example. Do they simply provide guidelines to love, guidelines which are to be rejected whenever love is so inclined? Or must we look for a closer relationship between love and law?

Two Experiences

There are two human experiences which serve to underscore the problematic nature of love's relationship to law. The first is the experience of having to make moral decisions when there simply are no moral rules to guide us. The second experience is when the moral rules themselves are present and clear enough, but in a given situation two moral rules appear to be in conflict with one another. Contemporary developments in science and technology are producing many situations of these two kinds. We have no moral rules, for example, guiding the donation of organs for the purpose of transplants. Should I donate my bodily organs to medicine for transplant purposes upon my death? Does love require this, so much so that to fail to donate is to fail to love my neighbor as Jesus loved me? We have no rules to answer those questions. Love has to decide. In a similar way, we do have moral rules governing both the conduct of war and the right of a nation to self-defense. But in an age of nuclear weapons, the rules of proportionality and discrimination in warfare seem to be in conflict with the rules of just cause and right intention in the defense of human freedom. Again it is love which must decide which rules are to prevail, but how is love to do so?

If we recognize that love is an open or a growing moral notion, we realize that it will never be possible to say all that love means and requires ethically. Love will always outstrip what law can command. Even if we scrupulously observed every moral rule ever articulated, love would still invite us to go further. Jesus himself did not invite his followers to follow the law but to follow him, a much more open-ended invitation. The Christian moral life, therefore, cannot expect to confine itself within the framework of law or moral rules, nor within a fixed, static world of rights and obligations. To try to confine the moral life within such limits is to miss the challenge of Christian ethics which summons us to love as Jesus loved.

Two Kinds of Rules

If we also recognize that moral rules are of two kinds, positive and negative or commanding and prohibiting, we will begin to suspect that love's relationship to moral rules is also of two kinds. Positive moral rules which say do this, do that—e.g., honor your father and mother, keep holy the sabbath day—are pointers to the demands of love, but clearly never exhaust what love demands. Such rules are always situational and relative in their application. One might call positive moral rules the stimulation or goad of love's imagination. Such rules do not call for literal obedience but for loving and intelligent interpretation. The person, for instance, who ignores an urgent need of the neighbor to attend church on Sunday can hardly be said to be keeping the sabbath holy. Positive moral rules will always have exceptions to their literal requirements, or, more exactly stated, will always require an interpretation relative to the situation in which we find ourselves.

Negative moral rules, on the other hand, are statements about what is not compatible with loving one's neighbor. The "shalt nots" of the commandments, for example, tell us what love excludes—killing, stealing, bearing false witness, coveting. Exclusion invites the question as to the absoluteness of these negative prohibitions. Are there some actions so foreign to love that they ought never to be done under any circumstances or in any situation for any reason? It is not my intention here to try to answer that question—I will make an effort to do so in the next chapter. For the moment I wish to explore the meaning and the implications of the question as a preparation for the question central to the next chapter: How do we know what is morally good and morally evil.

ABSOLUTE RULES

Educational psychologists tell us that young children react to all rules as if they were sacred, absolute, and unchangeable. It is only as they develop cognitively and morally that they begin to see that rules have a pragmatic purpose, that they can be changed, and that their value is relative to the situation. But is this the case with all rules of every kind, even those negative moral rules such as "thou shalt not kill," "thou shalt not steal," "thou shalt not commit adultery,"and so on? Are all attempts to hang on to at least a few absolute negative prohibitions merely remnants of an old childhood need for security?

From the Christian perspective, it must be remembered, it is love, not rules, which is the real issue. We have already seen that our inability to say all that love means renders our positive moral rules relative to the situation in which we act. Negative moral rules are attempts to delineate the sorts of behaviors that are foreign to love. Certainly we can say, in general, based upon human experience, that love does not steal or lie or practice adultery. But if any of these negative prohibitions are to be taken in an absolute sense, that is to say, that never, under any circumstances, for any reason, can any of these actions be loving, some formidable theoretical problems must be faced. I will mention three of those problems here, and in order to make our discussion concrete, I will use the Roman Catholic Church's teaching on the practice of artificial contraception.

As is well known, the modern Popes have consistently and repeatedly and explicitly taught over the past fifty years that the use of artificial contraceptives is always a grave evil and a seriously disordered action. In short, such an action is not and cannot be a loving action no matter what the circumstances of the couple or their psychological intentions. I ask the reader to notice that the teaching is not that the practice is always a sin. Subjective reasons like invincible ignorance may well diminish or even abolish personal responsibility and culpability. The action may be subjectively loving, i.e., personally well-intentioned and conscientious, but objectively it misses the mark—it fails to be true, authentic love. If the action misses the mark, it does not and cannot realize the full, self-transcendent value of love to which Christian parents are called.

Intention and Action

This teaching has been found to be a hard, even incomprehensible teaching by many people, for both practical and theoretical reasons. It is the latter sort of reasons we will consider here. First, the teaching insists that no human intentionality, however well-meaning, however deeply concerned for the welfare of one's spouse and other children, can give the practice of artificial contraception the form of love. This is a claim which surely flies in the face of the psychological experience of many couples. Hence, the first theoretical problem is to explain how human intentionality relates to the real world of action and relationship, or, in the context of the present example, where the distortion in intentionality, the missing of the mark in the use of artificial contraceptives, is to be found. A similar problem confronts many Christians today in regard to the problem of using lethal violence in personal or national self-defense. Even granting the justice of one's cause, how can a Christian aim at killing another human being with a right intention, i.e., out of love? In the birth control example, right intention seems simple enough, a concern for one's spouse and children without any harm befalling anyone else. Indeed, the same intentionality appropriate to natural family planning seems to apply to artificial means of birth control. In the self-defense example, right intention seems close to impossible since the action of killing is aimed at personal or national survival and death to the enemy. Yet the Church's teaching is exactly the opposite. It insists that the intentionality of artificial contraception always misses the mark, while the intentionality of self-defense is both a right and a duty. Consequently, there is the need to clarify the relationship between intentionality and the action that is done.

Virtually Exceptionless Rules

A second theoretical problem arises because the Church's teaching on birth control insists on an absolute ban on the practice of artificial contraception in spite of any circumstances, situations or consequences that might seem to warrant the practice. From a purely theoretical perspective, it is clear that no one person or group of persons can know or imagine all possible circumstances or situations in which human action might take place. If that is the case, how can anyone insist on absolute prohibitions? It would seem to say more than we human beings are capable of knowing. So weighty is this objection that many contemporary moral theologians have given up the notion of absolute negative prohibitions, preferring, instead, to speak about "virtually exceptionless rules." A virtually exceptionless rule would be one which functions practically as an absolute prohibition since we cannot, at the moment, imagine a situation in which a reasonable love would ever over-ride the rule. But, theoretically, one has to allow for the possibility of an exception to the rule because of unforeseeable or unimaginable circumstances. It would, then, be up to the individual conscience to judge when such circumstances occur. The moral prohibition against rape would be a good example of a virtually exceptionless rule since it seems practically impossible to imagine a situation in which love for the neighbor would rationally lead to an act of rape. So also might the American Catholic bishops' ban on the use of nuclear weapons be considered a virtually exceptionless rule, since they argued in their pastoral letter that it is presently impossible to imagine a realistic situation in which the use of nuclear weapons could meet just war criteria.

Rules and Infallibility

The third theoretical difficulty confronting absolute negative prohibitions is that one must advance a claim to an infallibility of some kind in order to sustain such rules. In some cases this is not as difficult as it may first appear. For some of our negative prohibitions are expressed in such a way that they are simply true by definition. To understand the meaning of the rule is infallibly to grasp the truth of it by reason. Prohibitions against murder and lying are clear instances of this. Once one defines murder as "the unjust taking of an innocent life," or lying as "the deliberate telling of a falsehood with intent to deceive to one who has a right to the truth," it is beyond question that such actions are certainly always morally wrong. Into such definitions there have been placed a number of situational and intentional factors which decide the morality of the practice by definition. What such definitions do not decide are the concrete actions which fall under the definitions. Such definitions, therefore, remain formal definitions and so give us formal norms which require material application. Hence, the application of the rules remains relative to the situation of the moral agent.

But not all absolute negative prohibitions are so defined as to be self-evidently true to reason. Certainly the Roman Catholic Church's prohibition on artificial contraception is not so defined. Consequently, the authority invoked to support the *absoluteness* of the prohibition is not the infallibility of reason before self-evident truths, but the authority of faith. This faith may be placed in some book, some person, some office or some process. There are fundamentalist groups, for instance, who call upon the Bible to support an absolute prohibition against homosexual behavior. For many Catholics it is the teaching office of the Church or the person of the Pope that is the authority for the ban on artificial contraceptive practices. Some sectarian groups invoke the charismatic authority of their leaders or a process of communal discernment for their assurance of absolute prohibitions against drinking or dancing or participating in war.

The point here is neither to praise nor to criticize the reliance on the authority of faith, but simply to point to its necessity if one wishes to hold to absolute negative moral rules. The same point can be expressed more simply, perhaps, in religious lan-

guage. Only God can know that some action is always and everywhere wrong. If human beings claim to know the same truth, it
can only be because God has revealed it to them in one way or
another. Therefore, the need arises to give some accounting of
how we know moral truth or God's will, or, in more technical language, the need arises to address the question of ethical methodology. Because love wants to hit the mark, it also wants to know
the mark to be hit. And so love needs to know *how to know* what
the loving action is in various circumstances. So we turn at last to
the final foundational question of moral theology, the question
of moral method. How do we know God's will? How do we know
what love should do in order to love one another as Jesus did?
How do we know what is morally right and morally wrong?

STUDY QUESTIONS

1. What is the difference between *philia, eros* and *agape?* Has the
   contemporary usage of love in songs and books and movies
   tended to reduce love to *eros?*

2. What do you think about the question raised in the text on the
   relationship of justice to love? Are they identical, complementary or contradictory virtues? How would you apply your view
   to the punishment of criminals?

3. Can you offer examples from your own experience where
   moral rules have been helpful in guiding your behavior toward
   neighbor love? Do you have examples where such rules have
   not been helpful?

4. Analyze each of the ten commandments. Can you imagine a
   situation in which breaking the commandment would be
   required in order to do the loving thing?

5. Give some examples of virtually exceptionless rules. What are
   the advantages of thinking in terms of virtually exceptionless
   rules instead of absolute prohibitions?

BIBLIOGRAPHY

Adams, Robert Merrihew. "Pure Love," *The Journal of Religious Ethics,* 8, 1 (Spring 1980), pp. 83–99. A clear discussion of the human possibility of a pure or disinterested love in which the author argues that all human love has a degree of self-regard. In the same issue John Giles Milhaven, "Response to Pure Love by Robert Merrihew Adams," pp. 100–104, further clarifies the relationship between *eros* and *agape.*

Evans, Donald. "Paul Ramsey on Exceptionless Moral Rules," *Love and Society: Essays in the Ethics of Paul Ramsey: JRE Studies in Religious Ethics,* 1 (Scholars Press, 1974), pp. 19–46. This article affords an excellent introduction to the problem of absolute negative prohibitions and indicates why virtually exceptionless rules are favored by many ethicians.

Fuchs, Josef, S. J. *Personal Responsibility and Christian Morality.* Washington, D.C.: Georgetown University Press, 1983. This collection of previously published essays by an eminent German theologian touches on a number of themes covered in this and other chapters. A difficult work that rewards careful study.

Maguire, Daniel C. "The Primacy of Justice in Moral Theology," *Horizons,* 10, 1 (Spring 1983), pp. 72–85. A very readable article that deals with the relationship of love and justice. The author argues for the biblical unity of the two virtues and presents many concrete examples.

Ramsey, Paul. *Deeds and Rules in Christian Ethics.* New York: Charles Scribner's Sons, 1967. An excellent introduction to the problem of moral rules and Christian love by one of America's leading Protestant theologians. An older but still useful study.

8 The Natural Moral Law

A great deal of energy has been expended by theologians over the past twenty years in trying to discover the distinctive character of Christian ethics. The reader was briefly introduced to this extensive discussion in Chapter 2. The efforts of the theologians have been focused on trying to understand and to articulate the proper relationship that should exist between Christian faith and Christian moral practice. In reading the literature on this topic, it appears that there are any number of substantive concerns underlying these efforts, but three concerns in particular are most prominent.

THE CONTEXT OF THE QUESTION

The first concern is an ecclesiological one. There is a desire to understand the authentic self-identity of the Christian community, the Church, in contrast to the self-identity of both other religious communities and of the secular society, the "world," as a whole. This ecclesiological concern encompasses two closely related issues: the life-style or manner of living that is normative for the members of the Christian community, and the proper mission of the Church to and for the world. In brief, this concern focuses on the Church's own questions of who are we and what are we about in the world.

The second concern is an anthropological one. In this particular focus there is the desire to understand human dignity, to know what constitutes human dignity and to discern the requisite expressions of and safeguards for this dignity. Since human dignity is commonly considered to be rooted in the moral autonomy of the human agent, the anthropological concern asks about the relationship of human freedom to the power and authority of God. As part of the same question, it also inquires into the media-

166

tion of divine authority to human beings through various human authorities like the state and the Church. Most basically, it is a concern to grasp the relationship between human nature, human freedom and God's grace.

The third prominent concern behind the search for the distinctive character of Christian ethics is an epistemological one. Here there is an interest in the sources, methods and norms of moral knowing, in how human beings come to recognize in both formal and material ways what, in religious language, they call the will of God. Do Christian believers have a source of moral knowledge that is unavailable to non-Christians? Do they have some method of discerning moral right and wrong that is unique to Christian faith? Do they have some distinctive norms by which to make moral judgments?

These three concerns are clearly related to one another. Although it is the last of the three that will occupy our main attention in this chapter, before engaging the epistemological question directly, it seems important to stress that the question of method is not asked in a vacuum. It is asked in the context of a prior eschatological, ecclesiological and anthropological understanding. It is because we have a sense of our origins and a hope about our final destiny (eschatology), a sense of ourselves as a people with a mission in the world (ecclesiology), and a sense of our capacity for moral agency and moral responsibility (anthropology), that we ask ourselves what, then, we should do here and now with our material goods, with our sexuality, with our children, and how do we know. I would further suggest that our choice of moral method should also not ignore the context of the question but be deeply influenced by it.

The Old Testament Method

Historically, both the Jewish and the Christian traditions of ethical thought developed and were handed on in the form of laws or commandments. The reason for this is worth some consideration. One of the most striking features of the Hebrew Scriptures, taken as a whole, is the vivid sense of distinctiveness which marked the self-consciousness of Israel as a people. This was certainly due, in part at least, to Israel's interpretation of her existence as the chosen people of God (Dt 7:6), with a definitive and distinctive mission in the world. The covenant relationship which was thought to exist between God and Israel put a unique stamp on Israel's existence which took a primarily ethical form. Israel was a people with an ethical task, a people called to be holy, summoned to covenant-fidelity to Yahweh, their God. In this calling and relationship was to be found the whole point and purpose of Israel's existence.

Furthermore, what holiness or covenant-fidelity meant in practice was spelled out in the law, so that the gift of the law came to be seen as one of Israel's most cherished blessings, and as one of the things that marked her as unique among the nations. This is particularly evident, by way of illustration, in the prayers of the psalmist who praised Yahweh repeatedly for, among other things, the law. "He reveals his word to Jacob, his statutes and rulings to Israel: he never does this for other nations, he never reveals his rulings to them" (Ps 149:19–20). Or again, "How blessed are you, Yahweh! Teach me your statutes! With my lips I have repeated them, all these rulings from your own mouth. In the way of your decrees lies my joy, a joy beyond all wealth. I mean to meditate on your precepts and to concentrate on your paths. I find my delight in your statutes, I do not forget your word" (Ps 119:12–16).

To be sure, the law was by no means the only thing that made Israel unique in her own eyes, but the realization of the unique mission and destiny of the people was repeatedly related to the observance of the law. The Deuteronomic historian, for one instance, saw Israel's existence in this light. "All the commandments I enjoin on you today you must keep and observe so that you may live and increase in numbers and enter into the land that Yahweh promised on oath to your fathers, and make it your own" (Dt 8:1). So also did the author of Chronicles, writing in the context of the renewal of the Davidic convenant with David's son, Solomon. "For your part, if you walk before me as David your father did, if you do all that I order you and keep my statutes and my ordinances, I will make your royal throne secure, according to the compact I made with David your father . . ." (2 Chr 7:17–18). The same interpretation of Israel's existence was a staple of prophetic proclamation, for which Jeremiah may serve as one example.

Who is wise enough to understand this? Who has been charged by Yahweh's own mouth to tell why the land lies in ruins, burned like the desert where no one passes? Yahweh has said this, "This is because they have forsaken my law which I put before them and have not listened to my voice or followed it, but have followed the dictates of their own stubborn hearts, followed the baals as their ancestors taught them (Jer 9:11–14).

Israel's distinctiveness among the nations, then, consisted in her chosenness which was intimately linked with the law that shaped and guided her ethical existence. Morality for Israel was a matter of clear understanding of and wholehearted obedience to God's will which was revealed to her in the law. Accordingly, Israel's ethics came to be expressed primarily in a politico-legal metaphor. Yahweh was the King who made the laws, enforced the laws and punished those who violated the laws. Israel's task was not to question the laws or to make new laws, but simply to listen to and obey the law. We have here a form of divine command ethics in which the way to know what is morally good is to listen to what an external authority commands. To sin, to miss the mark, is to act in violation of the law or in contradiction to the commands of authority. In such a view the very essence of morality is obedience. What remains unasked and unanswered is how one knows that the law is in fact God's law.

The New Testament Method

This politico-legal metaphor for ethics was clearly recognized and adopted for use by the authors of the New Testament. The evangelist Matthew was concerned to stress the role of Jesus as the one who fulfilled the law and the prophets (Mt 5:7), and as the one who, in his role as the new Moses, revealed the law of the new covenant. The author of the Johannine Gospel portrayed Jesus as one whose very food and drink was to do the will of his heavenly Father (Jn 4:34), and who also brought the new commandment for the new covenant (Jn 13:34). The author of the First Epistle of John could say quite directly: "Anyone who sins at all breaks the law, because to sin is to break the law" (1 Jn 3:4). Even the converted Pharisee, Paul, continued after his conversion to regard the law as among the gifts given to Israel which had made her, and continued to make her, unique (Rom 9:4–5). And he certainly expected the new Christians to follow the ethical imperatives of the law (Gal 5:16–22) as well as to "fulfill the law of Christ" (Gal 6:2).

It has been noted by scholars that the content of the law Israel believed she had received as a revelation from Yahweh, as well as the ethical content of her wisdom tradition, was not, in fact, as distinctive or unique as the authors of the Hebrew Scriptures appear to have thought. The specific ethical imperatives laid down in the ten commandments (Dt 20:1–17), for example, are not without parallel in other societies, cultures and religions. If Israel came to know God's will through the law revealed to Moses, other peoples came to know the same moral truths in some other fashion. Nevertheless, the law, as interpreted and lived in the context of Israel's religious self-consciousness, did produce a distinctive and lasting self-identity and way of life.

The same sense of distinctiveness, of having a special calling, which marks the Old Testament also characterizes that part of the Christian Scriptures called the New Testament. One reason for this is undoubtedly the acceptance of Jesus as the Promised One of Israel, the Messiah, who does not deny or abolish the law, but fulfills it. Hence, the Gentile Christians have been, in Paul's expressive phrase, "grafted" onto the root that is Israel and continue to be nourished by that root (Rom 11:17–19).* Since there is this basic continuity between the two Testaments, Israel's self-consciousness and identity properly become a part of authentic Christian self-consciousness and identity. Israel's story is part of the Christian story and Abraham remains the common father of the faith.

The Newness of Jesus

But there is also a recognition throughout the entire New Testament that in Jesus something new has been effected. The Christian believer has, as it were, been born again (Jn 3:5), so that "for anyone who is in Christ, there is a new creation; the old creation has gone, and now the new one is here" (2 Cor 5:17). The law, as such, is no longer the center and the entire content of the ethical life because the demands of Christian discipleship go beyond the limits of the law. In the context of this new Christian self-consciousness, the ethical demands of Christian discipleship produced a distinctive manner of living that came to be referred to as "the way" (Acts 18:12–26). Yet the precise ethical content of "the way," especially after the acceptance of Gentile converts, remained unclear and a matter of some dispute. The dispute received only a tentative resolution at the Council of Jerusalem (Acts 15:22–29).

Biblical scholars have also demonstrated that we can no longer speak of a single or uniform New Testament ethic. Some have argued, with varying degrees of plausibility, that Jesus himself proposed no ethics of any kind beyond the single demand to act always out of agapaic love. Yet even if one allows for a distinctive Christian emphasis on love as the supreme form of moral motivation and intentionality, as well as the primary human virtue, and one points to the person of Jesus as the paradigmatic instance of love in practice, still the two great commandments of love of God and neighbor which exhaust the whole law are not unique to the Christian Gospel. They can be found literally in the Hebrew Scriptures (Dt 6:5; Lv 19:18), and in other religious contexts, albeit Jesus radicalized neighbor love by shifting its primary expression from love for the widow, orphan and stranger to love for the enemy (Mt 5:43–48; Lk 10:29–37). Nor is the story of Jesus laying down his life for his friends unique in the annals of religious narratives.

It would seem, then, that however Israel and the early Christian Church came to know God's will as centered on love of God and neighbor, neither the content nor the motivation of ethical action was unknown to other less privileged or "unchosen" human beings. Nor was the close link established in both the Old and the New Testaments between religion and morality unique to the religious faith shaped by the biblical narrative. It was a common conviction among the vast majority of human beings until well into the nineteenth century that religion and morality were inseparable, and that no sense of absolute obligation in conscience could exist apart from belief in God.

Given this commonality in ethical motivation and content, and given the traditionally inseparable link between religious faith and morality, it seems likely that the distinctiveness of a people's understanding of morality is to be found, not in the specific content of their ethical codes and norms, but in the way they understand God to reveal himself and his will. It is this suggestion I wish to explore here.

THE PRIMACY OF GOD

Both the Old and the New Testament writings understand and make vividly clear that what is properly asked of human beings in regard to their free, responsible activity in the world is intelligible only as a response to God's prior word to them. Since God's word is ever-living and effective, human moral activity is understandable only as a response to what God has done and continues to do in his providential care to shape the human story and lead it to fulfillment. That is to say, the biblical authors uniformly present a picture of the basic structure of human moral existence which a number of contemporary moral theologians have described as invitation and response, gift and demand, action and reaction. They have tried to develop this structure in the language of dialogue, responsibility and relationality.

COVENANT

In singling out the people of Israel as his very own people, Yahweh entered into a special relationship with them which we call covenant.

> Say this to the House of Jacob, declare this to the sons of Israel: You yourselves have seen what I did with the Egyptians, how I carried you on eagles' wings and brought you to myself. From this you know that now, if you obey my voice and hold fast to my covenant, you of all the nations shall be my very own, for all the earth is mine. I will count you a kingdom of priests, a consecrated nation (Ex 19:4–6).

This alliance between God and Israel, as expressed in the Mosaic covenant, meant that God's gifts and promises to the chosen people—his continuing to be God for them and hence their well-being as a people—were contingent upon their fidelity to the demands of the covenant. If Israel chose not to hear God's voice and not to observe his precepts, should Israel harden her heart (Ps 95:8–11), then instead of being the beneficiaries of God's saving promises, the people of Israel would experience the curses of the divine wrath. In short, the covenant emerged on the part of the Israelites as a contract to observe the divine law in the interests of receiving the divine blessings. As such, it specified for them the very meaning of morality. "For us right living will mean this: to keep and observe all these commandments before Yahweh our God as he has directed us" (Dt 6:25).

This conditional understanding of the covenant lived side-by-side in the Old Testament texts with the unconditional covenantal promises of God to Noah (Gn 9:8–11), to Abraham (Gn 12:1–3), and to David (2 Sam 23:5). Here the ethical demands of the covenant were less explicit and specific but still present. Both understandings of covenant called for a human response to God's prior action and made continuous moral demands which were also religious demands. To respond to the moral demand was at the same time to respond to the God who made the demand in the very process of revealing himself. Morality was in origin and in essence both religious and historical. It was encounter with and response to the Divine Actor in history. So we find Yahweh prefacing the revelation of the decalogue with a revelation of himself and his saving works: "I am Yahweh your God who brought you out of the land of Egypt, out of the house of slavery" (Ex 20:2; Dt 5:6). God's self-revelation and the revelation of the saving path he has marked out for Israel's well-being are united. It is in the very process of revealing his saving will for his people that God reveals himself. It is in the very process of revealing himself that he reveals his will for his people.

Consequently, in biblical understanding religion and morality are not conceivable as being separate or even separable. Even so, non-religious motivations can also be given for moral behavior and non-religious sources can supply some of the content of moral action, as is especially evident in the wisdom literature of the Israelites. But the heart of the matter in morality is that the two great commandments of love of God and love of neighbor become one. The religious response to God and the moral response to the neighbor are inseparably related and make one another intelligible. That and that alone is the biblical meaning of morality, discernible alike in the story of Israel and the story of Jesus.

For an essentially religious morality the will of God becomes, of course, the central and decisive issue. God's will is the very content of the covenant relationship and specifies the substance of human ethical behavor. Biblically, this was not a will that could be known by detached philosophical speculation or by distinterested observation. It was divinely revealed to Israel in what God had done and was continuing to do in his providential care for all creation. Unlike Greek philosophical ethics which had for its aim the relationship of the individual and the community to impersonal ideals and values, Hebrew and Christian ethical reflection was concerned to relate the individual and the community to a person. For Israel this was the personal will of Yahweh; for later Christian believers it was to the mind and heart of Christ.

It is also important to note that, while biblically God's ways were not human ways, the will of God, unlike that of the gods of the pagans, was neither strange nor arbitrary. It was characterized above all else by steadfast love which reflected the very being and character of God. For that reason, not only the saving events of history but all created reality bore witness to the glory and goodness of God (Ps 19; Ps 104; Rom 1:17–20). Because the world was God's creation, the product of his love, it spoke to human beings of God and goodness. It was precisely because God himself was good that he revealed to humans what was for their good, and what he revealed to them was, in fact, good because God was good. The law of the Lord was holy and perfect because it was God's law and God was the Holy One. The question as to how one comes to know what is morally good is answered by urging people to a deeper knowledge and love of God. By contemplating God's law for the Israelites, or God's word, Christ, for the Christians, the devout believer would be led to identify the way of wisdom revealed there with the right ethical conduct of his or her own life. What are really being addressed in such views are the questions of moral motivation and character formation. The epistemological question is as yet unformulated.

God, Faith and Morality

What can we conclude from this brief reflection on the biblical and early Christian understanding of morality? One clear conclusion to be drawn is the intrinsically religious meaning of morality for them. Religion and morality, God's activity and the human response to God, were inseparably connected. Such a link is easily sustained when the existence and providential activity of God are not serious questions, and when the central ethical focus is not on how we know God's will—the law is taken for granted, as it were—but rather on how we grow in our desire to know and do God's will and how we train ourselves to be able to discern and do that will. That is to say, when questions of ethical epistemology are analytically divorced from the spiritual quest, as they have been in the modern world, the link between religion and morality is quickly called into question and the very method and content of ethics becomes problematic. For while it remains clear that religious faith, through its stories and symbols, can still provide the believer with reasons for wanting to know and do the good, the relevance of these stories and symbols for knowing what is the morally good thing to do in a given situation becomes highly doubtful, at least on any grounds other than authoritarian or intuitionist ones. In addition, it also is evident that other reasons, non-religious and specifically this-worldly, can be advanced for being moral from a variety of philosophical, psychological, sociological or political perspectives. The result is that morality no longer appears, logically, rationally or in practical fact, to be dependent upon religious faith. Any morality that claims such dependence is seen as either irrational or idiosyncratic. In the modern age, therefore, religious morality is faced with a challenge that biblical morality did not have—to give a rational accounting of its moral knowlege, an accounting that is faithful to the biblical witness and faithful to the canons of human reason.

New Methods

One method of doing Christian ethics which developed historically as a result of Christian interaction with pagan philosophies and which accepted the challenge of giving a rational account of moral knowledge is the ethical method known as natural law thinking. Often associated in Christian circles with the thought of Thomas Aquinas and adopted in the Roman Catholic tradition as the dominant ethical methodology, natural law theory makes explicit appeal to natural reason as the vehicle for knowing what is morally good and evil. One of the supposed strengths or advantages of doing ethics in this way is said to be the more universal appeal of its method, since it is not dependent upon any particular stories or symbols of a specific religion. Indeed, its conclusions were once said to stand independently of the existence of God, so that it was thought to afford us a human morality, one common to all human beings and capable of being known by them.

The question of ethical method has also been addressed extensively by contemporary philosophers in a way that is explicitly secular and oriented to human life in its temporal framework. Their work has spawned a number of theories of ethical methodology about which there is no widespread consensus, though many of the theories have made helpful contributions to the analysis of moral reality and moral knowing. Space does not permit an extended discussion of any of these theories here, but by way of a simplified summary, they may be reduced to the following four general categories: emotive theories, consequentialist theories, deontological theories, and mixed consequentialist theories. A brief word on each of them will be in order before propounding the method I judge most compatible with Christian faith and life.

Emotive theories of moral knowledge deny the objective validity of such knowledge. Moral judgments are said to be no more and no less than personal statements of one's own emotional preferences in regard to human attitudes and actions. To say that adultery is wrong means only that I personally do not approve of adultery or that I do not like the practice for a variety of subjective reasons. Emotive theories regard moral judgments as statements of taste, little different than one's stated preferences in food and drink. Such theories are correct, at least to the extent that they recognize the subjective dimension of all moral judgments, as we saw earlier in regard to the particular judgment of conscience. But they seem seriously inadequate to what most people think they mean when they make a moral judgment. Most of us simply do not mean the same thing when we say we do not like walnuts and think abortion is wrong. Furthermore, emotive theories are not compatible with the Christian idea of a personal God of goodness and love and justice, whose will is the norm of morality. God's will cannot be identified with the subjective whims and tastes and preferences of any or all human beings.

Consequentialist theories of moral knowledge argue that the consequences of an action, and only the consequences, are the sole right-making feature of the action. We know what is right or wrong by looking at how the foreseeable consequences of an action affect the people involved in or touched by the action. Consequentialist theories can take a great variety of forms depending upon the range of consequences they wish to consider (short-term, long-term, necessary, probable, likely, possible, personal, social), the general norm they use to assess the effect of the consequences (pleasure, utility, physical survival, emotional well-being, wealth, etc.), and the number of people they wish to take into account (those immediately affected, society as a whole, future generations, etc.). The strength of consequentialist theories is that actions do have consequences and the consequences are of fundamental importance in our moral knowing. To simply ignore or disown the consequences of our actions is the height of moral irresponsibility. Even more, it is the consequences, at least the intended and foreseeable consequences, of our actions that render human activity intelligible and enable us to judge actions to be either rational or irrational. In other words, the rational meaning of our actions is to be found in the relationship between the act and the result that the act is capable of achieving. We understand the actions of a person who works at a job fourteen hours a day when we realize that he wants to make money and is paid by the hour. It makes sense to us that people forego foods they enjoy when we realize that the doctor has told them to lose weight for the sake of their health. Most consequentialist theories hold that the end justifies the means. Even if it is not true that the end justifies the means, it is true that the ends of human action make the means intelligible to us. To this extent consequentialists are on to something very important.

The weakness of consequentialist theories from a Christian perspective is, it seems to me, twofold. The ends or the consequences of human action which are mandatory or required ends, i.e., morally obligatory, are seen to be products of the human will, desires of the human heart, ends that seem good to us but which lack the transcendent reference to the mind and heart of God. The ends that most consequentialists appeal to for justification are ends extrinsic to the action itself. The model is a model of working for money in order to get something else. The ends are results achieved after the action, not ends realized in and through the action itself. Hence, one has an extrinsic morality relative always to the whims and desires of human beings.

Second, the end of life is not the justification and achievement of our own actions. The end of life, eternal communion with God in Christ through the Spirit, is a gift freely given to us. We do not earn salvation and justify ourselves by our actions. What human action needs is not justification but authorization, and it finds authorization in the present, not in the future, not in terms of consequences. For we act in the present and we do not always know or control the consequences of our actions. That does not mean that consequences are of no importance for our moral knowing, but they are not of exclusive importance. Hence, I reject consequentialist theories as a method appropriate to Christian ethics.

A third general method for knowing what is good and evil may be called deontological theory. Such theories put their major focus on the obligations that are fundamental to human existence and stress the binding force of these obligations despite the consequences of fulfilling the obligations. Deontological theories generally develop in the form of law or commandments, or in more contemporary fashion in the form of rights and duties. It is not possible in the brief space we have here to give even a summary evaluation of deontological theory. Suffice it to say that, since the love to which Jesus summons us bursts the bonds of law, goes beyond the strict assessment of rights and obligations, I reject the deontological method for Christian ethics.

The fourth general ethical method for knowing what is morally good and evil I have referred to as mixed consequentialist methodology. The name refers to the fact that this methodology insists that there is more to knowing moral truth than an evaluation of the consequences, important as such an evaluation is. When pressed, however, to say what this more is, mixed consequentialists often grow vague and indecisive. Nevertheless, it is a version of mixed consequentialism that I wish to propose here as a method for knowing concretely the moral good and moral evil in specific circumstances. It is a natural law method, a form of teleology, indebted to the thought of Thomas Aquinas though not in thrall to it.

NATURAL LAW

Since all human actions are means to some end, an understanding of the moral meaning of our actions must begin with the end or goal or purpose or good those actions aim at. We all realize this, at least implicitly. When we come upon a person doing something we do not understand and ask "What are you doing?" we are inquiring into the purpose or goal of the action. Until we understand the connection between the action and the goal or good it seeks to realize, we do not know the meaning of the action. The goal of our human existence, the end or purpose of life, is eternal communion with God and with one another (Jn 17:21–26). This goal or end is not humanly comprehensible to us. It is not only beyond our ability to achieve by our own efforts; it is beyond our ability to imagine or comprehend (1 Cor 2:9). Nevertheless, this goal serves as the transcendent horizon and norm of all our deeds and as the one absolute good around which the many relative goods of human life are understood and ordered.

This way of expressing the matter is designed to indicate how the end gives intelligibility to the means. We come to understand and properly evaluate lesser goods in relation to higher ones. We recognize means to an end only in the light of the end that the means is able to achieve. In addition, by acknowledging God as the Supreme Good and the Creator and Sustainer of all other goods, it becomes clear that we human beings are not the creators of the goods and values that are the end or goal of our intending. We rather discover them by reason. The goods are offered to us as gifts and are discovered by us as realities that correspond to the dynamic tendencies of our own nature. As we come to self-awareness, i.e., as we come to understand who and what we are, we recognize the non-voluntary, pre-determined inclinations and tendencies of every reality, including ourselves. These tendencies and potentialities refer to what makes things work or function as they do, or to what we loosely call their nature. These non-voluntary, pre-determined tendencies make possible the scientific and rational study of reality. They provide the basis on which we can distinguish between what is normal and what is abnormal development, what is health and what is sickness, what is functional and what is dysfunctional.

Human Goods

In Chapter 3 we saw that these tendencies and potentialities provided the grounds for distinguishing between animate and inanimate life, between animal and vegetable life, and between human and non-human life. They enabled us to say that this reality is a cat and that reality is a tree. They were the clues to the nature of things. But these tendencies also enable us to say more than that. In the human context with which we are presently concerned, we can recognize, for instance, that health is a good of the human organism and disease is not. Sight is a good and blindness is not. Parental concern for children enables them to flourish; parental indifference and neglect are handicaps to their flourishing. These judgments are not affirmations of some subjective whim or emotive preference, but statements about the way human life works. This is the way things are whether we like it or not.

Of course, in the recognition of these goods of human life, we are not yet at the level of moral good and evil. Health, sight, parental concern are ontic goods, goods that are real and present to us for our choosing, but not yet chosen. As we come to self-awareness we also recognize the uniquely human dynamisms or tendencies, the dynamisms toward knowing and loving, or toward rationality and freedom. We discover that human beings enjoy a unique participation in Divine Providence precisely because we are a providence for ourselves and also for all other created realities. All of creation is taken up into the moral responsibility of human beings to a limited degree because we have the ability both to remember the past and to look forward to the future. Hence, we are able to take care for our own becoming and the future well-being of all creation to some degree.

In the process of discovering who and what we are, then, we human beings, made in the image and likeness of God, find that we are endowed with rational and spiritual capacities. We can know that we have such capacities and we can rejoice in them and choose to cultivate them. We can say yes to our own being and becoming. Not only do we have an inner dynamism toward our own rationality and freedom; we also have the capacity to know that we have such a dynamism and to understand the demands of our rationality and freedom to be both rational and free. In short, we have the capacity to know the natural moral law, or to know what God has made us to be and become. For the natural moral law is nothing more or less than the rational creature's participation in the eternal law or in the eternal wisdom of God.

The discerning reader will have noted the repeated use in the above paragraph of the language of possibility. The claim is that we can know, not that we do, or will or inevitably must come to such knowledge. We can say yes to our own freedom and rationality, yes to our own being and becoming, but we can also act irrationally and unfreely by saying no or by remaining indifferent to the gifts of God. And this possibility of self-determination is also something we can come to know about human nature.

The natural moral law, then, is discovered by reason's comprehension of what it is to be human in its basic structure, and is elaborated by practical reason to guide human action and human becoming toward fuller rationality and freedom. Or in religious language, the natural moral law reveals to us the path that God in his eternal wisdom and providential care has laid down for our human fulfillment and well-being in the very structure of creation. The moral law is, then, not a set of rules we must follow under threat of punishment. It is simply the dynamic ordering principle of our human being and becoming. Or, as we saw in our reflections on conscience, "in the depths of his being man discovers a law not of his own making," urging him to be what he has been made to be, fully human, fully alive, fully rational and free.

Practical Application

The method that we use to elaborate the more specific requirements of the natural law involves asking what the intrinsic purpose of any reality is, toward what goal or good the reality is dynamically ordered. One then attempts to articulate the goods that realize the purpose. In this way we come to know which goods are the proper objects of our intentionality. The task of elaborating the moral law is not always an easy one. The more particular and specific we become, the more difficult the task is and the less certainty we will have. The official teaching office of the Roman Catholic Church has always claimed a special grace as the interpreter of the natural law, not because it is especially gifted in moral reasoning, but because the Christian vision of the human person as created in the image and likeness of God, fallen but redeemed in Christ, and destined for eternal communion with the Trinitarian God affords it the most adequate view of human nature. Still, no religious view of the nature of the human person allows us to bypass the knowledge of ourselves derived from empirical observation and human experience. Nor does it allow us to ignore the historical and social rootedness of all human knowing. All of these considerations must be kept in mind as we try to understand the demands or the specific norms of the natural moral law.

Truth-Telling

How the methodology actually works in practice can be illustrated briefly if we consider the question of truth-telling. Human beings speak; they have the need and the inclination to express their inner thoughts and feelings to themselves and to their fellow humans. We must ask, then: What is the purpose of speech? What are the goods that realize this purpose? To what is speech of its very nature ordered? We speak to express and to communicate with others what we think, feel, believe, hope. The goal of speech, the good which it intends, is communication, a kind of communion or oneness with the other in mind or in heart or in faith or in common aspirations. An essential requirement of such communication is truthfulness—truthfulness understood both as subjective sincerity and as objective accuracy. More concretely put, if I am to share my thoughts with another person, I must express what I really think and my expression must accurately capture what my thoughts really are.

Now, not everyone at all times can lay claim to a right to know the thoughts, feelings and hopes of another person. The nature of the relationships we establish with others defines the rights and obligations of communications. Patients, for example, have a right to know from the doctor the true state of their own health. But they have no right to know the state of some other patient's health. A wife has the right to know the true state of her family's financial situation. She has no right to know the financial situation of her neighbors. Hence, as natural law thinking reflects upon the nature of human speech and the good at which it aims, it can define the moral evil of lying as "the speaking of a falsehood, with deliberate intent to deceive, to someone who has a right to the truth." That is what it means to miss the mark morally in the human activity of speaking.

Such an elaboration of the natural moral law, then, takes into account not only the nature of human speech, but also the situations, consequences and relationships in which human communication occurs. It recognizes four essential aspects in every human action: the intention of the agent, the circumstances in which the action takes place, the consequences of the action, and the nature of the act itself. It argues for a harmony, an integral compatibility among all four aspects for any action to have moral worth or moral integrity. It is not sufficient morally simply to have a good intention or for the action to effect good consequences. The action must be appropriate to the circumstances and must respect the intrinsic nature of the act itself. The first three points are not matters of great dispute or complexity. Certainly it is clear that morally we need to have a good intention, the consequences of the action should benefit human beings and the action should fit the situation. The fourth point, however, is more subtle and requires a word of explanation.

THE NATURE OF ACTION

There is a traditional notion in Roman Catholic moral theology, one that has been largely discredited today, that some actions are of their very nature intrinsically evil. To intend such actions for whatever reasons is, therefore, to intend evil, and that is always morally wrong. If there are, in fact, actions that are intrinsically evil, no circumstances, no consequences, no intentions can change the fact, and there would then be absolute negative prohibitions. Any action that is evil of its very nature ought never to be done or even intended.

This notion has been largely discredited today because we recognize that actions in themselves, apart from human intentions and actual historical and social situations, are abstractions. They simply do not exist in reality. As we saw in Chapter 7, certain actions can be described in such a way that the intention of the agent and the circumstances of the action are built into the description of the act so that the action is wrong by definition. Lying and murder and rape were offered as examples. But in such cases it is not the action of killing or speaking a falsehood or having sexual intercourse that is intrinsically wrong. It is rather the intention and the circumstances of the action that give the action the form of moral evil.

Nevertheless, the nature of the action itself is not irrelevant to moral analysis and moral behavior. For actions are not simply pieces of clay that can be given any moral form we choose to impose upon them. All human actions are forms of human self-expression, and so they have consequences not simply in the world outside the agent but they have consequences also for the character of the moral agent who performs them. Lying, for example, may have unhappy consequences for other people or it may not. It is quite possible that no one will be hurt by a particular lie in certain circumstances. But lying always affects the moral character of the agent, rendering him or her a liar, and so less free, less rational, less human. The goods and values we seek to realize in and through our actions are not all external to the action itself, not products, as it were, which are realized only at the end of the action. The most significant values are often realized in the very doing of the action, which is why it is essential to pay attention to the nature of what one is actually doing.

The Example of Work

It is not easy to give clear and simple examples to illustrate this final point, but let me try to give one brief example here. In his encyclical letter on human work, *Laborem Exercens*, Pope John Paul II pointed out that the work we human beings do to earn our daily bread has both an objective and a subjective meaning. The objective meaning and worth of our work is determined by the results it produces, by the social usefulness and desirability of what we do. This finds its objective measurement in the salary, prestige and status we receive for the work. From this objective perspective it is the work that is valued, not the worker; the worker's value is measured by the value of his or her work.

This objective perspective of the human activity of work is not false; it is merely one-sided and incomplete. If the only important thing about human work were the rewards received for it, then how it was done and what was done would be of no significance. It would make no difference whether one lied and cheated, did the work with care or with indifferent neglect, produced pornography or food, so long as the rewards were forthcoming. But work also has an inescapable subjective dimension; it is a form of human self-expression and self-determination. In this perspective it is the worker who is more important than the work, the producer who has the priority of value over the product. The subjective meaning and value of work are not measured by the reward the work receives, but by the manner of the doing itself and by what that doing is. What one does and the way in which one does it is of more significance than what one receives for the product of one's labors. It is in this sense that natural law theory insists that we pay attention to the nature of the act itself and its impact upon the moral character of the agent as central to all moral analysis and moral evaluation of human behavior.

The New Testament Witness

There are a number of New Testament passages which illuminate and, in turn, are illuminated by the understanding of the natural moral law being proposed here. In the Sermon on the Mount we read the following.

> That is why I am telling you not to worry about your life and what you are to eat, nor about your body and how you are to clothe it. Surely life means more than food, and the body more than clothing. . . . So do not worry; do not say, "What are we to eat? What are we to drink? How are we to be clothed?" It is the pagans who set their hearts on all these

things. Your heavenly Father knows you need them all. Set
your hearts on his kingdom first, and on his righteousness,
and all these other things will be given you as well (Mt 6:25,
31–33).

In the Gospel according to Mark we find the following condition
for true Christian discipleship.

If anyone wants to be a follower of mine, let him renounce
himself and take up his cross and follow me. For anyone who
wants to save his life will lose it; but anyone who loses his life
for my sake, and for the sake of the gospel, will save it. What
gain, then, is it for a man to win the whole world and ruin his
life? And indeed what can a man offer in exchange for his life?
For if anyone in this adulterous and sinful generation is
ashamed of me and of my words, the Son of Man will also be
ashamed of him when he comes in the glory of His Father
with the holy angels (Mk 8:34–38).

Finally, in Luke's Gospel we read, "If any man comes to me without hating his father, mother, wife, children, brothers, sisters, yes
and his own life too, he cannot be my disciple" (Lk 14:26).

At first glance these passages seem harsh, almost inhuman.
Are food and drink and clothing not goods of human life? Are
we wrong to intend them and seek them? Indeed, is life itself not
a good but something to be renounced and lost? Is the love of
family not a precious good to be protected and cultivated, but an
obstacle to faithful Christian living? A closer examination of the
passages, however, makes clear that their central emphasis is on
seeking first and above all else the kingdom of God, despite whatever worldly consequences this search might entail. All other
human goods, all other things and relationships which meet
human needs and fulfill human longings, are relative to this one
highest good. It is, then, the quality of our moral agency or the
rational and free ordering of our loves that is the most crucial
moral consideration and task. It is such an ordering of human
goods that the natural moral law attempts to articulate in order
to assist love to hit the mark.

No doubt the reader is still unhappy and unclear about the
ethical method of natural law theory. By way of a conclusion to

this chapter, then, let me present a summary statement in as concrete a way as possible. Recall the question with which we began. How do we know what is the right and good thing to do in the actual time and place of human decision? Natural law theory answers that we know by the use of reason, based upon our ability to know and understand who and what we are. We can discover the basic tendencies and inclinations of our nature and the real goods which correspond to these inclinations and tendencies. Most basic to human beings is their dynamic orientation to freedom and rationality and personal communion with others. Natural law theory bids us to act in accord with our dignity as free, rational, social creatures.

In terms of more specific questions natural law theory seeks the purpose or end inherent in any reality. This is not always easy to know. It requires both experience and reasoned reflection. Many realities have multiple purposes which are related to one another in complex ways. Sexuality, for example, serves a variety of purposes and is capable of realizing a number of human goods. The relationship among these goods is highly complex. But always natural law theory bids us to return to the nature of the human person for whom these goods are good. How do our proposed actions enable the human person to become more fully human, more fully rational and free, more deeply and truly centered on loving God above all things and the neighbor as oneself? The method of natural law theory is not a mechanism for grinding out pre-packaged answers to human questions. It is rather a method, a way of exercising our human capacity for rational thought and self-understanding in the light of God's providential care for us in the creation, redemption and sanctification of his people.

What a natural law methodology yields is not a static, fixed view of the world that can be expressed in terms of absolute do's and don't's, though that mistake has been made. What it yields is a developing, growing set of mutual rights and obligations essential to the dignity of human persons, whose concrete meaning is always relative to the time and place of human living. The natural law yields both formal norms which prescribe the intentions and virtues that are always and everywhere appropriate to human life. So, for instance, human beings should always intend justice, truthfulness, respect for others, peace, fidelity, and so on. These formal norms are certain and absolute, demanded by the dignity of human being. Natural law also yields material norms which prescribe the kinds of actions we should and should not do. The meaning of these material norms is always tied to specific situations, and so their application is always relative and lacks the certainty and absoluteness of formal norms. For example, employers should pay their employees a just wage, one that is sufficient to enable them to meet their basic needs and to support their families in dignity. But the amount of money that counts as a just wage is relative to the time and place of work. The final two chapters of this book will deal briefly with some fundamental goods of human life and are meant to assist in the further clarification of the method of natural law theory.

STUDY QUESTIONS

1. In the biblical and early Christian view of morality, why was moral motivation the chief focus of concern? How does calling the laws God's law advance or help this concern?

2. Take any one of the ten commandments. How would each of the four methodologies mentioned in the text explain its knowledge of this commandment?

3. Choose one of your strongest moral convictions about an action that is always or almost always wrong. Can you give a rational account of how you know what you know? If you cannot, how do you account for your conviction?

4. Natural law theory claims that it is possible for us to understand the basic goods which correspond to basic human needs. Does this claim seem concretely true to you? Why or why not?

5. Apply the analysis of truth-telling and lying in the text to the practice of taking or using possessions that belong legally to another person. How, then, would you define stealing? Why or why not, for example, is the practice of a progressive income tax an act of stealing?

BIBLIOGRAPHY

Fletcher, Joseph. *Situation Ethics*. Philadephia: Westminster Press, 1966. This is the most popular and clearest effort to develop Christian ethics in a pure consequentialist style. It is plausibly deceptive, but worth wrestling with, especially the examples.

Gula, Richard M. *What Are They Saying About Moral Norms?* New York: Paulist Press, 1982. A fine introduction to the problem of moral norms. It includes a discussion of the various kinds of norms, the derivation of norms and the uses of norms.

Gustafson, James M. *Protestant and Roman Catholic Ethics*. Chicago: The University of Chicago Press, 1978. Not a work for beginners, this is a scholarly and careful delineation of the differences and similarities in historical origins, philosophy, theology and practical moral reasoning of Catholic and Protestant ethical method.

Hauerwas, Stanley. *Vision and Virtue*. Notre Dame: Fides/Claretian, 1974. In this series of essays, the author elaborates a number of the themes pertinent to this chapter and the previous one. The author's chief concern is the formation of moral character and the role of faith in the formative process.

McCormick, Richard A. and Paul Ramsey. *Doing Evil To Achieve Good*. Chicago: Loyola University Press, 1978. The essays in this volume are scholarly and challenging. McCormick's two essays in particular are excellent examples of what mixed consequentialists are trying to do.

O'Connell, Timothy M. *Principles for a Catholic Morality*. New York: Seabury Press, 1976. Chapters 12–17 present a fine historical account of natural law, some of the problems and objections to the traditional understanding of natural law, and a useful modern exposition of the theory.

9 The Counsels of Perfection: A Path to Love

For Christian faith the example of Jesus dying on the cross to save all human beings from sin and death has become the paradigm of what it means to love our fellow human beings. The New Testament itself holds up the crucified Christ as the supreme expression of love. "A man can have no greater love than to lay down his life for his friends" (Jn 15:13). Paul takes this love even further than the author of John's Gospel. "It is not easy to die even for a good man—though of course for someone really worthy, a man might be prepared to die—but what proves that God loves us is that Christ died for us while we were still sinners" (Rom 5:8).

In the light of such an example it comes as no surprise that, in the early Church, martyrdom became the clearest sign of Christian discipleship and the pre-eminent way of following Jesus' footsteps. And the martyrs themselves became the first Christian heroes and saints, for they were the most obvious manifestation of the triumph of God's grace over the forces of sin, selfishness and death. Here, in the death of the martyr, willingly accepted and courageously endured, was a sign of the love with which Jesus had loved his own.

The opportunity to die as a martyr, however, does not come to everyone. The literal losing of one's life for the sake of the Gospel or the literal taking up of one's cross to follow Jesus is not a realistic possibility for most Christians, however willing they might be to do just that. Already in the New Testament we find the idea of carrying the cross being taken metaphorically to refer to the struggles of everyday living (Lk 9:23). In time, with the cessation of persecution and the acceptance of the Christian faith as the religion of the Roman Empire, a way of life developed in early Christianity which was seen as a substitute for the martyrdom which was no longer a likely possibility. It, too, was seen as a form of witness to the Gospel and to the power of grace and the new creation in Christ. It was a kind of mini-martyrdom, as it were, since the literal meaning of the word "martyr" is witness. This way of life initially centered on virginity, the renunciation of worldly goods and a rejection of worldly pursuits and worldly power. It saw a radical difference between the life of the world and the new life in Christ, reflecting in this view the words of the first Johannine letter. "You must not love this passing world or anything that is in the world. The love of the Father cannot be in any man who loves the world, because nothing the world has to offer—the sensual body, the lustful eye, pride in possessions—could ever come from the Father but only from the world" (1 Jn 2:15–16). Thus was spawned the beginnings of the monastic way of life.

Experience with the failures and excesses of early monasticism gradually led to a more orderly, community based form of monastic living, centered on the three evangelical counsels of poverty, chastity, and obedience, and given its concrete expression by the unique charism of the monastery founder. In Roman Catholicism the way of life based on the three vows came to be known as "the religious life" and has been held up to the faithful for the last fifteen hundred years as "the more perfect way."

NEW TESTAMENT FOUNDATIONS

The New Testament origins of the evangelical counsels are somewhat dubious. The counsel of consecrated celibacy rests essentially on three texts (Mk 12:18–27; Mt 19:10–12; 1 Cor 7:1–7, 25–35), and the presumed celibacy of Jesus himself. The strongest support for a life of consecrated celibacy as a higher calling comes from the testimony of Paul who, by his own admission, had no directions in the matter from the Lord (1 Cor 7:25). Paul offered an essentially pragmatic justification for the celibate way of life. The celibate person, he assumed, was able to devote himself or herself wholly to the affairs of the Lord. The married person has to worry about pleasing his or her partner and about other worldly affairs. In any case, the celibacy praised by the New Testament is not simple abstention from sexual activity for its own sake, but a celibacy embraced positively for the sake of the kingdom of God. Nor is there any suggestion of any kind that marriage excludes a person from the kingdom or makes Christian discipleship impossible.

The counsel of voluntary poverty would seem to have a much stronger New Testament foundation. The classic text to support it is the story of the rich young man (Mk 10:17–22). But the New Testament is simply rife with warnings against riches and the pursuit of wealth. (Mark 10:23–27; 12:41–44; Luke 1:53; 6:24–25; 9:57–58; 12:13–21; 13:33–34; 14:33; 16:13–15; 2 Corinthians 8:6–15; Colossians 3:5; 1 Timothy 6:17–19; James 2:1–9 are but a few instances.) In addition, the idealized picture of the early Church presented by Luke favors the common ownership of goods and equality in their use (Acts 2:44–45; 4:32–35). The thrust of the warnings against riches points consistently to the danger of a divided heart. Greed is a form of idolatry leading the person to serve mammon rather than God. The value of poverty is seen to lie in the spiritual freedom and single-heartedness it affords the individual. It also keeps envy and class distinctions out of the community of believers, thus fostering Church unity and love.

The counsel of obedience, at least as it became enshrined in religious life, has no explicit New Testament basis. The Gospels and the epistles are very clear on the Christian duty to obey legitimate authority as a matter of conscience (Mt 23:1–3; Mk 12:13–17; Rom 13:1–7; Eph 5:21—6:9), but this is a matter of obligation, not of counsel. The rationale for obedience is, of course, for the sake of doing God's will, although Paul suggests that it will also enable us to live in peace with one another. Most pertinent to the vow of religious obedience is Jesus' insistence that, among his followers, authority was to take the form of humble service, not domination and control (Mk 9:33–37; 10:41–45; Jn 13:1–15). Obedience, then, in its voluntary forms, is related to the unity and peace of the community as well as to service to and for the community. Obedience is a communal virtue and a form and manifestation of love for others.

A Way of Life

The vows of religion taken in response to the evangelical counsels structure a form of life in community which is said to have a witness value. Many religious orders and congregations also adopt a specific mission or form of apostolic service to accompany their religious witness and to embody that witness more clearly. Nevertheless, it is not the apostolic service which has been held up by the Church as "the more perfect way," for non-vowed people also teach, minister to the poor and the sick, and exercise any number of other ministries of service. It is the vowed life of eschatological witness which has been put forth as the ideal, embodying in its objective structure the more perfect love. It was never claimed, of course, that any person who took the religious vows was, therefore, a better person or a more perfect lover than those who did not take vows. Rather, the claim was that the objective meaning of the religious way of life embodied central features of how to relate to the things of the world in a way that best enabled love. It is this claim, its meaning and implications, that I want to explore in this chapter.

Since the vowed life has been under serious attack since the time of the Protestant Reformation, which mistakenly rejected it as a form of works righteousness, and since it continues under attack today as unnatural or irrelevant to real human concerns, it is important at the outset to clarify what is and is not being said about the evangelical counsels as a vowed way of life. No suggestion is being made that everyone should live the vowed way of life. It is not normatively the Christian way of life. Even if most of us do not share St. Paul's self-confidence in holding ourselves up as models for others to imitate, we recognize the wisdom of his observation to the Corinthians: "I should like everyone to be like me, but everybody has his own particular gifts from God, one with a gift for one thing and another with a gift for the opposite" (1 Cor 7:7). Nor is there any assertion being made here that the vowed life is first-class Christianity and the non-vowed life second-rate. There may well be first-rate and second-rate Christians, but that distinction is not based on whether or not they have taken religious vows. It is based upon the quality and extent of their love for their neighbors, a judgment best left to God.

In proposing the life of the religious vows as the more perfect way, the Church historically was pointing to an ideal that
reflected the way of life in the kingdom of God and that afforded
here on earth a symbolic witness to the primacy of the kingdom.
In the perfect reign of God there will be no mine and no yours,
no haves and have-nots, no economic and social class distinctions.
Our radical dependence upon God for all good gifts will be clear,
as will the graced character of all goods. In the kingdom of God
there will be no giving and taking in marriage (Mt 22:30), no birth
and no death, no jealous or possessive love. And in God's kingdom his will will be done by all, joyfully, freely, without question
or complaint. The religious vows attempt to structure a way of
life that is a symbolic anticipation of life in the kingdom. To that
extent, as an objective ideal, it can indeed be called the more perfect way.

Vows as Virtues

There is a sense, however, in which the evangelical counsels
are not counsels at all, but fundamental Christian obligations.
Understood as formal norms of morality, the counsels prescribe
attitudes and dispositions that are appropriate to all Christians in
regard to three fundamental areas of human existence. The spirit
of the evangelical counsels should inform every Christian's attitude and shape every Christian's intentionality toward the material goods of the world, toward sexuality, and toward the structures and uses of political and social authority. To put the same
idea in other words, poverty, chastity and obedience are proper
and essential virtues for all Christians. The material realization of
those virtues will differ, of course, depending on one's state in
life, but some realization of the virtues is a central demand of
neighbor-love.

The importance of the evangelical counsels is that they guide
love in the three temporal concerns central to human life—
money, sex and power. It is in learning how to deal responsibly
with these areas of human concern that we become caring and
responsible persons. Indeed, there is a danger and a very real risk
involved in the vowed life, for that way of life can easily bypass
the human involvement in the struggles of self-support and
other-support, interpersonal love and responsible freedom. To

escape these struggles may look appealing and provide the illusion of greater availability to serve God and his people. But the
result of avoiding these struggles is rather the continuance of a
childish dependence and emotional immaturity. In one way or
another human maturity and Christian love must pass through
the school of learning that the struggle with money, sex and
power affords.

POVERTY

Poverty is the Christian virtue appropriate to the human
relationship to material goods. The virtue is, perhaps, badly
named since in our day and age poverty more commonly refers
to a state of economic and cultural deprivation which is in no way
a human or Christian good. "How happy are you who are poor;
yours is the kingdom of God" (Lk 6:20b), the evangelist Luke
proclaims. Matthew changes the beatitude slightly:"How happy
are the poor in spirit: theirs is the kingdom of heaven" (Mt 5:3).
While the two evangelists do not mean the same thing by what
they write, they both see some virtue in poverty of some kind, and
so it is that poverty enters the lexicon of Christian virtues. It is
too late to change the name of the virtue now.

It is not my intention here to enter upon a lengthy discussion
of what the two evangelists mean or of the various types of poverty in the world. I am concerned with how love finds its way in
dealing with material goods, and I want to suggest that it is the
virtue of poverty which provides guidance for love's search. Earlier love was spoken of as the inner form of all virtues. It is only
love, so only the free choice of poverty, that gives it the moral
form of virtue. But it is the task of reasoned reflection to supply
content to that form.

One of the central ways we all learn responsibility and love
is in the use we make of money and all the things that money can
buy. A great deal of our time, talent and energy goes into the task
of earning money, and a considerable amount of the time and
energy we have left goes into spending it. Money, of course, is
not something we desire for its own sake, but for what it can buy.
But because it is able to buy so many things, it is able to satisfy a
great many of our needs and desires, as well as creating the illu-

sion that it can satisfy many other desires and needs. Consequently, money, and the things money can buy, develop a strong hold on the human heart and mind. This hold on the heart and mind is not altogether unjustified. We do have real needs for food, shelter, clothing and recreation which the instrumentality of money enables us to satisfy. Much as we may deplore the fact, polls repeatedly show that there is a direct correlation between people's level of material well-being and their degree of satisfaction and joy in life. The desire, then, for a share of the material goods of the world and a delight in them is not, on the face of it, un-Christian. But it can easily become so.

Poverty is the Christian virtue which properly orders our attachment to material goods so that they may be put at the service of life and love and not become our master. Negatively, poverty may be described as detachment from material things so that they do not get an unholy hold upon us, do not deprive us of the spiritual and moral freedom to love others. Again in a negative sense, poverty may also be described as a lack of dependence upon money and the things money can buy for one's happiness and well-being in life. The virtue of poverty inclines us toward a radical dependence upon God who is the true source of all good.

But virtues are positive realities; they are human strengths. They enable us to act in freely chosen ways, and so they deserve a more positive definition. Poverty, then, may be described positively as the virtue which enables human beings to see and use money and all material goods for what by their nature they truly are, means to higher and more important ends. Poverty moves us to embrace material goods as purely instrumental values whose whole worth is in the ends they serve. Poverty is the virtue which enables the corporal works of mercy such as feeding the hungry, clothing the naked and sheltering the homeless. It is the virtue which overcomes our greed, our envy, our possessiveness, and enables us to share freely and responsibly what we have been blessed to receive. Poverty is the virtue that inclines us to use our material goods to serve people in need, including ourselves, rather than to achieve and protect the false goods of social and cultural status and prestige.

More globally, the virtue of poverty, in its hunger and thirst for justice, is the essential prerequisite for social justice. It recognizes that the goods of the earth belong to all people by God's gift and each one of us has an equal claim to a share of these goods. What we struggle to learn in our dealings with the material goods of this world is how to love our neighbors and ourselves in ways that are concrete, respectful of human freedom and dignity, and devoid of strings. There is, perhaps, no area of our lives more suited to learning what it means to love one another as the Lord has loved us, regardless of gratitude, appreciation or worthiness, without seeking anything for ourselves in return. The virtue of poverty does not renounce the possession and use of material goods so much as it renounces the control and domination of others which wealth often makes possible.

Poverty and Sacrifice

It seems unlikely, from a personal perspective, that the spirit of poverty can pervade our lives without some real material sacrifices being made. Children, for example, need to forego the occasional toy or ice cream cone and give the money saved to the starving children's fund. Teenagers need to surrender some new records or stereo equipment and give the money saved to soup kitchens serving the hungry and unemployed. Adults, too, need to make similar sacrifices in order to make real both their professed detachment from material goods and, more importantly, their love for the needy neighbor. Without such sacrifices we only fool ourselves about our freedom and our love.

At a deeper level, however, poverty cannot be a real virtue in our lives unless it enables us to be self-critical about our own life-styles in a positive and liberating way. What I mean by such a comment is that our delight in and gratitude for the good gifts of God's earth, which delight and gratitude is a fundamental aspect of the virtue of poverty, must also move us to work so that others may also enjoy our good fortune. Poverty means a glad willingness to share the world's goods with others, a desire to help others realize their own equal share of these gifts. The virtue of poverty does not sentimentalize the economic and cultural deprivation of the poor. It seeks ways to overcome that deprivation and so guides neighbor-love into the concerns of and the struggle for social justice in the world.

Poverty, as we have discussed it here, is a virtue, and virtues, let us remember, are human strengths. Strengths intensify or else they grow weak, and that is the case with the virtue of poverty. It is hard to set down practical norms or to give concrete examples to illustrate the virtue in practice. Many Christians follow the practice of tithing, which they take to be a biblical norm, giving one tenth of their income to the Church or other charitable causes. This may be laudable for some and an initial guideline for others. But I would suggest that the spirit of poverty is best developed through reflection upon and actions in accord with the great Matthean parable of the last judgment (Mt 25:31–45), until we are able to give freely what we have freely received. Perhaps most simply stated, the virtue of poverty enables us to prefer persons to things.

CHASTITY

Chastity is the Christian virtue appropriate to the human relationship to sexuality, both one's own and that of others. In many ways the virtue of chastity is also in ill-repute today. It often seems to smack of prudery, or of unresolved psychological hang-ups, or of some antiquated moral code based largely on ignorance or superstition. But such things are not the same as the moral virtue of chastity. Another reason for chastity's poor reputation is that it is so often defined in negative terms. Chaste people don't sleep around, don't read pornography, don't indulge in sexual fantasies, don't masturbate, don't tell or laugh at off-color jokes, don't give in to their sexual urges. Even marriage is sometimes regarded as a license to do unchaste things, as if a legal contract could make right what would otherwise be dirty and unholy. When defined in such a negative fashion, it is little wonder that many people conclude that the virtue of chastity involves a denigration of sex and a rejection of the goodness of sexual pleasure and intimacy. This is unfortunate, as well as false, for the virtue of chastity has great esteem for human sexuality and for the high possibilities of growing in love through sexual expression. What may contribute to the negative understanding of chastity and the negative assessments of the virtue is the fact that vowed virginity or consecrated celibacy includes abstention from overt sexual expression and sexual relationships. In popular parlance, priests and nuns renounce sex and marriage. But such abstention hardly begins to exhaust the meaning of the vow or the virtue, though it always runs the risk of doing so in a given individual's life.

In a more positive sense, chastity is the virtue that enables sexual beings to love other sexual beings in a way that is fully human, i.e., rational and free, and promotes their human development. For many human beings the greatest school for learning how to love will be the sexual relationship we call marriage. And there is probably no single human experience closer to the passionate and intense love of God for us than the experience of a committed, caring relationship celebrated in the experience of sexual intercourse.

We have previously reflected upon that form of human love called *eros* and pointed out its powerful drive toward interpersonal intimacy as well as its demonic possibilities for jealousy, possessiveness and violence. Sexual attraction, sexual desire, sexual passion can easily get out of hand and become personally and socially destructive. But they are not evil in themselves for all that. The human problem with sexuality is to learn its human meaning and purpose and to enable its free and responsible use. That is precisely what the virtue of chastity informed by love inclines human beings toward.

Unlike money, which is of its very nature an instrumental value, sex is not simply a means to an end, not merely an instrument whose whole worth is to be found in the ends it is capable of achieving. Sex is not a thing; it is an activity and, when engaged in by human beings, it has the chance of being a human activity, an expression and embodiment of one's very own self. Sex can, of course, be seen and used as if it were simply a means to an end. Human beings can and do use sex to make money (prostitution, pornography, advertising), to obtain pleasure (masturbation, voyeurism, recreational sex), to make babies (*in vitro* fertilization, surrogate motherhood, adoption sellers), to manipulate and control others. But they cannot do any of these things without dehumanizing both themselves and their sexual partners, without using their embodied selves as things or means. It is for this reason that traditional Christian teaching on sexual morality, however flawed and negative it has been at various times, wisely held together in an inseparable unity the various goods that sex can serve in the context of a committed human love.

Chastity and Human Dignity

The key to understanding both the virtue and the vow of chastity, I would suggest, is to be found in the notion of respect for human dignity, both one's own and that of others. Chastity invites and enables respect for oneself and others precisely as sexual beings. As a man, I have sexual powers and desires which open up various possibilities for my living and loving. The same is true for other human beings I encounter in life's journey. But human finitude requires me to make a choice, a choice guided by the grace I have received. One choice is to direct my sexual energy toward a universal love, to turn toward God as the immediate object of my erotic longing for personal intimacy. I choose to give myself directly and totally to the divine lover and in that process of giving to include in my love all his people without difference or distinction. This choice is given a visible and concrete expression in the religious vow of chastity for the sake of the kingdom. The vow excludes other choices and the goods which pertain to them, but it honors and respects both its own choice of celibacy and its demands (self-respect), as well as the choices of others and the demands entailed in such choices (other-respect).

A second choice is to direct my sexual energy toward a particular love, to turn toward another human being as the immediate object of my erotic longing for personal intimacy. In this choice I may or may not find a person who calls forth within me the needed desire, or who is the willing, mutual partner of such desire. I choose to give myself totally to a human lover and to receive in turn his or her love, and in this relationship I discover the divine love mediated to me in and through our two-in-one-flesh unity. This choice is given concrete and tangible expression in the marriage vows, vows which exclude the goods of other choices, but which honor and respect both one's own choice of marriage and its demands as well as the demands of other people's different choices. In religious literature this is often expressed by saying that celibacy and marriage need one another to understand both the goods one has embraced and those one has foregone.

Both of these two choices or commitments demand of their very nature a total and permanent self-giving. In either choice we remain human beings, subject to temptation and doubt, prone to failure, in need of and capable of many other forms of inter-personal intimacy. In both choices we continue to need the psychological and emotional intimacy we experience with friends, the social and intellectual intimacy with our neighbors and co-workers, and the spiritual intimacy of our fellow believers and our intimacy with God in prayer. The virtue of chastity is the guide of all these intimate relationships, setting the healthy boundaries within which these relationships may flourish while respecting the dignity of one another's choices and obligations.

But there is a form of intimacy proper to each of the two choices mentioned, which gives the choice its distinctive character. The intimacy proper to the vowed life of celibacy is total personal union with God which has its symbolic or sacramental expression in the prayer of mystical union. The intimacy proper to the vowed life of marriage is total personal union with one's spouse in a fully shared life which has its symbolic or sacramental expression in the act of sexual intercourse.

God and Chastity

There are a number of difficulties with what has just been said that need to be addressed at least briefly. One difficulty is that married couples also pray and seek personal union with God in prayer, and such personal union may well find expression in mystical prayer. Many celibates, of course, live a life of shared minds and hearts in religious community, never experience mystical union in prayer, and feel strong desires for sexual intimacy with close friends. Conversely, some people experience the ecstatic delights of sexual union without the personal commitment of marriage and a shared life, or are married and find little that is shared and nothing that is ecstatic about sexual intercourse. A final, obvious difficulty is that the two choices proposed here seem to ignore the vast number of people who make neither choice and who remain single either by choice or necessity. What can be said about these obvious situations?

Chastity has been described as the virtue which guides and enables sexual human beings to love one another precisely as sexual. The virtue is learned and strengthened in and through our struggles with the power and the demands of our own sexuality. As we struggle to bring *eros* under the sway of *agape*, two temptations constantly beset us. The first is to deny and stifle our erotic yearnings as incompatible with agapaic love. The result of yielding to this temptation is to turn our personal relationships cold and formal and our actions into exercises of duty rather than expressions of love. The impact is felt both in our relationship with God and in our relationships with others. Our lives lack an ecstatic dimension; they are without joy and spontaneity. Chastity is then understood in a largely negative way, as the unending struggle for a self-control that does not really free one to love and relate to others. Ultimately one is left alone. This temptation may befall anyone, married, celibate or single, though it is more likely to beset the celibate and the single person.

The second temptation in the struggle to bring *eros* under the sway of *agape* is to abandon the struggle as misguided or impossible. The result of yielding to this temptation is that we give unbridled rein to our erotic longings and so quickly confuse lust with love. Sexual desire and activity finds its meaning in tensions relieved, desires satiated, and the number of conquests one can boast of. In the process sex is divorced from love and ceases to be an occasion for the learning, expression and enhancement of love. The self surrenders to its own emotional and bodily longings rather than bringing them under free and rational control. Chastity is still understood negatively but is now evaluated as an unwarranted limitation on the desires of the self. This temptation, too, may beset anyone, celibate, married or single, but it is more likely to befall the single person or the unhappily married person.

It seems to me that the only way anyone, married, celibate or single, will come to understand the meaning of sexuality and the virtue of chastity is to grasp their dynamism toward a mutual love that serves life and human well-being. Our sexuality tells us that we have been made for intimacy with one another and with God. Sexual activity should serve this purpose and the virtue of chastity enables it to do so. No person who seeks only the satisfaction of his or her own sexual desires, curiosity, or power serves life and love. Whatever specific material norms may be developed to guide sexual conduct, chastity finds its moral meaning in the human ability to love others freely, joyfully, with respect for their dignity, in fidelity, and in life-giving ways. That is the worth of both the virtue and the vow.

OBEDIENCE

Finally, the virtue of obedience is that virtue which enables and guides the responsible use of our social freedom. Its deepest meaning and manifestation are to be found in our total submission to the will of God. But since God's will is not directly and immediately revealed to us, but is mediated to us in a variety of ways, our obedience requires a discerning submission to any number of human authorities. We are called by love to obey authorities such as teachers, parents, civil and religious leaders, employers, as well as the laws which structure their authority. I have called this a discerning submission, for none of these authorities can be simply identified in an absolute sense with the will of God. Obedience, therefore, as a virtue has two essential characteristics. It sees clearly that one's own will is not to be identified with God's will, that there are submissions to the will of others that I should freely and gladly make even when I do not wish to do so. The virtue of obedience enables this use of my freedom. Second, it recognizes that the human search for God's will is a cooperative venture, requiring the full and free participation of all human beings, reflecting an awareness of the social nature of the human person.

The virtue of obedience, then, calls us not to silence, not to a passive resignation or meek docility before authority and its claims. Rather it calls us to dialogue and participation, to social and political responsiblity for our social groups and organizations. What precisely is involved in the religious vow and the virtue of obedience can be seen if we contrast the religious basis of social obligation to the secular basis of social obligation in the two dominant political ideologies in our modern world, democratic liberalism and Marxist socialism. These two political ideologies have quite different bases for obedience to authority.

Political Ideologies

In Marxist-socialist versions of obedience to social authority, obedience is due to the state or the party because the social body is supreme over the individual. It is the social body which enables life, grants rights, protects and promotes human well-being. So, too, it allocates goods, work, and the obligations of its members. The central purpose of the efforts of public authority is to insure the real equality of the members of society, an equality which is inevitably purchased at the price of social conformism and restrictions on individual freedom.

In liberal democratic versions of obedience to social authority, obedience is owed to authority because the social body and the authority it has are the products or creations of the mutual consent of the individual members of the body social. Human beings freely choose, for reasons of their own self-interest, to form social groups and to endow these groups with certain rights and obligations in regard to the members of the group. Human beings obey the social authority because they have agreed, tacitly or explicitly, to obey. Obedience is due because of this mutual consent. But what human beings have consented to, they may also dissent from at any moment for any reason. To ensure the stability of the group, therefore, all agree that the majority will should be the basis for authority's claim to obedience. The central purpose of the efforts of public authority is to insure the maximum degree of individual freedom for the members of the social body to pursue ends of their own choosing as long as they do not unjustly interfere with others' pursuit of their own purposes.

Consequently, Marxist-socialist ideology which stresses and seeks human equality finds itself at odds with liberal-democratic ideology which emphasizes individual freedom as its highest goal. Marxist-socialist ideology reveres a scientific, technical reason that finds little place for the individual choice of ends and values, while liberal-democratic ideology worships individual choice that rejects anyone's right to ask for a public, reasonable account of its choices. Both ideologies find no public significance and no public place for religious faith. Religion becomes a private matter, a matter of emotive preference.

Religious Obedience

The religious basis of obligation is quite different than either of the two ideologies would suggest. Christian faith acknowledges God as the Author of life, as the all-good, all-wise, all-loving Creator and Sustainer of life. He alone has any right to tell anyone else what he or she ought to do. It is, then, the very nature and character of God which grounds every human obligation to obey, for all free obedience to his will is both rational and enabling of our humanity. Christian faith summons people to acknowledge God as the Author—the Authority—of human existence and so to obedience to him. It calls upon people to honor and respect the very structures of creation, including the gift of life itself and their own nature as free and rational and social persons. Hence, the religious virtue of obedience will not grant to the social body, to the will of the majority, or to any other human agency what belongs to God alone. Religious obedience, if it is truly a human virtue, is always discerning, discriminating and critical, knowing that "obedience to God comes before obedience to men" (Acts 5:29).

Curiously enough, then, the virtue of obedience enables human freedom rather than restricting it. The virtue makes possible family life, free political and social life, free academic and cultural life, and one day, we may pray, a life of peace and freedom in one world as one people. The virtue of obedience guides and serves neighbor-love because it sees authority not as domination and control, but as service to the community. Authority that seeks domination and control loses its moral claim to obedience; it becomes tyranny, which requires, instead of obedience, our criticism and our courageous refusal to obey.

The evangelical counsels, then, understood first of all as human character strengths and formal norms of morality, necessarily must guide and order every Christian love that seeks to love as Jesus first loved us. The counsels do, indeed, set us on the path to love, to a love that is more than sentiment and good intentions. One essential feature of the counsels is their recognition of the social nature of the human person. So they place the individual person in a relationship to material goods, sex and power which seeks to use these realities to serve persons and human well-being. Material goods, sexual pleasure and the use of power

can all be vehicles for self-satisfaction and responsible indepen-
dence. These, too, are human goods not to be slighted or scorned
and rejected out of hand. But from a Christian perspective they
are neither sufficient unto themselves nor adequate pursuits for
a truly human life. They must be brought to bear on service to
the neighbor.

Material wealth, or money as we have spoken of it here, must
serve greater justice, equality and freedom in human life, not just
for oneself but for others outside one's immediate circle, if it is
to serve love. Sex must serve human and divine intimacy,
strengthen it and stabilize it, as well as serve new love and new
life, if it is to realize its Christian possibilities. Power must serve
to promote and protect human life, human freedom, and the
social order and unity essential to both, if it is to reflect the source
of all power and authority. It is to both the present possibility of
these goods and to the hope of their future realization in the
kingdom of God that the vowed life of the evangelical counsels
bears witness. In less formal and less public ways, but in ways no
less real and demanding, so should the life of every person who
seeks to love his or her neighbor as Jesus loved his own.

STUDY QUESTIONS

1. What are your personal feelings about the religious life? Do
   you find it irrelevant or indifferent to life, challenging, an
   escape, a form of witness, or simply incomprehensible? Why?
   Have the changes in the life-style of religious following Vatican
   II affected your views?

2. Is the spirit or virtue of poverty real in your life? What is it
   about the possession and use of material goods that causes you
   the most perplexity? Do you find it hard to share your goods
   with the so-called "undeserving" poor? How can you be sure
   they are undeserving?

3. What do you think is the purpose of sex in human life? Why is
   sex such a concern and problem for our culture? Can you recognize the temptations mentioned in the text in your life?

What would it take to develop a positive sense of the virtue of chastity in your own life?

4. Many people find authority to be a real problem in their lives. Why do you think this is so? Can you indicate how, in your experience, obedience to authority promotes human freedom and love?

5. If obedience is to be discerning, then at times we will refuse obedience to public authority. Can you specify the conditions and possible occasions when civil disobedience would be a moral obligation for you?

BIBLIOGRAPHY

Gremillion, Joseph. *The Gospel of Peace and Justice: Catholic Social Teaching Since Pope John.* Maryknoll: Orbis Books, 1975. An excellent collection of papal and episcopal documents on the pertinent economic, social and political problems of our times. The author has provided a very useful introduction. A superb way to enter into the problems and principles of economic and political responsibility.

Hanigan, James P. *What Are They Saying About Sexual Morality?* New York: Paulist Press, 1982. A brief, readable review of what contemporary theologians are teaching about sexual morality. The accent is on the positive meaning and possibilities of sexual love.

King, Martin Luther, Jr. "Letter From Birmingham Jail," *Why We Can't Wait.* New York: The New American Library, 1964, pp. 76–95. This classic letter by Dr. King, written in the midst of the civil-rights struggle, is still a fine introduction to the problems and principles of civil disobedience.

Marstin, Ronald. *Beyond Our Tribal Gods.* Maryknoll: Orbis Books, 1979. A readable and radical argument that mature Christian faith terminates in a commitment to social justice and a corresponding change in one's life-style. The argument is challenging if not always convincing.

Metz, Johannes Baptist. *Poverty of Spirit.* New York: Newman Press, 1968. A prayerful, reflective essay on poverty as a spiritual attitude and condition. The author, an eminent German theologian, takes the incarnation as his starting point and concludes with prayer as the most fundamental expression of human poverty and truthfulness.

10 No Longer Servants, But Friends

In the famous Last Supper discourse in the Johannine Gospel, the evangelist has Jesus speak the following words as part of his farewell statement to his disciples.

> As the Father has loved me,
> so I have loved you.
> Remain in my love.
> If you keep my commandments
> you will remain in my love,
> just as I have kept my Father's commandments
> and remain in his love.
> I have told you this
> so that my joy may be in you
> and your joy may be complete.
> This is my commandment:
> Love one another,
> as I have loved you.
> A man can have no greater love
> than to lay down his life for his friends.
> You are my friends,
> if you do what I command you.
> I shall not call you servants anymore,
> because a servant does not know
> his master's business;
> I call you friends,
> because I have made known to you
> everything I have learned from my Father (Jn 15:9–15).

This is a most suggestive passage, for it points quite directly to the ultimate goal of the moral life and declares that goal to be capable of at least a partial realization even before the arrival of the final reign of God. It proclaims, rather surprisingly perhaps,

that morality is really about friendship, even friendship with God
in Christ.

Earlier, in discussing the form of love called *philia,* we mentioned that friendship is based upon shared or mutual interests.
Jesus calls his disciples no longer servants but friends because he
has now fully shared with them the secrets of his Father's heart.
He has shared with them the Father's love, the Father's commandments, the Father's mind, the Father's whole business. And
he promises to share with them also "the Spirit of Truth who
issues from the Father" (Jn 15:26), who will join the disciples as
witness to Jesus. The disciples have become friends of the Trinitarian God and will remain friends if they but continue to share
the mind and heart of Christ.

Here is the startling good news of the Gospel. God wants us
not as his slaves or his servants, not as pawns to be deployed in
some cosmic chess game, nor as fragile vessels whose weaknesses
show off his infinitely greater power and wisdom. He wants us as
friends, to sit around the table with him, eating, talking, singing
and celebrating the divine-human friendship and our mutual joy
in it. As with any good friend, God wants to share with us what is
important to him. He would introduce us to his other friends in
the hope that the circle of friends will be expanded. And he rel-
ishes our sharing with him in return our hearts and minds. It may
be staggering to think that God loves us; it is sometimes even
more astonishing that he likes us as well.

THE CONDITIONS OF FRIENDSHIP

As the evangelist portrays this friendship between Jesus and
his disciples, it seems to have one condition attached to it—that
the disciples do what Jesus commands them. Such a condition
may appear to be something of a contradiction. Real friends do
not put conditions on their friendship, especially such a one-sided
condition as this one. It almost sounds like: "I'll be your friend
as long as you do things my way." A demand like that is hardly
the basis for a friendship; it is the very antithesis of friendship. If,
then, we are to grasp the meaning of this condition, and the real-
tionship of morality to the goal of friendship, we had best explore

the objective conditions of friendship, for the evangelist's condition is surely to be understood in that way.

We have already seen one objective condition of friendship, the existence of a shared interest. But a closer look at this condition, precisely as an objective condition of friendship, is warranted. To call shared interests an objective condition of friendship means that it is simply impossible to be friends with someone with whom you have nothing in common. This is not a case of not wanting to be friends with the other person, not a matter of subjective preference or personal taste. It is a real inability that is objectively based in reality. There simply is nothing that seizes our joint interest. Think, for instance, of the difficulty we all have in simply conversing with another person when we cannot find a topic of common interest. We find, literally, that there is nothing to say and no relationship is possible.

Shared Interests

Now it is theoretically the case, to be sure, that we have some things in common with every human being. We all inhabit the same planet, have bodies, experience the weather, eat food, recoil from pain, get tired, ask questions, laugh, and shed tears. Any of these things, as well as a host of others, could be the basis of a mutual interest. But we cannot will ourselves to be actually interested in what does not in fact really catch our interest. We can study and eventually acquire an interest in some things, but in that case there was already something about the matter that at least tickled our initial interest and led us to pursue the matter.

In the case of Jesus and his disciples, their mutual interest arose from a shared religious faith in the God of Israel and his will for his people. Initially this shared interest bound them together in a relationship of master and disciple: "You call me Master and Lord, and rightly; so I am" (Jn 13:14). So it is evident that a shared interest alone is not sufficient to constitute a relationship of friendship. However essential they may be for a friendship to develop, mutual interests can lead to a variety of relationships other than one of friendship. These other relationships include parent and child, teacher and student, employer and employee, co-workers, co-conspirators, and so on. Something more is needed for a friendship to result from shared interests.

Freedom

A second essential objective condition for friendship is the freedom of both parties willingly to enter into and sustain the relationship. A coerced friendship is a contradiction in terms, whether the coercion be deliberate or accidental, psychological or social. Indeed, one of the joys of friendship is precisely the absence of any bonds of psychological, social or legal compulsion. Friends find they are free to be themselves with one another, free to speak or be silent, free to come or to go, free to laugh or to cry, free to succeed or fail, without imperiling the friendship. Friends find that the bond that supports them is supportive but not restrictive. The bond of friendship liberates friends from the grip of isolation and self-absorption, enabling them to enter into new relationships with new friends. As a friendship deepens and solidifies, jealousy and possessiveness increasingly disappear.

The pattern of mutual freedom is clear in Jesus' relationship with his disciples. He invites them to believe in him and follow him, and they freely choose to do so (Lk 5:1–11). They are also free to refuse the call (Mk 10:17–22), or to leave him after a time (Jn 6:66–71). While the refusal of the invitation and the early departure bring sadness, they do not bring recriminations or threats. The disciples are free to speak their minds (Mt 16:21–23; 19:10–12; 19:27; 20:20–23), just as Jesus is free to speak his own mind in return. Yet the freedom proper to the master/disciple relationship requires the disciple to submit to the instruction and discipline of the master, to accept the master's authority in a way that is not quite appropriate to a friendship. Friends do not try to make one another over in the way that the Lord and Master properly tries to do to his disciples. So it again appears that freedom is a necessary condition of friendship, along with shared interests, but together they are not sufficient conditions. Something else, objectively, is still needed.

Equality

The third and final objective condition essential to friendship is equality. Friendship is possible only between equals. This is a particularly difficult condition to comprehend, especially in the context of the divine/human relationship. For surely no one of us wishes to lay claim to an equality with God. Yet it is the most important condition of friendship, giving the relationship its unique character. Shared interests and freedom can be present in many other kinds of human relationships, but only friendship has the additional mark of equality. Hence we need to explore the meaning and the possibility of this condition to some degree.

In an earlier chapter we discussed the three conditions of freedom as space, power and authority. Power was defined as the human ability to act to achieve purpose. Understood in this initial and limited way, power is obviously an essential and basic human good. It is an ontic good of which the moral quality depends on the uses we make of the ability, on the purposes we strive to achieve and our manner of achieving them. To be and to become human is already to be powerful to some degree, and every increase in the human ability to act is a form of empowerment, an increase in ontic goodness. It is good, then, that human beings "seek to do more, know more and have more in order to be more," as Pope Paul VI expressed it in his great encyclical letter, *Populorum Progressio.* It is only in this way that they become more fully human.

The ability to act to achieve purpose has both a collective and an individual form. The individual ability to act may conveniently be called strength to distinguish it from the collective form which is a different ability and which is more properly called power. Strength is always the property of an individual. As such, it cannot be given to or conferred upon another person. My ability to write beautiful poems, to fix mechanical gadgets or to lift heavy packages is and always remains my ability, my strength. It may, of course, be used in the service of others, but it still remains my ability. Strength may be used to assist other people to develop their own strengths, as, for instance, by teaching someone the art of poetry writing or weightlifting. To this extent we may say that it is possible to empower other people. More accurately and realistically, however, people empower themselves with the help and guidance of others. Good parents, good teachers, good coaches know they are not the agents of human empowerment but only assist at and oversee the development of another's strengths.

Good doctors know they are not the agents of physical healing but only shepherd the body's own curative powers.

Manifestly human beings differ in strength in all sorts of ways. Some sing beautifully; others croak like frogs. Some solve complicated mathematical problems with ease; others cannot balance a checkbook. From one perspective this wide difference in the range and degree of human strengths is fortunate in that one person is able to do what another is not, and so the whole human community is enriched by the plurality of human strengths. This perspective enables us to delight in the gifts of both ourselves and others without envy or jealousy. But from another, equally valid perspective this difference in human strengths is something of a problem, for it makes free and equal relationships often difficult and sometimes impossible. Freedom and friendship are fully possible only between those people who are roughly equal in regard to the interests which bring them together.

Imagine a relationship in which there is a great inequality of strength between the two parties to the relationship. Such a relationship will inevitably be one of domination and submission. Lacking the ability to do anything else, I have no choice but to submit to the domination or to break off the relationship, a choice that is not always possible or wise. The domination may be friendly, benevolent and helpful, even welcome to the submissive party, as is the case at times in the parent/child, teacher/student, master/disciple, doctor/patient relationships, for example. But in these cases we should have no illusions about freedom and equality, or about friendship. Parents are not and cannot be the friends of their dependent children; teachers are not the friends of their students. All parties to these kinds of relationships, if they have any sense at all, want the relationship to end—the children to grow up, the students to graduate, the disciple to embrace a way of life of his or her own, the patient to get well. With such enhanced strength, with achieved equality, friendship will now be a possibility.

The same analysis that we have made of strength could also be made of the collective ability to act to achieve purpose. It would show the same difference in power in various social groups and the possibility of freedom and friendship only between social groups where there is a rough equality of power. Where the difference in power between social groups is great, the relationship between them can only be one of domination and submission, and can only be experienced as such, no matter how well-meaning the dominant partner may be. It would be helpful to think out our foreign policy positions in these terms.

If this analysis of strength and power is even approximately correct, it follows that our love for others, if it is to be substantive and not merely symbolic, calls us to aid them, insofar as we are able, in their own empowerment. In doing this we render them capable of being our equals, establish the possibility of real friendship between us, and show respect for their human dignity. It is not a question of earning their friendship, for friendship is not earned but freely given. It is a matter of making friendship a real possibility.

THE TEMPTATIONS OF FRIENDSHIP

In the task of helping others toward their own empowerment, there are two temptations to be alert for and to resist. I shall call them the temptations to paternalism and sentimentalism. The temptation to paternalism in the Christian life wells up in hearts that have been touched by the compassion of the good shepherd (Jn 10:1–16). Recognizing the plight of the poor and the oppressed of the earth, knowing of the callous indifference toward the deprived of too many of the powerful and well-to-do, such hearts see the need to care for, protect and guide the weak of the world safely through life. Taking upon themselves the pastoral burden to love and care for others, it becomes all too easy to accept the role of parent to child, helper to client, teacher to student, ruler to ruled, shepherd to sheep, as something permanent rather than as a transitional stage of a relationship.

Paternalism

Paternalism, of course, is not all bad. If it were, it would not be a temptation. There is, after all, a place and a time for parenting, teaching, helping, shepherding. But these are only transitional roles whose purpose is to move those we help and care for to a place where freedom and friendship can flourish. Jesus is, indeed, Lord and Master, Teacher and King, but in the long

run he prefers to be Friend and Brother. The dynamics by which
he tries to realize his preference are clear and establish a pattern
for his disciples to follow.

> His state was divine,
> yet he did not cling
> to his equality with God
> but emptied himself
> to assume the condition of a slave,
> and became as men are;
> and being as all men are,
> he was humbler yet,
> even to accepting death,
> death on a cross (Phil 2:6–8).

Sentimentalism

This act of self-sacrificing love to become as men are, to
share the misery of the human condition, must not be sentimen-
talized, which is the other temptation of Christian love. Jesus did
not embrace the oppression and alienation of the human condition as something good in itself, nor was he particularly eager to
experience the agony of death on a cross (Mt 26:38–45). He
became like one of us and accepted death to set us free from our
weakness, to enable us to overcome the oppression and alienation
of the human condition. Death on the cross leads to resurrection
and ascension and Pentecost, not to the sentimentalizing of
human poverty and deprivation as blessed conditions. If Christians are called in this life to have a preferential option for the
poor, and they are, it is not in order to hallow the conditions and
consequences of poverty, but to help people overcome those conditions and consequences.

> But God raised him on high
> and gave him the name
> which is above all other names
> so that *all beings*
> in the heavens, on earth and in the underworld,
> *should bend the knee* at the name of Jesus
> and that every tongue should acclaim
> Jesus Christ as Lord,
> to the glory of God the Father (Phil 2:9–11).

But Jesus did not cling even to his resurrected glory. He invited his disciples to share his glory, to be his friends: "Father, I want those you have given me to be with me where I am, so that they may always see the glory you have given me because you loved me before the foundation of the world" (Jn 17:24). Jesus could call his disciples friends because, by sharing his own life and his Spirit so fully and so freely with them, he had empowered them, individually and collectively, to be the sacrament of his continued presence in history. His followers become members of his body, the Church. They are now able to perform the same works as he himself performed and even greater works (Jn 14:12).

THE VIRTUES OF FRIENDSHIP

The significance of the Christian moral life, then, lies in this empowerment to love as Jesus loved to the extent that we are able to enjoy the friendship of the Triune God. The moral life is the path to the shared interests, freedom and equality which make that friendship with God possible for us. That is the chief and over-riding work of God's grace.

If freedom and equality are essential conditions of friendship, mercy and compassion are its life-blood, the indispensable virtues for friends. Without the ability to feel with, suffer with, experience with the other, which is the literal meaning of compassion, there will be no bond of friendship, no mutuality of mind and heart. This, of course, points us back to the importance of mutual interests for friends, for we learn compassion in and through these shared interests. We come to understand the joys and sorrows, hopes and fears of another only as we share them and feel them with our friends.

Compassion

The bond of affection and mutual support that compassion creates between human beings is vividly illustrated in close personal friendships. My friend's success in a task brings me joy just as her failure brings me pain and disappointment, not for myself but for her and with her. Her illness brings me dis-ease; her return to health brightens my day as well as hers. Or as John the Baptist explained the matter to his jealous disciples, "The bride is only for the bridegroom; and yet the bridegroom's friend, who stands there and listens, is glad when he hears the bridegroom's voice" (Jn 3:29).

Compassion is not unique to the relationship between friends. The same affection, support and shared joy and sorrow are also manifest between teammates who play a common sport, between actors and actresses who put on a play together, between soldiers who endure the shared hell of war, between alcoholics who have experienced the struggle for sobriety. But it is basic to all friendships because it is the route to knowing the friend for who he or she really is, and not as we would like the friend to be. It is compassion which enables us to love the friend as other, as a unique and independent personality and not merely as an extension or reflection of ourselves.

Compassion, of course, does not just happen. We must be willing to let it occur, be willing to listen to the other, be willing to enter into the life of the other and experience the world through his or her eyes. In doing this we increase our own capacity and likelihood for pain and anxiety, but also for joy and wonder. Friends find themselves inhabiting a wider and richer world than before they were friends, and more capable of compassion and concern for others. And so it was also with the Lord Jesus: "The Word was made flesh, he lived among us" (Jn 1:14), "so that he could be a compassionate and trustworthy high priest of God's religion, able to atone for human sins. That is, because he has himself been through temptation he is able to help others who are tempted" (Heb 2:18).

Mercy

A corollary of compassion is mercy or the willingness to forgive others, and it is equally basic to friendship, both human friendship and our friendship with God. That the Christian God is understood to be preeminently a God of mercy needs little elaboration. Among the most touching of the parables in the New Testament are the three Luke records about the lost sheep, the lost coin and the prodigal son (Lk 15:1–32). This chapter in Luke's Gospel is sometimes referred to as a Gospel within the Gospel, so central is it to the good news of our salvation. Fur-

thermore, we have Jesus' own example of forgiving his execution-
ers as he hung on the cross (Lk 23:34), his instructions on forgiveness in the Sermon on the Mount (Mt 6:12–15), and his
admonition to Peter to forgive his brother without limit (Mt
18:21–22). As the psalmist in the Old Testament was already well
aware, without God's mercy the human enterprise is hopeless. "If
you never overlooked our sins, Yahweh, Lord, could anyone sur-
vive? But you do forgive us: and for that we revere you" (Ps
130:3–4).

But it is not only God's readiness to forgive and show mercy
that fuels and sustains friendships. Human friends must be ready
and willing to forgive one another and to be forgiven. And all of
us must also learn a willingness to forgive God. It may be that the
need for human friends to show mercy to one another is fairly
obvious. No human being is perfect; we all fall short from time
to time. To hold another human being to some standard of per-
fection without any possibility of forgiveness for an occasional
failure is not the sign or the task of a friend. It may at times be
the proper task of a teacher or an employer, but it also makes
friendly relations impossible. But why does God need our forgiveness? Surely God does not fall short or miss the mark in his
relations with us. How, then, can we speak of forgiving God? To
answer that question a brief, additional reflection on friendship
and mercy is required.

Friends invest a great deal personally in friendships; consequently, they have a great deal to lose if the friendship is betrayed
or goes sour and dies. It may very well be that friends do not put
explicit conditions or requirements on their relationship. But
they do inevitably count on one another. Tacitly, implicitly, perhaps even unconsciously, to declare oneself a friend to another
human being is to say that I am for you. If I can ever help you in
any way, I will do so. But since we are limited and sinful human
beings, sooner or later we will fail in this pledge, wittingly or
unwittingly, deliberately or by chance, in small ways or in major
ways. The failure may not be at all deliberate. It may be due to
the pressures of work or personal worry, to oversight or lack of
attentiveness, even to physical absence at a particular time. Whatever the cause of the failure, the friend is hurt, disappointed,

wounded by our failure. Even if we are in no way morally or legally responsible for the failure, we grieve at our friend's hurt and we are sorry for our part in causing it.

Friendship, then, if it is anything more than superficial acquaintance, will necessitate that one learn to say "I am sorry." It will require an honest acknowledgement and sincere repentance for our human shortcomings, both deliberate and indeliberate. To live as a friend, to sustain a friendship over time, we will have to both ask for and receive mercy. The role of the prodigal son will at some time be ours.

But for mercy to be received, it must also be given and given freely. This forgiving is no easy task and is certainly not a simple matter of words. The closer a person is to us, the higher are our expectations of being able to count on that person, and the more painful are our wounds when those expectations are disappointed. Our expectations may be unrealistic, unfair, and unspoken even to ourselves. Or they may be perfectly reasonable and clearly understood both by our friend and by ourselves. But in either case, when these expectations are ignored or violated, we are hurt, angered and resentful. A wall is thrown up between ourselves and our friend, destroying the comfortable intimacy we once knew. There is nothing that can remove the wall except the genuine offer of mercy expressed in the words "I forgive you."

We can now see why mercy is the corollary of compassion, for mercy will not be possible for us unless we are able to enter into and share the perceptions and feelings of our friend. We need to grasp our friend's grief at our own pain, her incomprehension of our expectations, her inability to meet our unrealistic expectations, her integrity of conscience which forbade her meeting our unfair ones. It is not only the role of the prodigal son that a friend will sometimes have to play. Friendship will also require us to act at times the role of the forgiving father, at other times to deal with the anger and resentment of the older brother. For however fair or unfair our expectations may be, whether we are in the right or in the wrong in our expectations, we are still hurt and the anger and resentment must be dispelled for the friendship to continue.

Here, then, is the reason why we must also be ready and willing to forgive God. For despite the fact that God does us no wrong in his dealings with us and never truly lets us down, he may often fail to meet our expectations and we are hurt and angry. Like the older brother of the prodigal son we become resentful that our life is not quite as we would have it be, that others seem more fortunate or more blessed than we are and yet somehow less deserving. Such resentment is like a cancer eating away at our ability to love. Only compassion and mercy, given and received, can restore us to health and life.

Jesus' revelation of God as the Father of mercies and his admonition to Peter to forgive his brother seventy times seven times, then, are not frills on our moral existence. They strike at its very essence, for they proclaim both the possibility of and the path to friendship, both with God and with our fellow human beings. Mercy, the willingness to forgive which is the fruit of compassion, has not only personal and religious significance; it is also fundamental to political and social life for its contributions to public peace and civility as well as to the possibility of a human future. The poor and the oppressed of the world do not need to forget the past, but they do need to forgive the oppressors for it. Those people who will not forgive and who will not show mercy are the same people who will not accept forgiveness or ask for mercy. As the Sermon on the Mount tells us, such people reject both human and divine friendship. "Yes, if you forgive others their failings, your heavenly Father will forgive you yours; but if you do not forgive others, your Father will not forgive your failings either" (Mt 6:14–15).

PRAYER AND FRIENDSHIP

Human friendships have their objective possibility because of shared interests, mutual freedom and equality. They are given life by mercy and compassion, and are nourished and sustained by personal presence and personal communion. I have been making the case in the previous pages that the same is true for our friendship with the Trinitarian God. But since we do not have a direct, material experience of God as an embodied object of our senses, personal presence to and communication with God are something of a problem. I can visit my human friends in their homes, call them on the telephone, write them letters, meet them for lunch, share a vacation with them, and remember them on special occasions with a card or a gift. There are numerous ways in which to communicate and to share personal presence with each other within the constraints of our time and energy. But how do we do the same thing with God so as to nourish and sustain our friendship with him? One answer is, of course, prayer, and so I would like to conclude this study of human moral existence with some brief comments on prayer as the nourishing and sustaining factor in the moral life of the divine-human friendship.

Prayer may be defined in general terms as the raising of the mind and heart to God. This definition is an old catechism definition which I learned in my youth. It seems to me to be still as good a definition as any I have heard since. The basic premise for all personal prayer is the existence of a personal, caring God, the presence in the world of a Subject who wants to enter into personal communication with me, to whom my mind and heart are of some interest and who, in turn, wishes to share his mind and heart with me. If this is not the case, if the premise is invalid and there is no such presence, then prayer is merely self-reflection, or a form of fantasizing, or talking to oneself. It would be foolish and deceptive to give such practices another name like prayer.

The conviction that underlies the practice of prayer in both the Hebraic and the Christian traditions is that God has called each one of us personally by name (Jer 1:5), and wishes to enter into intimate personal communion with each one of us. This personal communion as we may experience it here and now is but a pledge and a foretaste of the eternal communion we will have with him when we will know as we are known (1 Cor 13:12) and see God face to face.

The Purpose of Prayer

This conviction points us to the purpose of prayer: intimate, deep, personal communion with God in Christ which leads to an ever-present awareness that I am not alone in the universe. There is Someone to say yes to, to be with, who knows me more intimately than I know myself, who is the very source and goal of my being. This awareness of the presence of a loving Subject has led Christians, following the example and teaching of Jesus, to give this Subject the name Abba, Father (Mt 6:9; Rom 8:16–17). The same conviction directs us to the different kinds of prayer possible for human beings. That is to say, the kinds of prayer can be distinguished on the basis of or according to the different things one can do in prayer. Prayer forms may also be distinguished by the way one prays, e.g., vocal or mental prayer, private or public prayer, liturgical or spontaneous prayer, but that distinction is not a focus of concern here. Its relevance to the moral life seems small.

The kinds of prayer I am interested in for the purpose of this study basically come down to the kinds of responses the human heart can appropriately make to the presence and activity of the Divine Subject. These responses can be usefully ordered under four headings. There is, first, the prayer of praise and thanksgiving in which we express our awe, wonder, joy and gratitude for the many marvels and gifts of creation as well as for the blessings of our own personal and social history (Pss 8; 103; 104; 135; 136). There is, second, the prayer of petition and intercession, in which we express our needs and the needs of others, acknowledge our dependence and poverty, and ask for God's grace and blessing on our lives and the lives of those for whom we intercede (Pss 20; 25; 28; 31; 40). Third, prayer can take the form of sorrow and repentance. Here we acknowledge our faults, our lack of gratitude and generosity, express our sorrow and grief for the shallowness and tepidity of our love, and affirm our resolve to be more faithful in the future (Pss 32; 38; 51; 106; 130). Finally, there is the prayer of personal communion, a form of prayer in which we simply enjoy and rest in the presence of God, share our hopes and fears, and allow God's word to speak to our own hearts.

In ordering the forms of prayer according to these four headings, I do not mean to suggest that these forms of prayer are simple techniques indicating what one might do in order to pray well. I do mean to say that a healthy prayer life will include all these expressions of prayer, just as any intimate personal friendship does. The key to prayer is not the form of prayer one uses, but the authenticity and sincerity of the prayer. Is the prayer an honest, genuine expression of what is really in one's mind and heart? That is the critical point. The usefulness of distinguishing these four forms of prayer is to test the breadth and depth of our relationship with God. Prayer that is exclusively petitionary, or repentant, or grateful betrays an unfortunate narrowing of who and what God is in one's life and restricts the possibility of real friendship with God. In the worst case, it betrays a fashioning of God in an image of our own making.

The Prayer of Friends

While all four forms of prayer have a place in every Christian's life, the one that is most pertinent to the moral life is the prayer of personal communion in which we most directly foster our personal friendship with God. The prayer of personal communion has two distinct aspects to it, just as any form of interpersonal communication does: speaking and listening. The speaking to the Lord, telling him of our cares and anxieties, our delights and our doubts, requires from us only subjective truthfulness and sincerity. We must mean what we pray and pray what we mean. But the listening to the Lord, the process of allowing one's own mind and heart to be shaped by the word of God, is usually a more difficult and complex prospect. It is, after all, generally a more difficult task to learn to be a good listener than to say what is on one's own mind. What, then, is required and what may be expected from efforts to listen to and commune with the word of God?

The first requirement for listening to God's word is that we open the Bible and allow the stories and events recorded there to shape our moral attitudes and stimulate our moral imagination. The stories of God, the stories of Jesus must become the framework for our own personal story, giving form to our moral dispositions and intentions and providing the interpretive context of our self-understanding. Such stories must tell us who we are and what we are about in the world, rather than the dominant stories and symbols of the secular culture. Our ideas of success, happiness and well-being, of failure, shame and sin must develop from the biblical context and not from the slick promotions of the mass media.

A second requirement for listening to God's word is that we listen seriously to the responses of our hearts to the biblical stories to find where they challenge us, convict us, and also comfort us. What, for example, is my honest response to the story of the rich young man (Mk 10:17–22), or to the parable of Lazarus and the rich man (Lk 16:19–31), or to the tale of the widow's mite (Mk 12:41–44)? Do these stories challenge or confirm us in our use of material goods?

Finally, we must bring the events and experiences of our lives into contact with the biblical stories to see what light is shed on the ambiguities of our existence, what blessings we have ignored or abused, what possibilities for loving service to others await us. It is our lives that we need to share with God in prayer, our whole lives, not some small piece or fragment of them. If we meet these requirements of the prayer of personal communion, we will find much to discuss with the Lord in prayer, much to be healed, much to be grateful for, much to repent of. More importantly, however, the bond of intimacy with God will grow ever stronger.

And what may we expect from the prayer of personal communion? Surely we should not expect to see visions or hear voices or find an end to moral complexity and struggle. In the beginning of this book it was mentioned in passing that prayer is not an objective source of moral knowledge. Prayer does not provide us with information. It does not give us the relevant facts of a situation, does not teach us how to evaluate those facts, nor does prayer make decisions for us. Prayer can, however, deepen our motivation and strengthen our desire to do God's will, give form to our attitudes and intentions, and provide confirmation or challenge to decisions we have made and now offer to God in prayer. For if it is in the depths of conscience that we are alone with God, then the prayer of personal communion is an essential part of all conscientious decision-making. By the same token, all conscientious decision-making is, explicitly or implicity, an encounter with God and a form of the prayer of personal communion.

We conclude this study, therefore, with the promise and the challenge of Christian ethics: to be and to become a friend of God who has reached out the hand of friendship to us in Christ. Would you have God for your friend? Does personal friendship with Father, Son and Holy Spirit appeal to you as the desirable goal of life? Christian ethics or moral theology serves no other purpose than to help people say yes to the offer of divine friendship, to help them hit the mark in doing what Jesus commanded his followers to do: "Love one another as I have loved you."

STUDY QUESTIONS

1. What interests do you share with God? What interests of yours do you think God does not share? What interests of God are of no interest to you? Why do you think this is so?

2. What do you think of freedom and equality as conditions of friendship? Do they seem to be present in your own personal friendships? In what ways does God make us his equals?

3. Discuss the relationship between mercy and compassion. Do you find it hard to forgive others when you do not understand how people can act as they do? Does forgiveness mean you approve of a person's actions or don't really care about what people do one way or the other?

4. Do you feel the temptations of paternalism and sentimentalism present in any of your relationships? What are the signs by which you can detect the presence of either of these temptations?

5. Do you find prayer difficult? Could you implement in your own life the steps outlined in the text for listening to God's word? If not, why not? If you think of God as the ever-present friend, does it help in understanding St. Paul's admonition to pray without ceasing?

BIBLIOGRAPHY

Dufresne, Edward R. *Partnership: Marriage and the Committed Life.* New York: Paulist Press, 1975. An excellent view of the marital relationship as one that should be marked by friendship, with practical suggestions for achieving the freedom and equality essential to the ideal.

Gutierrez, Gustavo. *We Drink from Our Own Wells.* Maryknoll: Orbis Books, 1983. A treatise on spirituality by one of the outstanding liberation theologians. It stresses the importance of the concrete events of one's own history for discerning the presence and call of God in our lives.

Hanigan, James P. "Spiritual Life and the Uses of Power," *Studies in Formative Spirituality*, V, 3 (November 1984), pp. 335–344. A brief article which has proved helpful to a number of students in understanding their own talents and goals and how to use their gifts to empower others in parenting, teaching, and pastoring.

Hellwig, Monika K. *Jesus: The Compassion of God.* Wilmington: Michael Glazier, Inc., 1983. A somewhat novel approach to Christology which portrays Jesus as God's compassion for human beings and so helps to illuminate the central importance of mercy and compassion for all relationships.

Johnston, William. *Christian Mysticism Today.* San Francisco: Harper & Row, Publishers, 1984. A personal illuminating account of mysticism and mystical experience from a Catholic perspective. Rooted in Scripture, it also brings mysticism to bear on the issues of peace, power, poverty and social concern.